THE COMPLETE
ILLUSTRATED
GUIDE TO
CRYSTAL
HEALING

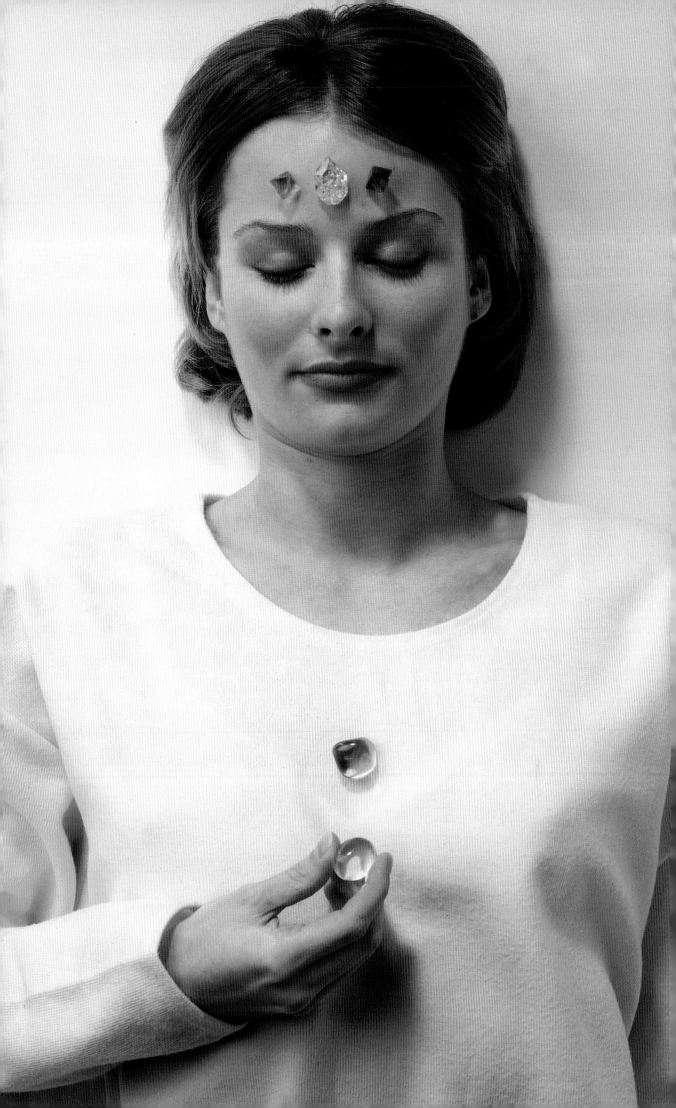

THE COMPLETE
ILLUSTRATED
GUIDE TO
CRYSTAL
HEALING

The Therapeutic Use of Crystals
for Health and Well~Being

SIMON LILLY

ELEMENT

Shaftesbury, Dorset • Boston, Massachusetts • Melbourne, Victoria

© Element Books Limited 2000

First published in Great Britain in 2000 by
ELEMENT BOOKS LIMITED
Shaftesbury, Dorset, SP7 8BP

Published in the USA in 2000 by
ELEMENT BOOKS INC
160 North Washington Street, Boston, MA 02114

Published in Australia in 2000 by
ELEMENT BOOKS
and distributed by Penguin Australia Ltd
487 Maroondah Highway, Ringwood, Victoria 3134

Designed and created with
The Bridgewater Book Company Limited

ELEMENT BOOKS LIMITED
Editorial Director Sue Hook
Managing Editor Miranda Spicer
Senior Commissioning Editor Caro Ness
Project Manager Shirley Patton
Production Manager Susan Sutterby
Production Controller Fiona Harrison

THE BRIDGEWATER BOOK COMPANY
Art Director Peter Bridgewater
Senior Designer Caroline Marklew
Designers Jane Lanaway, Sheilagh Noble
Editorial Director Fiona Biggs
Managing Editor Anne Townley
Project Editor Caroline Earle
DTP Design Chris Lanaway
Picture Research Caroline Thomas
Illustrations Guy Passey, Vicky Emptage and Derek Lee

Printed and bound in Great Britain by Butler & Tanner Ltd

British Library Cataloguing in Publication
data available

ISBN 1–86204–372–2 Hardback
ISBN 1–86204–326–4 Paperback

Dedication
For my parents, Janet and Ken

Acknowledgments

With thanks to
Maria Anderson, Gavin Bates, Clare Bayes, Jane Elliot, Linda
Fleischman, Maggie de Freitas, Anette Gerlin, Louise Gorst,
Trevor Gunn, Caroline Hasler, Justin Huckle, Pat Infanti,
Amy Jeavons, Mette Lauritzen, Kay Macmullan, Avlla
Macphail, Lucy Phillips, Emma Scott, Francesca Selkirk
for help with photography

With thanks to:
Booth Museum of Natural History, Brighton
Curioser and Curioser, Brighton
Andrew James Designs, Lewes
K Harrison, Evolution, Exeter
Winfalcon's Healing Centre, Brighton
for the kind loan of props

Picture Credits

Abode: 139, 170–1b.

AKG London: 24l, 44b, 58bl, 59tr, 64t, 84bl, 149, 182bl, 192,
192–3, 193, 194.

Bridgeman Art Library: 184t, 186b (© The British Museum),
187b.

Fortean Picture Library: 188b, 189t.

The Hutchison Library: 168t, 184b, 189b.

The Image Bank: 36t, 40, 60t, 65bm, 140–1b, 183tr, 188t.

Images Colour Library: 11tr, 27mr, 35tl, 43tr, 44t, 48, 49tr, 58t,
66l, 66tr, 68, 70, 82bl, 88, 106t, 141tr, 148, 151t, 167b,
171mr, 172tr, 173bl, 176t, 182–3, 190t, 191 (backdrop),
195tr.

NHPA: 67l.

Science Photo Library: 10t, 34 (both), 37tl, 37tr, 37br, 57b, 61t,
63t, 67tr, 172bl.

Steiner Waldorf Schools Fellowship: 166tl.

The Wellcome Centre Medical Photographic Library: 101, 185tr.

Werner Forman Archive: 143tr, 186t, 187t, 190bl, 190br.

b = bottom; l = left; m = middle; t = top; r = right

Contents

How to Use this Book

The present-day interest in crystal healing is a continuation of mankind's constant fascination with gemstones and minerals through the ages. In *The Complete Illustrated Guide to Crystal Healing*, I show the reader how to make use of crystals to enhance the body's own healing abilities, reduce stress, and improve the quality of life.

This book gives an account of the formation and structure of crystals and introduces the basic procedures of crystal healing, together with practical advice on choosing and storing crystals. It clearly outlines the seven main chakras, detailing how particular crystal layouts can strengthen and support these energy centers.

Next, the reader is encouraged to develop their intuitive skills using methods of assessment such as pendulum dowsing and muscle-testing procedures. Then there are descriptions of advanced healing layouts to balance the human body's subtle energy systems and ways to make crystals a part of everyday life by using them to enhance our surroundings.

The book includes a unique survey of the history of crystal healing, demonstrating that, from earliest recorded history, different gemstones have been associated with particular virtues and properties. Finally, the Gemstone Directory identifies some of the most useful stones for crystal healing.

Because crystal healing is a new area of alternative therapy that uses non-orthodox systems of subtle anatomy, there is a shortage of accurate terminology. The vocabulary of crystal healing has its origins in the Sanskrit, Tibetan, and Navaho languages, so the words just do not exist in English to cover the nuances needed. Thus, in this book, terms like "energy," "subtle," "level," and "vibration" are used quite extensively. The word "body" refers to the complete energy systems of the physical and subtle anatomies. "Physical body" is used to denote the actual physical attributes of the individual. The term "healer" or "crystal worker" has usually been chosen in preference to "therapist," and the person receiving crystal healing is called the "patient."

There is no established system within the field of crystal healing yet, and in this book I have tried to cover those aspects of the subject that seem worth-

Simple layouts are clearly explained, identifying the preferred crystals to use and where to place them.

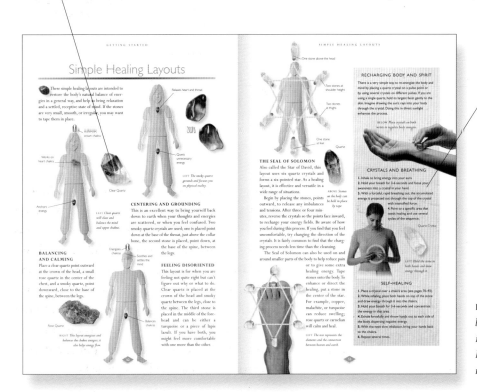

There are numerous easy-to-follow crystal healing techniques that can teach the reader how to reenergize and recharge body and spirit.

LEFT *Part Two of the book gets you started by introducing simple healing layouts which can help restore energy and balance.*

RIGHT Part Seven
explores the methods
of crystal healing further,
by introducing more
advanced techniques.

In addition to crystal
placement, this book
indicates other crystal
healing techniques to
try, such as meditation,
goal balancing, and
emotional stress release.

This section shows you
how to develop intuitive
skills by using different
methods of crystal healing.

Learn how the careful
placing of crystals around
the home can have a
beneficial effect by
neutralizing negative
energies from the earth or
electrical appliances.

ABOVE Part Eight shows us how
crystals can become an integrated
part of our existence, enhancing our
surroundings and everyday lives.

Find out how crystals can
help environmental stress,
plants, and animals, and
how they can be used in
astrology and divination.

while and are accepted as standard practice. However, each therapist brings their own expertise and develops personal work methods. I have chosen a more structured approach to the healing process for two reasons. First, I have a personal background that evolved from kinesiology and related testing techniques; second, I believe that in a learning situation, it is vital to begin with a clearly discernible working structure within which personal experiences can be firmly set or measured.

A distinction needs to be made between "healing with crystals" and "crystal healing." Many healers use crystals as an amplification of their healing skills – as an adjunct to personal energy. While crystals do seem to work in this way, crystal healing – applying crystals in the right place at the right time – will initiate profoundly positive life-changes, despite the belief or skepticism of the people around them. I hope this book will encourage experimentation with crystals to bring you lasting benefit.

PART ONE

CRYSTALS
The beginnings

When we hold a crystal, we are instantly in touch with the forces that shape our planet and the elements that first formed eons ago in the heart of distant stars. Current scientific knowledge of the chemical structure and properties of crystals is comparatively recent. It was only a few hundred years ago that curious minds began to look at what crystals were made of and why they exhibit such unique characteristics. That flurry of investigation during the eighteenth and nineteenth centuries has led to our pre-

ABOVE *Earth's riches: sparkling crystals formed from mixtures, liquids, or vapors in the Earth's crust.*

sent-day technological dependence on a variety of both naturally occurring and synthesized crystals. Our modern world would not be possible without such crystals. From computers to car engines, lasers to space shuttles — all have vital components that use these unusual bits of stone.

Structure of the Earth

It is important to place the mineral kingdom and its crystals in a larger context in an attempt to lead to an understanding of the unique properties of crystals and an acceptance of their use as a healing tool. The composition of every planetary body depends upon what sort of matter formed it and where it is placed in relationship to other gravitational bodies.

The Earth is believed to be about 4.6 billion years old. From early in its existence it is thought to have consisted of the same four layers that exist today: the outer crust, the mantle, and the outer and inner cores. It is nearly 8,000 miles (13,000km) in diameter.

ABOVE *The outermost layer of the Earth is the crust, where there are three types of rock: igneous, sedimentary, and metamorphic.*

The outermost layer, the crust, is proportionately very thin. Under the oceans it is only about 5 miles (8km) thick, increasing on the continents to an average of 20 miles (30km), and, at its deepest, 55 miles (90km) under the Himalayas. The crust makes up only 0.4 percent of the planet's mass! Nearly all the rocks in the crust are crystalline, and of these, the majority are formed of oxygen and silicon. The rest are composed primarily of six other elements – aluminum, iron, calcium, sodium, potassium, and magnesium.

The thin crust floats on the mantle – nearly 70 percent of the Earth's mass. The mantle is over 1,800 miles (2,900km) thick and consists of different layers of swirling, very hot, thick melted rock called magma (lava). Little is known for certain of the core except that it is mainly iron and nickel. The outer core seems to be liquid, and the inner core is thought to be solid.

THE ROCK CYCLE

Continental drift – the slow sliding of the massive tectonic plates that make up the Earth's crust – is responsible not only for making mountains as the continents collide, but also for creating many stress fractures, folds, and faults in the surface rock. This allows new material to well up from far below, changing the nature of many minerals through heat and pressure, while at the same time creating the perfect condition for new minerals to crystallize. Plate tectonics is the engine that drives the continental process of rock formation and crystallization known as the rock cycle. Understanding this cycle enables us to see how crystals are created and how the Earth's huge variety of minerals is made. Three types of rock are created: igneous, sedimentary, and metamorphic.

Igneous rocks are formed when continental drift creates areas of stress deep in the Earth's crust. These cracks release some of the enormous pressure placed on the semifluid magma by the crust's moving plates. There is then a huge increase in tem-

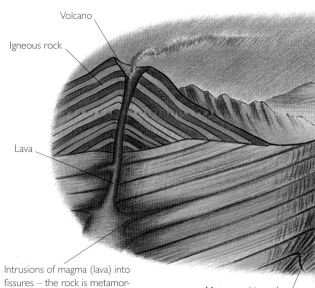

Volcano

Igneous rock

Lava

Intrusions of magma (lava) into fissures – the rock is metamorphosed by heat from lava intrusion.

Metamorphic rock – rock metamorphosed by pressure and resulting from heat movement in the Earth's crust.

ABOVE *The rock cycle of change: rocks are pushed up, eroded, transported, compressed, and sometimes metamorphosed.*

RIGHT *Igneous rock starts off as hot liquid rock called magma, deep in the Earth. Pressure can push it upward, and when it reaches the Earth's surface, it is known as magma (lava).*

perature, liquefying the magma so that it flows upward through the cracks. If this superheated, highly pressurized magma reaches the surface, it either forms a volcano or spreads out as a lava flow. Sometimes the magma is stopped by a solid layer of rock so that it spreads out, and then cools within the earth. As the magma solidifies, well-defined crystals may form in hollow spaces such as those left by gas bubbles. The majority of crystals are created from super-heated, mineral-rich gas and water released as the rocks solidify. These solutions rise higher through crevices and cracks in the rock, crystallizing wherever the conditions of temperature and pressure are right. Depending on the elements in the solution, different crystals will grow.

Metamorphic rocks have been changed from their original state by heat or pressure or both. Existing rocks close to an igneous intrusion may be altered by a high local temperature that can drive off elements or add some new ones. Other metamorphic rocks are created by incredible pressures within the crust. The most common form of metamorphosis occurs when there is both heat and pressure. Usually the greater these factors are, the greater the change in the rock structure. The types of crystals found in these rocks will depend on the original material and the metamorphic conditions. For example, garnet and corundum are found in igneous rock, but, under the right temperature and pressure, they will also crystallize in metamorphic rocks.

Once a crystal bed has formed, it may stay intact for millions of years, or it may undergo radical changes as dynamic processes within the Earth introduce new mineral solutions and new conditions. Wherever rock reaches the surface of the planet, it will be eroded by wind, water, and temperature changes. Debris from this rock may be deposited far from its original site, and over millions of years thick layers will build up and are gradually compressed to form new rocks. Crystals within these sedimentary rocks tend to be soft because they form at much lower temperatures and pressures, but they crystallize very rapidly and can create huge deposits of, for example, calcite and halite (rock salt). Sedimentary rocks are subject to metamorphosis as well. Limestone, for example, under heat and pressure turns into marble.

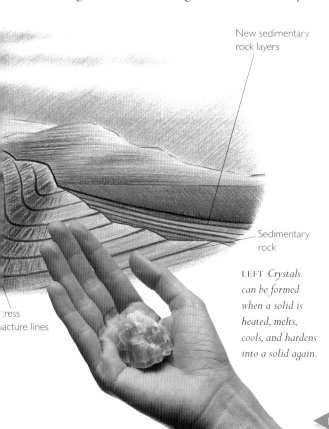

New sedimentary rock layers

Sedimentary rock

ress
acture lines

LEFT *Crystals can be formed when a solid is heated, melts, cools, and hardens into a solid again.*

Crystal Structure

Every crystal consists of a single chemical compound; one molecule is repeated throughout, forming a geometric internal structure. A crystal is defined by its internal structure, which directly influences its exterior form. It is made up of atoms that have bonded together into regular repeating patterns, and it is these patterns that create a crystal's solid form with flat faces, which are arranged in a precise geometry. This is known as a crystal lattice.

Crystals can form only from a gas or liquid solution because only in this state are atoms free to arrange themselves into stable relationships with each other. Depending on what elements are combined within the gas or liquid solution, different types of atoms will bond together into mineral crystals.

A crystal will always have the same fundamental internal order of atom structure lattices, no matter what it looks like — whether it is perfect, misshapen, battered, chipped, or eroded, or if it is perfectly clear, cloudy, or colored. A crystal lattice is built up very rapidly when one or two atoms take up a set pattern of bonding together. The shape of the original molecule, dictated by the size of the atoms of the elements involved, establishes the unit cell that is the smallest part of the crystal lattice. Other atoms of the same elements are attracted to this cell, and so the crystal builds up layer upon layer of repeating parts.

When all the available elements have been used, or when temperatures and pressures change in the surroundings, the crystal's growth stops, leaving its outermost atoms as flat external faces. The speed at which the liquid flows and the space available for growth tend to create distorted shapes so that some crystal faces become larger

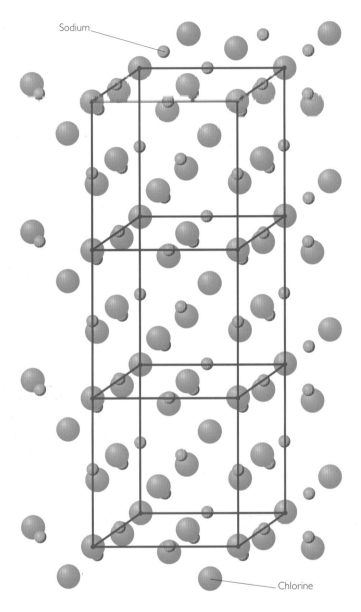

Sodium

Chlorine

ABOVE *The atomic structure of a salt crystal, showing the repeating geometric arrangement known as a crystal lattice.*

than others. Every crystal is unique in appearance, but the angle between corresponding plane faces will be the same in all crystals of the same substance and structure. It is often possible to identify a mineral according to the shape of its crystals and the way that the crystallization has taken place. A single crystal can vary in size from a minute, submicroscopic particle to a mass as much as 100 feet (30 meters) long.

Granite contains a mixture of crystals.

LEFT Granite is made up of quartz, feldspar, and mica crystals.

RIGHT A soft environment like clay or volcanic tuff, can allow the development of perfect crystal faces such as double-terminated crystals, Herkimer diamonds, etc.

Volcanic tuff

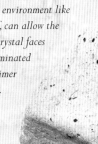

Amethyst geode

Crystals grow into the center.

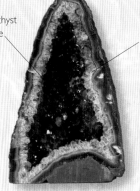

Natural faceted termination

Clear Quartz

Gypsum cluster

ABOVE When a cluster of crystals grows in a confined space, they crowd each other and prevent each others' full development. If the rock wall is curved or round, crystals grow into the center and a geode is formed.

ABOVE The external shape of a crystal, its flat sides, and characteristic facets reflect the inner structure of its atoms.

ABOVE In rock crevices, crystals can only develop faces in the open space of the center of the cavity. This produces a crust of crystals lining a rock cavity called a druse.

Crystals grow in different directions.

Quartz crystal cluster

RIGHT If a growing crystal gets entangled in a neighboring crystal, it cannot grow any further in that direction, but it is able to expand in other directions.

Unique Properties of Crystals

When a crystal grows, the lattice is very rarely perfect. Sometimes there are gaps in the structure, sometimes extra atoms are squeezed in or an atom of a slightly different size enters the lattice. This means that, although it is in a state of equilibrium, the crystal has a reservoir of extra electrons. Because they are not all used up in the making of bonds between atoms, some electrons have nothing to do. When energy is put into the crystal, these electrons become excited and begin to flow through the lattice structure. This means that crystals can act as transducers or change one form of energy into another.

One possible effect is that light energy may stimulate the electrons to become conductors, thus generating an electric current. Heat can create the same effects. Sometimes heat or friction will produce light in a crystal   pieces of quartz when rubbed together in a dark room will show triboluminescence. A sugar cube crushed in darkness will display flashes of green light. This is called piezoelectricity and happens when a crystal lattice is deformed enough to create a large electric current or an electric current deforms the lattice structure. This latter effect is the driving force behind quartz watches. The battery stimulates a minute expansion of the crystal in regular pulses and this drives the mechanism.

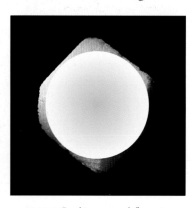

ABOVE *Crushing sugar deforms its crystal lattice and creates flashes of green light known as piezoelectricity.*

Another interesting possibility is that pressure in the form of sound may create a unique electron excitement in a crystal structure, leading to the entrainment or storing of a word, phrase, or event. It may be that the perceived atmosphere of a place is caused by the local crystal-bearing rock, or even the crystallike structure of a body of water, somehow retaining a pattern, imprint, or a memory of events. Within the stable structure of each crystal lattice, there are potentially vast vortices and currents of energy held in place until some kind of extra input allows them to manifest in various energetic guises. The growth of technology can largely be seen as an exploration and utilization of the properties of stone, from flint arrowheads to nuclear reactors. Stones as sources of energy have also been used to heal and empower us. Today, solid state physics is beginning to reveal the mechanisms that healers and sensitives have subjectively experienced for millennia.

CRYSTAL STRUCTURES

▲ A crystal is a mineral in its most stable form.

▲ A crystal has a recognizable internal structure made up of repeating arrangements of atoms, known as a crystal lattice.

▲ The geometrical form of a crystal, with symmetrically arranged plane faces, is an expression of its internal atomic structure.

▲ Every crystal of the same mineral will have flat faces meeting each other at identical angles.

▲ Crystals can grow to a huge size or appear as microcrystalline masses where each crystal is too small to be seen with the naked eye.

▲ Crystals will only form from a gas or liquid solution at the correct temperature and pressure.

▲ Once crystallized, a mineral can remain unchanged for millions of years.

▲ Subjected to extreme conditions of heat and pressure, a crystal may alter its form or become another mineral altogether.

▲ Crystals are the most organized and stable matter in the universe.

Quartz crystal cluster

LEFT *A macrograph of a cut diamond showing the exceptional light dispersion emanating from the crystal. Diamond is the hardest known mineral; it is the structure of its atoms that make it unique. This crystal is invaluable for industry because it is hard but very lightweight compared to steel making it perfect for grinding, shaping, and cutting.*

BELOW *Piezoelectricity is utilized in quartz watches. The watch battery causes the quartz crystal to expand in regular pulses, thus driving the watch mechanism.*

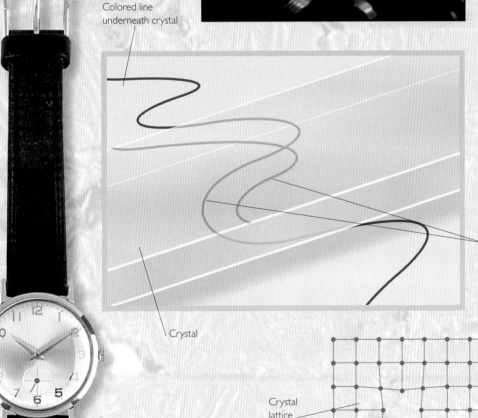

Colored line underneath crystal

LEFT *As light passes into a crystal, it is usually bent (refracted). Some crystals — for example, a variety of calcite known as Iceland spa — are double refractive. In this case, when a ray of light hits the crystal, it vibrates in two directions at right angles to each other.*

Line appears double as the light is refracted in two different directions

Crystal

Crystal lattice

Distortion in lattice

RIGHT *Piezoelectricity occurs when the crystal lattice is distorted, usually by heat, light, or friction. In quartz crystal, positive silicon ions move to one side of the crystal and negative silicon ions to the other, resulting in a strong electrical charge.*

The Crystal Systems: Their healing geometry

There are a maximum of 14 different ways in which points can be arranged in space. These correspond directly to seven main crystal systems. Each system contains minerals whose constituent atoms have been arranged into regular lattices that have the same axes of symmetry in the same relationship to each other. This means that all of the crystals within a group tend to have similar basic shapes.

Most crystal healers do not pay much attention to the geometrical systems of crystallography. Without the correct equipment, angle faces are difficult to measure, and the huge variation within each system can make visual identification both confusing and difficult. A crystal's geometrical form, however, is the essence of why it does what it does, both in terms of its physical properties and its potential for healing.

Geometry is the knowledge of how things arrange themselves in space. Every physical object follows geometrical laws and is built upon three-dimensional patterns. Crystals just happen to be clear evidence for this fundamental organization of matter. Richard Gerber, M.D., in his book, *Vibrational Medicine* – written in 1988 as a survey of alternative methods of healing – gives an interesting analysis of the subtle qualities of crystal systems. Every crystal in a system will share certain energetic properties and ways of working. Like a crystal's color, its symmetry provides another method by which a stone's potential can be assessed.

Fluorite

CUBIC SYSTEM

Crystals of the cubic system have all axes of symmetry at right angles to each other. The cubic system is noted for the qualities of foundation and stability, and can be used where structural and physical repair are needed in the body systems. Their solidity and simple symmetry help to organize things in a straightforward, clear manner. This system is the only one of the seven that does not distort or alter light rays as they pass through. It leaves everything as it is and so can be of great value in exploring the reality of a situation. Examples of the cubic system include gold, diamond, copper, fluorite, halite (rock salt), sodalite, garnet, and pyrite. No matter what other properties these stones exhibit, they will always be anchored at the level of practical reality.

Zircon

TETRAGONAL SYSTEM

Crystals of the tetragonal system have all axes of symmetry at right angles to each other, but here one axis is longer. These crystals are associated with the characteristic of balancing and working well with opposites. Tetragonal crystals can be both absorbing and reflecting. Many can absorb unbalanced or negative vibrations and transmute them into life-supporting energy. They create a link between the physical structures on the Earth and finer dimensional levels. Crystals of this system tend to grow as short prisms based on the three-sided pyramid of the tetragon. Examples are rutile, zircon, and apophyllite.

HEXAGONAL SYSTEM

The hexagonal system comprises forms with three angles at 120 degrees and often appears as six-sided prisms and pyramids. Hexagonal crystals are characterized by growth and vitality. They emanate energy that may be used in healing, energy balancing, and communication. They help to focus on particular areas of need and develop creativity and intuition. Useful as meditation and self-development stones, crystals of this system include emerald, aquamarine, quartz, and apatite.

Aquamarine

Amazonite

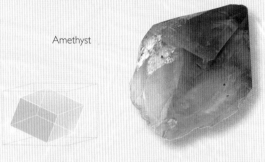

Amethyst

TRIGONAL SYSTEM

The trigonal system is sometimes included with the hexagonal system. It has the same angles as the hexagonal, but is made up as rhombohedral and triangular prisms. These crystals continually radiate energy useful for balancing the body's subtle anatomy, particularly where lack of energy is the problem. Trigonal crystals are more dynamic and focused in their activity than the hexagonal. Examples include agate, amethyst, bloodstone, carnelian, calcite, rhodochrosite, tourmaline, ruby, and sapphire.

MONOCLINIC SYSTEM

The monoclinic crystals system has three unequal axes, two at 90° and one greater than 90°. It forms various shapes, but often has long prisms. In them, there is a continual expansion and contraction, a constant pulsing, that is stabilizing but encouraging to activity on some level. Monoclinic crystals are directional and can clear away obstructions. Clarity on deeper levels of perception can result from their cleansing action. Among the monoclinic crystals are azurite, jade, malachite, moonstone, selenite, lepidolite, amazonite, and kunzite.

Topaz

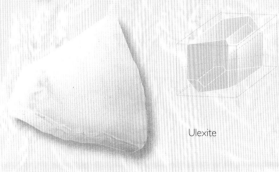

Ulexite

ORTHORHOMBIC SYSTEM

The orthorhombic system has three unequal axes at right angles making prismatic or tabular crystals. They can be useful for bringing perspective and focus, clearing away unnecessary patterns and unwanted energies. Orthorhombic crystals have a protecting, encompassing quality to them in which purification and cleansing can safely take place. Examples are peridot, topaz, sulfur, celestite, danburite, and staurolite.

TRICLINIC SYSTEM

The triclinic system has three unequal axes of symmetry, none the same as any other. This produces variable crystal forms, notably tabular ones. These crystals naturally tend to integrate different states of energy. They help to merge and harmonize polarities where there is loss of balance. This can be of particular use in situations when beliefs and attitudes give rise to personality problems. Triclinic crystals can often work as vehicles to access different states of consciousness and finer nonphysical dimensions. Crystals found in the triclinic system include turquoise, rhodonite, sunstone, labradorite, ulexite, and kyanite.

PART TWO

GETTING STARTED

The best way to learn about crystals is to begin working with them in simple ways. You can build up a basic set of stones and continue to add to it over time by looking for crystals in jewelry stores and gem and mineral suppliers. Once you know how to cleanse crystals and are able to ground and center yourself, you will be well-equipped to explore the fascinating world of crystals. Grounding is the state of being mentally focused and in control, while centering occurs when all physical, mental, and emotional energies are in harmony.

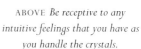

ABOVE *Be receptive to any intuitive feelings that you have as you handle the crystals.*

Following basic procedures will help you make sure that you become aware of the beneficial changes that crystal healing can bring. Learning to notice slight shifts of awareness, subtle feelings, and intuition are important keys to becoming an effective crystal healer.

Choosing and Storing Crystals

Many people become interested in crystal healing due to one or two stones or crystals that attracted their attention, which they acquired as simply beautiful or interesting objects. Some people simply collect a few crystal clusters to decorate their homes, while others become fascinated with the their variety of shapes and colors. It is easy to find yourself with a quickly growing collection of rocks and crystals of all shapes and sizes.

LEFT *You are likely to find that you have a natural affinity with certain crystals.*

Choosing gemstones and crystals is a very personal matter because we are all drawn to different shapes and colors. Never be deterred from buying a crystal just because the information says it is good for an ailment you don't have, or because an author does not have any positive opinions about it. There is always a reason why one crystal is noticed among many, why one almost identical tumbled stone feels more comfortable than another. This is one of the first, and most important, lessons to learn: to appreciate our intuitive choices and balance the rational with the magical. Time and again, the same scenario is repeated in crystal shops. Someone comes in and picks up or touches a stone. They spend the next half hour exploring every shelf and display case looking for the right stone and finally buy the original crystal.

Some people have special ways in which they hope to identify the right crystal for their needs. A pendulum might be used to single out a stone, or a hand can be used to feel a subtle difference in energy. In some circumstances, such strategies might be useful, but generally speaking if you have your wits about you, your own senses will lead you to those crystals that will be of most use to you. We have, after all, evolved over millions of years making choices and using experiences, learning to recognize what may be of benefit to us. Your initial reaction to a crystal will usually provide a good clue as to how its energy interacts with your own.

Pay special attention to those stones that are very attractive to you because they will probably be ones that are in tune with the current state of balance and energy within your body. Similarly, notice those stones that seem unaccountably unappealing or that you instinctively dislike, since these will often represent qualities of energy with which you can't cope at the moment but will need to adjust to in time, or ones which begin a release of stress that creates a feeling of unease or discomfort in you as it occurs.

Following are some guidelines that may help you to build a working collection of stones for use in healing and self-development. Three different types of crystals may be found, and each type has its own particular place in crystal healing.

Specimen samples

Mineralogical specimens are usually fine and interesting examples of minerals in native bedrock. These can be large or delicate and are not easily used in healing situations, but they can add great energy and atmosphere to a room.

Natural single crystals

These are crystals that have been separated from their matrix and from any surrounding crystals but have not been worked or altered in any way.

Worked crystals

There are three main types of worked crystal. The most common form of worked gemstones can be found either in jewelry or in gem and mineral stores in the form of polished or tumbled pebbles of semiprecious stones. Buying tumbled stones is probably the most effective and inexpensive way to build up a broad-based crystal and gemstone collection. These smoother stones, which look like river pebbles worn smooth by the action of water, are made by taking damaged crystals or large, broken pieces of stone and then placing them in revolving drums of grit for many days until they become smooth and polished. It is usually only the harder stones that can be treated in this way since softer stones tend to disintegrate too easily.

CHOOSING CRYSTALS

▲ Use your intuition when choosing crystals – you will be able to sense which crystal is right for you

▲ Take note of the crystals you are instantly attracted to and those that you dislike

▲ Gradually build up a working collection of the three types of crystals

Single large crystals that are slightly chipped or have a rough surface are sometimes repolished or ultrasonically cleaned to reveal their internal clarity. A crystal may also be ground to give it a flat base upon which to stand upright. If this sort of work is done well, it has little effect on the usefulness of the crystal and indeed can serve to enhance its beauty.

Massive crystalline lumps may be carved or shaped into decorative statuary or natural-looking crystal shapes and tools such as massage wands (see pages 146–7) and spheres (see pages 137 and 178).

A WORKING COLLECTION OF CRYSTALS

NATURAL FLUORITE
A natural single crystal, found in sedimentary and igneous rocks. It can be transparent to translucent and white, blue, green, or violet.

AMETHYST
An unworked amethyst crystal of a dark hue. Amethyst is prized as a gem.

AMETHYST
A beautiful natural amethyst crystal. Its misty mauve color may come from traces of iron.

CALCITE CRYSTAL CLUSTER
An example of a mineral in native bedrock. Usually opaque, calcite may be tinged with impurities, providing a hint of yellow, orange, brown, or green.

CLEAR QUARTZ CRYSTAL
A fine clear quartz crystal. Such large crystals are rare. Clear quartz crystallizes thoughts and balances chakras.

ROSE QUARTZ CRYSTAL
A single unworked example of rose quartz. This stone usually occurs as a mass of crystals. Sometimes the cut stone reflects light in a starlike pattern.

BASIC SET

Consider acquiring the following stones as a basic working set for crystal healing:

I Tumbled stones, also known as tumblies or smoothies, can be found in a great variety of minerals. It is a good idea to select stones that will not be too heavy when placed on the body, and that are not so small as to get lost easily. Remember that flat stones will stay in place more easily than round ones. You will naturally be drawn toward certain types and colors of stone. So bear in mind that you will need at least two stones of each spectrum color (see pages 56–67), although they can be different minerals.

2 Small, natural crystals of clear quartz will always be of use. They do not have to be large: 1¾in (2–4cm) in length is fine. Twelve or more small quartz is a good number to have.

3 Small single crystals of amethyst quartz, smoky quartz, and citrine quartz are also worth looking for, although they are generally less common than the clear variety. It is often easier to find tumbled stones of these colored quartz.

Amber

Citrine

Clear Quartz

Amethyst

Smoky Quartz

Rose Quartz

Amethyst

Carnelian

Blue Quartz

4 Small, hand-sized clusters of clear quartz, amethyst, or other quartz varieties are very useful for recharging and cleansing your other stones and crystal jewelry.

5 Larger single crystals or tumbled stones that are easy and comfortable to hold in your hands make very good tools for meditation and other self-development work. These will be special, personal crystals that you will feel drawn to at certain times. It is worth spending a while getting to know these stones. It is quite usual to have several crystals around that haven't been used at all. Let your intuitive senses choose an appropriate time for an investigation.

Aquamarine

Amazonite

Ametrine

BUYING CRYSTALS

If you are lucky enough to have a selection of stores in your area that supply gemstones, it is a good idea to compare quality and cost. If no specialized crystal shops can be found locally, check the jewelry stores. Many have small selections of tumbled stones and inexpensive cabochons and cut stones, often at a lower price. (A cabochon is a stone cut in a convex form and highly polished, but not faceted.)

STORING CRYSTALS

Once you start a small collection of crystals and gemstones, you will need somewhere to store them. It is important to remember that even hard stones can be damaged by careless handling. Tumbled stones are the most robust because they have no delicate faces. Crystals on the other hand, have tips and corners and are prone to chips and scratches if knocked together. It is a good idea to keep hard and soft stones separate to avoid damage. Be aware of which stones will fracture easily. Fluorite and calcite, for example, will readily shatter if dropped. Some crystals – especially the softer varieties such as halite, which is rock salt, and selenite, a variety of gypsum – are very sensitive to humidity and may disintegrate completely in very damp conditions. Some, such as amethyst, may fade or change color if exposed to strong sunlight for long periods. Even quartz may shatter if internal flaws are exacerbated by rapid changes of extreme temperature.

If you own a crystal that is undamaged and perfect, remember that it may have been this way for many millions of years. It would be a shame to damage such ancient perfection simply through careless handling. However, many crystals do have chips, scratches, or rough surfaces. Not all crystals are beautiful and clear to look at. Whatever a crystal may look like, grubby or pristine, the internal structural harmony is the same for each example of that mineral. The external form might modify the way the crystal's energy manifests itself but the fundamental quality, and healing power, remains constant. Some people choose only to work with the finest examples of each mineral; others are happy with knocked and battered stones that feel comfortable and full of character.

An old printer's box, tool box, or fishing tackle box that has a lot of different-sized compartments is ideal for storing and carrying your healing stones. Small pieces of foam or tissue paper can help to protect more delicate pieces.

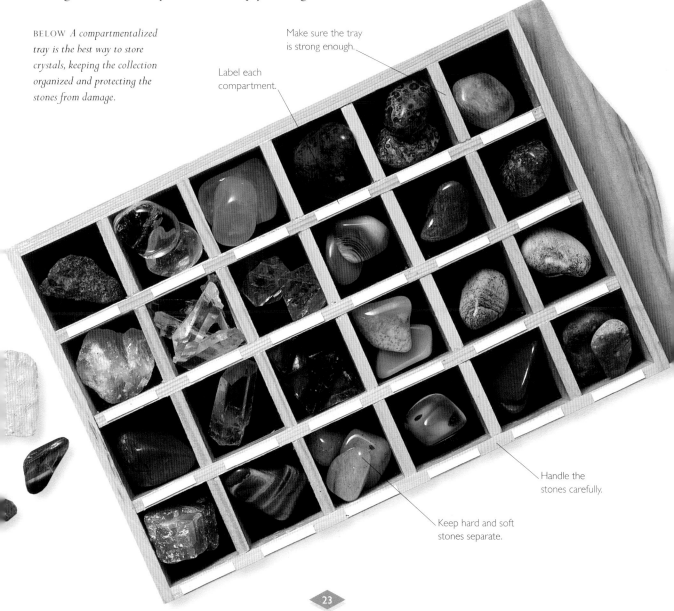

BELOW *A compartmentalized tray is the best way to store crystals, keeping the collection organized and protecting the stones from damage.*

Make sure the tray is strong enough.

Label each compartment.

Handle the stones carefully.

Keep hard and soft stones separate.

Cleansing Crystals

Before and after you use a stone, it is a good idea to cleanse it in some way. If the stone is new to you, a simple wash in soapy water will help to remove physical grime, fingerprints, and so on. Make sure the stone is not water soluble (see page 46)! Even more important is to remove any energy imbalances the stone may have picked up. Crystals have a tendency to absorb emotional stress and other strong energy patterns. Given time, a crystal will be able to restore its own internal equilibrium and neutralize the unwanted energy, but in a stress-filled environment the opportunity for rebalancing may not occur so readily. A crystal that needs cleansing may give the impression of feeling dull, heavy, or unpleasant. Regular cleaning is essential when crystals have been used for either healing or meditation. If you do not cleanse your healing stones, they will become less effective and may pass on their accumulated imbalances to someone else the next time you use them. Crystal cleansing should become a routine and automatic process after each healing session.

There are many different ways to clear your crystals. Try out these methods and use those with which you feel most comfortable.

LEFT AND BELOW *Let the natural energies of water and sunlight cleanse the crystals after a healing session before you use them again.*

SUN AND WATER METHOD
Hold the stones under running water for a minute or so and then put them in the sun to dry. You could hold the stones in both hands and imagine all imbalances being washed from the stone, flowing away with the water. Or while the water is running over the stones, imagine light gradually filling up the crystal until it is completely clear. A cloth or colander in the bottom of the sink will prevent breakage or loss down the drain.

This is an excellent method of cleansing newly acquired stones that are not water-soluble. However, if you have a lot of stones to cleanse, it can be a little tedious. A window ledge is fine if you don't have access to a safe spot outside. When putting crystals in the garden, it is a good idea to keep them out of the way of pets and small children.

BELOW *Salt absorbs imbalances and negativity.*

THE SALT METHOD
Salt itself is a crystal used for centuries as a preservative and protector from negativity. Salt has the ability to draw imbalances into itself, so if you use this method always throw the salt away afterward. Some people suggest using salt water, but this is only appropriate with harder crystals (it will damage and dull softer stones). Even with crystals such as quartz, it is difficult to wash away the salt from the little cracks and crevices, where it will recrystallize. The easiest method is to bury each stone separately in dry sea salt. Leave them for about 24 hours, then wipe the stones carefully.

RIGHT *Hold the crystals in the smoke from burning aromatic herbs in order to purify them.*

INCENSE SMOKE

Herbs such as frankincense, sandalwood, sage, and cedar have a long traditional use in purification rites. Any aromatic smoke will help to clean crystals that are held in the smoke. Solid incense, incense sticks, or smudge sticks will all work well.

ABOVE *Surround the used stone with a pattern or circle of quartz crystals.*

CRYSTAL CLUSTERS

Placing single stones on a large crystal cluster will help. Crystal jewelry can be left on the cluster overnight. Alternatively, surround a stone with clear quartz crystals, points toward the center, and leave for 24 hours.

SOUND

The vibrations of pure sound can quickly clean a stone. A singing bowl, one made of metal alloy that resonates when struck or rubbed along the rim is very useful because it can hold many stones at once and will clean stones thoroughly and quickly in a minute or so. The sound will also have a purifying effect on the surroundings. A bell, gong, or tuning fork can also be used. Sound them close to the crystals until they feel completely cleared.

BELOW *The vibrations of sound waves will wash the crystals clean.*

VISUALIZATION

Visualization can be useful where other techniques can't be used. Experimenting will help you choose which works best for you. The imagery is less important than your clarity of intent. Fill the stone with bright light, visualize water rushing through the stone or fire burning away all impurities, or imagine the stone as an animal shaking water off its fur after swimming. Use your breath to heighten the imagery. Take a deep breath, pause, and then forcefully blow over the crystal. As you do this, imagine all negativity clearing away from the stone. Repeat this until you feel it has worked.

LEFT *Use mind power to visualize imbalance being removed from each stone in turn.*

Gem Water and Gem Essences

The unique properties of water mean that it is possible to make simple, effective remedies of enormous value to healing processes. A gem essence is essentially a liquid version of a gemstone's energy patterns, and because it is liquid it can be used in ways that the stones themselves cannot.

Although the mechanics are not yet understood, it is thought that the particular atomic bonding between the hydrogen and oxygen atoms in a molecule of water allows much greater range of movement than in other substances. This means that water is able to hold a memory or an energy pattern of something placed within it.

TOXIC STONES

It is important what sort of stone is used for making gem water, particularly if you intend to drink it. Be aware that some minerals are toxic and should be avoided. The quartz family is sufficiently hard and is non-toxic, and has such a great variety that a stone for most purposes can be found from a quartz selection. Softer stones tend to be more water soluble than hard ones, so are more liable to form a chemical solution with possible toxic effects. If in any doubt, consult an expert or mineralogical textbook.

Keeping one or two clear quartz crystals in a water pitcher enhances the beneficial effects of the water. Try gem waters with different types of quartz, for example: clear quartz, amethyst, tiger's eye, or aventurine – and see how the taste varies!

GEM WATER

It is simple to make your own gem water.
◆ Put a cleansed sample of a gemstone or crystal in the bottom of a clean, plain glass tumbler or pitcher.
◆ Fill the tumbler with fresh water – spring water if at all possible.

Clear Quartz

Aventurine

Amethyst

Tiger's Eye

LEFT *These stones are all members of the quartz family and safe for making gem water.*

◆ Leave for 10–12 hours or overnight. Use immediately or store for a few days in the refrigerator.

GEM ESSENCES

Gem essences are made in a slightly different way and have the advantage of a longer shelf life than gem water. They use the energy of sunlight to activate the memory of water.

1 Place a cleaned sample of crystal in the bottom of an undecorated, plain glass bowl. Add spring water until it just covers the sample of crystal.

2 Place the bowl containing the crystal in full sunlight, perhaps on a window sill outside, for at least two hours.

3 Afterward, carefully pour the water into a storage bottle that contains at least 50 percent brandy or vodka to act as a preservative. If a dropper bottle is used, drops can be taken as necessary. This is known as the mother essence.

4 Put between 3 and 7 drops of a mother essence into a clean dropper bottle containing a 50/50 mixture of water/brandy for regular use. This is called the stock bottle.

5 If several essences are being combined, you can make one further dilution of a few drops from the stock bottle with 50/50 water/brandy. This is called a dosage bottle.

If necessary, alcohol can be replaced by cider vinegar as a preservative.

SUGGESTIONS FOR USE

Gem essences and waters are excellent for self help, and there are many ways of using them.

❖ Adding a couple of drops of gem essence to bath water will mean that the whole body and its subtle energy fields absorb the remedy very rapidly.

❖ Another way of bringing the essence into an auric field is to put a few drops into a diffuser sprayer with water, and then to spray it around the body. Spraying a whole room with a gemstone essence will really change the energy feel of a place and is a useful way to cleanse a space or to change its mood. Spraying pets and plants can help to maintain their health in a simple way. Pets and plants will also benefit from being given gem water to drink once in a while.

ABOVE AND BELOW
Use a diffuser to spray
pets and plants with
gem water to keep
them in good health.

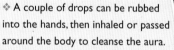

❖ A couple of drops can be rubbed into the hands, then inhaled or passed around the body to cleanse the aura.

❖ Rub a drop into the body's pulse points, such as the wrists, throat, and forehead.

❖ Add three or four drops to a glass of water, and sip it throughout the day.

❖ Place a couple of drops under the tongue once or twice a day, for example, upon waking or before sleep.

HOW GEM ESSENCES AND GEM WATERS WORK

The potent water of these essences holds the energy characteristics of the gemstone. When this is brought into a person's subtle bodies, it encourages positive change, probably through the principles of resonance (see pages 34–35). The advantage of essences and gem waters is that they allow the body to balance itself at its own pace and will not usually bring about unnecessary changes. They help the body to deal with the underlying stresses that may cause emotional or physical upsets.

Varieties of Quartz Crystal

Clear quartz is the most common crystal used in healing. Every stone is unique in its shape and growth, but there are certain characteristic types that have acquired particular meaning for many who work with them. Often the visual form of the crystal has symbolic significance or an association with a state of mind or experience. The accidents of crystallization can suggest a parallel with human experience that some believe will create a resonance to help them in those circumstances. For instance, quartz is a very coherent, resonant structure, and its outward shape tends to affect the less-organized structures around it, perhaps much more than another substance would.

The deep mind is a huge energetic ocean of which we have little conscious knowledge. It seems to be able to influence states of health and wellness and works by means of symbolic imagery. A crystal that reminds us of, or looks like, something else may be stirring deep forces of change within us.

Double terminated crystal

ABOVE *Quartz is one of the most common minerals in the Earth's crust.*

DOUBLE- TERMINATED CRYSTALS

When quartz crystallizes in soft conditions of mud or sand, it is able to form terminations in more than one direction. Also, when crystals begin to grow on the sides of other crystals, they are able to extend far beyond their support, forming faceted points in both directions.

These double-terminated crystals are useful healing tools because they are able to move energy in two directions simultaneously and can act as a bridge between two energy points. Double-terminated crystals have a special balanced feel and are used to help unblock negative energy. Complete in themselves, they have the ability to instill integration and poise, and can make wonderful stones for holding during meditation.

FACETED CRYSTAL

A second category of quartz crystal, known as a faceted crystal, is given special significance by the geometric characteristics of the facets of its terminations. The size and the relationship of the facets reveals the sort of healing tool each crystal will be. In crystal healing, the combination of shape and number carries great symbolic weight. A triangular face suggests a very different energy characteristic than a seven-sided face and so will be able to focus or channel energy in an entirely different manner. Ultimately, the usefulness of such categories must be determined by each individual healer. It may be that new or very personal associations will be found to be relevant or useful in certain cases.

Smoky Quartz

ABOVE *The shape of a crystal's facets may alter the way it works with energy.*

HERKIMER DIAMONDS

Herkimer diamonds are a variety of quartz named after their original location in New York. Formed in cavities of soft mudlike rock, Herkimer diamonds are generally small, very brilliant, double-terminated crystals of clear quartz. Similar quartz has been found more recently in Mexico and Spain. While other varieties of quartz seem to direct and move energy, Herkimer diamonds concentrate and focus the qualities of light. This makes the stone very effective for cleansing toxins and blocks on many subtle levels of the body. The absorbent quality of Herkimer diamonds means that they will need regular cleaning (see pages 24–25) to remain effective. As a result of their multilevel rebalancing abilities, Herkimer diamonds have been found to amplify and improve subtle energy perceptions, clairvoyance, lucid dreams, and astral travel. Areas suffering from tension may well benefit from this stone.

Herkimer Diamonds

ABOVE *Herkimer diamonds have a special ability to concentrate the qualities of light.*

BELOW *The striking form of an elestial is a good aid to meditation.*

ELESTIALS

Elestials, or skeletal quartz, often take a peculiar form. Like other double-terminated quartz, they crystallize in a soft matrix, but in this instance natural terminations occur over large areas of the crystals, both on its sides and major facets, looking like steps or etched layers. Many elestial quartz are smoky quartz, though other varieties can be found.

The key attribute of this quartz form is the revealing of hidden levels of situations or occurrences. Elestials make useful personal meditation tools both for holding and for looking at. They can help to bring emotional stability, increase energy levels, and clarify expanded states of awareness. They tend to balance chakras (see pages 70–92) and subtle bodies (see pages 114–5). Elestials often have a rough, earthy appearance and can help to link us more deeply to the forces of creation and to reveal the underlying causes behind an illness or life problem which Herkimer diamonds can then clear.

Smoky Quartz Elestial

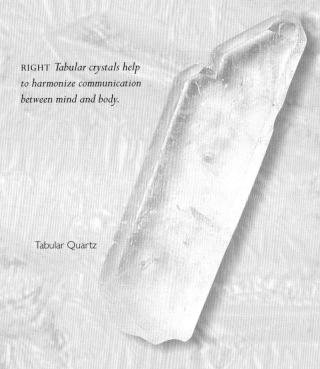

Tabular Quartz

TABULAR CRYSTALS

Tabular crystals form with two large flat planes,
making a wide, thin crystal. They can often be
double-terminated, and elestials may take a tabular
form. This quartz crystal shape allows a rapid flow
of energy to take place with little resistance. These
stones are said to be the finest ones to facilitate
communication between the levels within ourselves
and other areas of creation. Confusion, misinterpretation, and misunderstanding can be alleviated
by the use of tabular quartz. As meditation stones,
they allow an effortless flow of awareness to many
areas of consciousness. Their large flat surfaces
encourage people to gaze at and touch them.

SCEPTER QUARTZ

An unusual quartz form
is the Scepter crystal;
it is a larger crystal
which forms around
the top of a quartz
rod. These stones can
direct healing processes
to the center of a problem
area, acting as both amplifier
and a source of radiant energy.

LEFT *Use scepter quartz to
send healing energy into the
heart of an affected area, where
it will radiate outward.*

Scepter
Quartz

LASER WANDS

In contrast to the spacious quality of tabular
quartz, laser wands are crystals that concentrate,
accelerate, and focus energy passing through them.
They are easy to identify as they are long, thin
crystals with a pronounced tapering toward a very
small terminated end. Their sides are usually bent
or curved as if under great pressure. The greater
the contrast between their base and tip, the faster a
beam of energy from them may be projected.
Laser wands can prove extremely useful for precision healing. If a tight beam of healing energy
needs to be focused on a small area such as a
meridian point, or to stimulate an area hidden
within the body such as the pituitary or pineal
gland deep in the brain, a laser wand is ideal.
Wands can also remove extraneous debris from the
subtle bodies, break harmful links to other people
and things, and help to isolate stubborn areas of
imbalance. Laser wands are excellent amplifiers of
intention, so great caution does need to be taken.
Remaining attentive, fully centered and grounded,
open to intuitive direction, and knowing one's personal tendencies and limitations is always the best
approach to any tool or technique.

BELOW *Laser wands get their name
from their resemblance to actual
lasers, emitting deep, penetrating
energy with great precision.*

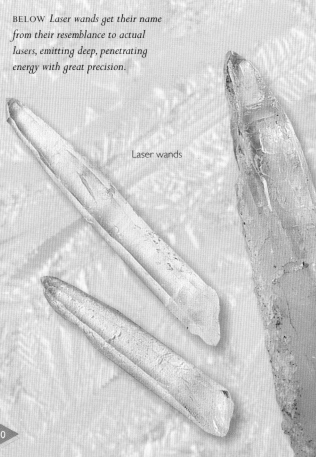

Laser wands

Phantom
crystals

ABOVE *Phantom crystals can help create
an understanding that every event, whether
pleasant or traumatic, is part of our
personal makeup and reality.*

INTERGROWN CRYSTALS

Where quartz crystals grow partly or
completely surrounded by another
larger crystal, they can express qualities of manifestation and protection.
Quite common are small crystals that
can be seen to grow a little way into
the main quartz. This brings the quality of
nurturing support and the development of new
understanding about the relationship of inner and
outer worlds to the crystal.

Much less common are whole crystals completely surrounded by another crystal growth.
These stones make fascinating meditation tools; the
enclosed crystal can represent aspects of the self.
Exploration of the many layers of reality and the
workings of creation can all be symbolically
accessed. These stones also give effective protection
from outside influences. A person who associates
with the inner crystal is thus surrounded by the
larger coherent field of the outer quartz. They
can also be helpful in bringing about wishes and
desires. Here the intention is the interior
crystal taking form on finer levels of reality
and growing out toward the physical.

PHANTOM CRYSTALS

Phantom crystals show the outlines and angles of
earlier stages in their growth. If the constituent
elements of the superheated solution changes
slightly during creation, small crystals of some
other mineral may form on the faces and sides of
the quartz. If there are still enough silicon and
oxygen atoms in solution, further growth can
occur. This can happen once or many times during a
crystal's formation, leaving permanent reminders
within the quartz. Some phantoms are clearly
visible, even opaque, shapes seen within the
transparent quartz. Others may be just
the faintest of lines that resolve into
planes when examined closely. The
angles and shape of a phantom will
always echo the final crystal form.
Phantom crystals make good meditation pieces. They encourage the
mind to dive to deeper levels of
awareness and can be helpful
tracing memories from long ago.
In a healing context, phantom
quartz can put past events into
correct perspective.

RIGHT *Intergrown crystals
have a particular affinity for
support and protection.*

Quartz Crystal Formations

Quartz crystals rarely grow in a perfect shape with six regular hexagonal sides meeting at a central point. The conditions of formation and environmental changes create a unique asymmetry and surface patterning. The size and shape of the resulting faces are thought to modify the sorts of energy each crystal can use.

GENERATOR CRYSTALS

A generator quartz has six equal sides and six faces meeting together at the apex. They are surprisingly rare. They have a general, all-purpose energy field useful for positively charging spaces and acting as a focus for healing.

ABOVE *The generator yields an all-purpose energy.*

TRANSMITTER CRYSTALS

This form has two seven-sided faces with perfect triangular faces between them. This combination of seven-three-seven enables it to receive information and transfer it to the user, either from the Higher Self or another source. After grounding, centering, and attuning yourself to the crystal, clearly define your purpose or question. Then project this thought into the stone through a triangular face held to your brow. Then leave the crystal in an upright position in a quiet place for a day. Later, sit with the crystal again, and in a receptive, quiet state place the triangle to your brow chakra (see pages 82–83), and absorb the information.

RIGHT *Use the transmitter to receive and transmit information.*

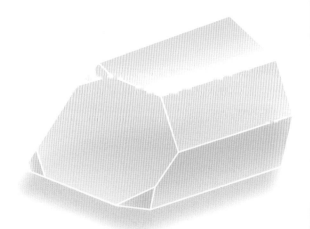

ABOVE *Channeling crystals are excellent aids to meditation, providing insight and inspiration.*

CHANNELING CRYSTALS

In this type of crystal, the largest face is seven-sided and is opposite a small triangular face. It can be used for meditation and for getting answers to specific questions. The large face of a channeling crystal helps to access the intuition and can be held to the brow chakra, or rubbed with the thumb. Where the crystal face is large enough, a channeling crystal makes a good tool for contemplation and scrying (see pages 176–179).

Occasionally it is possible to find a crystal that has characteristics of both transmitting and channeling crystals. These are known as trans-channeling or Dow crystals. They can be identified by their regular faces of equal proportions, with alternating seven-sided and triangular facets. Dow crystals are said to provide a continuous free flow of energy and information between all levels of creation and the self. These crystals can provide inspiration and a clear balancing environment wherever they are, and usually have a distinct personality.

WINDOW CRYSTALS

Many crystals exhibit small diamond or rhomboid faces between larger facets. Where the diamond is as large as other faces, with each angle joining the facet angles, it is known as a window crystal. Large window crystals are not common and are easy to identify. The diamond shape symbolizes both clarity of mind and the ability to reconcile information from different levels of the mind.

Window crystals are mainly used to assess the energies of another person or to look inside oneself. This can be done by holding the window toward the person for a while and then turning it to face the brow chakra allowing the images and impressions to register on your conscious awareness. For working with yourself, gaze into the window with the intention of understanding the issue of concern. Again, place the window to your brow chakra and gather impressions.

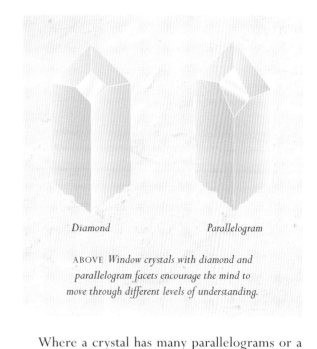

Diamond   *Parallelogram*

ABOVE *Window crystals with diamond and parallelogram facets encourage the mind to move through different levels of understanding.*

Where a crystal has many parallelograms or a combination of diamonds and parallelograms, each acts as a doorway to different levels of reality. To work with a window crystal, ground and center your energies (see pages 40–47) and quieten your mind. Gaze without effort into the window, and when there is subtle awareness of a wavelike motion or pulsing, close your eyes and breathe in time with the sensation. With a clear destination in mind, focus your awareness just above the top of your head and let the mind travel. As with all of this kind of work, have a grounding stone nearby for your return to normal consciousness.

ABOVE *Window crystals reflect thoughts and inner energies: useful for assessing others and for self-awareness.*

LEFT *Apply a crystal to the brow chakra to gain answers to a problem that has been troubling you.*

Where the window facet is not a regular diamond but a parallelogram, the quartz is sometimes called a time-link crystal. These crystals are used to shift awareness to different times, places, or dimensions. Some healers suggest a parallelogram skewed to the right will reveal futures, whereas one that leans to the left will view the past.

Crystals and Healing

There is no credible explanation why crystals and other gemstones should have any beneficial effect whatever on the human being from the point of view of Western medicine. Even though the properties of some minerals make possible the advanced technology that medical doctors use today, and they also are the raw materials with which pharmaceuticals are manufactured, there is no construct in mainstream science that allows for such an effect. This is hardly surprising. It is only in the last few years in the West that it has been recognized by modern medicine that the emotions and the mind may play a part in the healing process. Traditional healers, however, have known this through their own experiences for thousands of years.

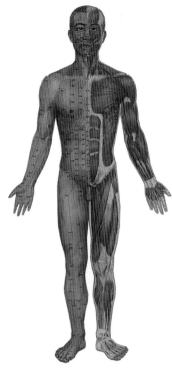

ABOVE *The meridians are invisible energy channels in the body. Blockages can lead to poor health.*

Crystal healers, together with practitioners of most other complementary and alternative methods of healing, view the human body in a completely different way from orthodox scientists and doctors. First, there is a holistic model where the physical body and its state of health are fully integrated with the emotional, mental and spiritual aspects of the individual. Health is seen more as a state of dynamic growth rather than a lack of symptoms. Second, subtle energy systems like electrical polarity, meridians, pressure points, chakras, aura, and subtle bodies are used to assess and correct what are perceived as energy imbalances. Not even the meridian system, used in healing for at least 3,000 years in the East, is acknowledged by most of the medical professions in the West, even though it is the most demonstrable of all the subtle body systems through sensitive electrical measurements.

Orthodox and complementary or alternative practitioners are speaking completely different languages. They have different maps of the human body where there is little or no correspondence. The only, and most important, shared viewpoints are the health and welfare of people.

Explaining how crystal healing might work in terms of accepted science is not going to convince many people. Until basic unbiased research is undertaken, the only evidence is subjective. However, it is possible to suggest by analogy how crystals might have such positive effects. Each crystal consists of a single chemical compound, that is, it has one molecule, which is repeated throughout its structure. It has inherent order and the ability to rapidly adjust to all kinds of environmental changes. A crystal has a fundamental stability and, at the vibrational level, can maintain a constant electromagnetic signature.

BELOW *From its basis as DNA, the complexities of the human body encompass myriad systems and interactions.*

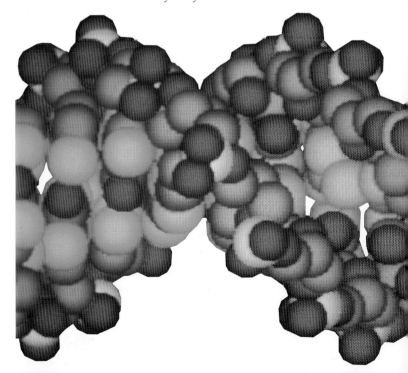

LEFT AND BELOW *In a body that is out of harmony, crystals sound a pure note amid conflicting vibrations.*

The human body, on the other hand, is built up from hundreds of thousands of different molecules, some simple, others of enormous complexity. Each molecule has its own vibratory pattern and way of interacting with surroundings.

The simplest unit of the body – the cell – contains DNA and RNA, each with thousands of molecules, as well as proteins, enzymes, and internal structures. Each of these has different electrical charges and biomagnetic fields and belongs to other systems of increasing size and complexity. By analogy, it may be possible to suggest the effects of a crystal upon the bioelectromagnetic field of the body.

Imagine the body as an enormous orchestra with millions of individual instruments representing different vibrational signatures. The instruments are all using the same basic score – like the sequences of individual DNA – but are following their own parts – the function of the cell, organ, system – and playing continuously without a break for a complete lifetime of 60, 70, or 80 years.

Over this length of time, one could imagine some players giving up altogether, some having their instrument go out of tune, and others losing their place in the score. When the body becomes stressed, there is an alteration in the functioning of the whole system, and this is like one instrument going slightly off-key or falling behind the others. A small disharmony enters the system.

The more disharmony there is, the more difficult it becomes for the remaining instruments to follow the score in front of them. Bringing a crystal into this cacophony of vibrations is like striking a tuning fork. One single, pure tone is constantly emitted with no change or variation, and this can act as a guide by which members of the orchestra can retune their instruments and reestablish local harmony.

Another view is that, since crystals are in fact the simplest forms of matter that exist throughout the universe, they may be seen to represent all possible combinations of energy. Since they reflect the basic harmonies of matter, it could be argued that crystals demonstrate the fundamental laws of nature. Because any state of disharmony within the individual is caused by an imbalance of these natural laws, then bringing the appropriate stones or crystals into the energy fields of the body can help to restore this harmony.

Wellness and Illness

The human being does not stop at the skin. Even orthodox science measures the thermal layer – equivalent to a planetary atmosphere – and a complex electromagnetic field generated by all the electrical and chemical processes in the body. This bioelectromagnetic envelope is extremely sensitive to all outside influences, which may only be registered subconsciously by the body.

Wellness can be understood as a stable state where every energetic influence upon us can be utilized in a positive way, or neutralized easily. Illness occurs when other patterns that don't belong to our own nature are so much stronger than our own and are in such contrast that they can disrupt our characteristic field patterns.

Where there is slightly less order in a system through inherent weakness or stress of some kind, there will be a place where the imbalance will begin to show itself. In the body there are many types of potentially life-threatening bacteria and viruses that do not cause any apparent ill effects until a stress of some kind disrupts the equilibrium of the body, giving them the chance to proliferate and cause health problems. Health is a delicate balance between a multitude of factors. Any one influence in our lives can increase the level of stress to such a degree that illness will manifest itself within the physical body.

ABOVE *Disease is like the tip of an iceberg: a whole chunk of associated problems may be submerged from view.*

As a holistic therapy, crystal healing does not concern itself primarily with physical symptoms or with disease. From a holistic viewpoint these are simply the tip of the iceberg. Removing the tip will not necessarily improve the situation. It cannot be seen, but the majority of the problem is still there, and there is a distinct probability that it will resurface.

We can visualize these stress factors as a series of steps or levels like sediments building up from an ocean floor. When the overall amount of stress rises to a certain height, it will appear above the surface of the sea. This is when symptoms of illness will appear. Health can be restored, and the symptoms will vanish once more if a therapy is able to reduce the amount of stress in one or more of these levels, thus reducing the total height. A sudden increase in any one level, such as emotional trauma or a buildup of environmental pollutants, may push us into a disease state. The form that the disease takes will very often be with the uppermost stress layer. If there is an underlying chronic infection of the throat, we will tend to get recurrent throat infections whenever the body becomes run down. Effective healing can thus be defined as any system that releases enough stress from the underlying energy structures of the body so self repair and self regulation can be restored.

It is important to address the particular type of stress that each individual has acquired in the largest amount. If lifestyle is a major stress-creating factor, balancing meridians might reduce symptoms for a while, but the lifestyle stress will continue to dominate and increase. Removing stress from the lifestyle will reduce the overall stress-loading by a much greater degree and is more likely to achieve lasting results.

Aquamarine

Moonstone

Blue Lace Agate

LEFT *Crystals superimpose a stronger coherent energy upon the body, causing it to regain health.*

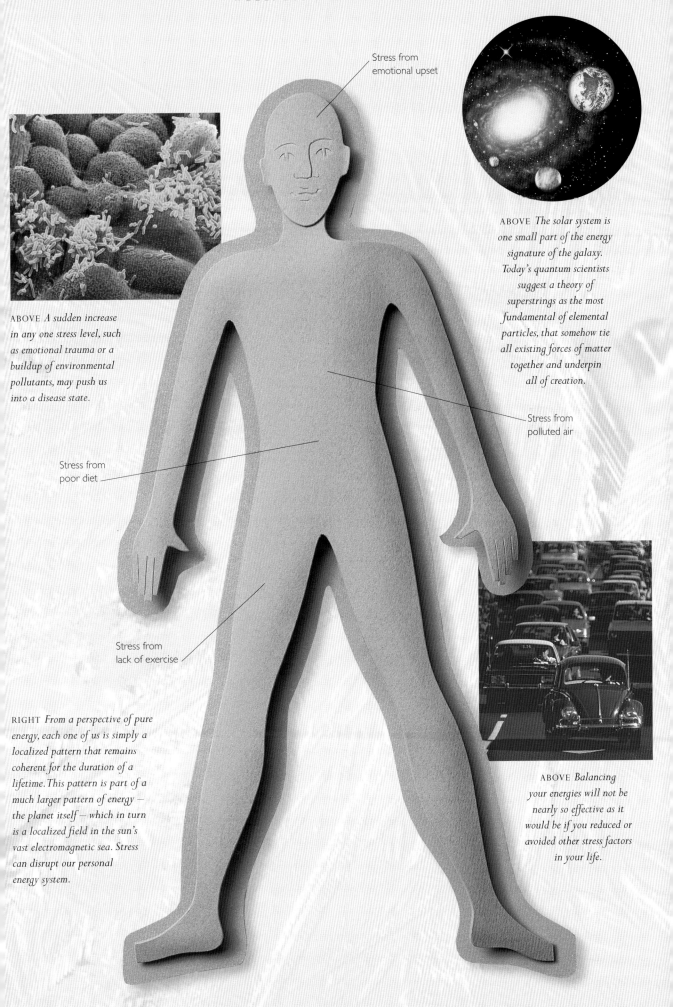

Stress from
emotional upset

ABOVE *The solar system is
one small part of the energy
signature of the galaxy.
Today's quantum scientists
suggest a theory of
superstrings as the most
fundamental of elemental
particles, that somehow tie
all existing forces of matter
together and underpin
all of creation.*

ABOVE *A sudden increase
in any one stress level, such
as emotional trauma or a
buildup of environmental
pollutants, may push us
into a disease state.*

Stress from
polluted air

Stress from
poor diet

Stress from
lack of exercise

RIGHT *From a perspective of pure
energy, each one of us is simply a
localized pattern that remains
coherent for the duration of a
lifetime. This pattern is part of a
much larger pattern of energy —
the planet itself — which in turn
is a localized field in the sun's
vast electromagnetic sea. Stress
can disrupt our personal
energy system.*

ABOVE *Balancing
your energies will not be
nearly so effective as it
would be if you reduced or
avoided other stress factors
in your life.*

Healing Session

Crystal healing is a very individual therapy. Healers work in a way most suited to themselves. Some use crystals as an adjunct to massage or reflexology; others use crystals combined with spiritual healing. At the first session, the healer will take the patient's case history. This will probably include asking about any serious illnesses, hospitalizations, broken bones, and accidents, as well as current medicines or treatments and whether other complementary help is being sought. The healer may also note any emotional or life trauma around the time of illness onset.

ABOVE Be prepared to give medical and lifestyle details to the healer.

Especially on the initial visit, many people find that it is the first time they have been given the opportunity to describe fully their circumstances and feelings about their condition. A crystal healer, unless also a doctor, will not give any medical opinions, nor will they comment on medical practices, but can offer support for the human and emotional aspects of the problems faced. After this talk, the crystal worker will begin the crystal healing work.

Before seeing the patient, the healer will have centered and grounded him- or herself (see pages 40–47), and may also have spent some time in prayer or in meditation. All stones will have been cleansed and charged, and the working space cleared of all imbalances before healing can begin.

It is best to remove shoes and wear light, loose, comfortable clothing. The patient may be asked to remove any jewelry to ensure the body energies are not masked by other electromagnetic fields. The healer may now assess what healing work is a priority using techniques such as dowsing or muscle testing or intuitively scanning the person's auric field with a hand. Stones will be placed on or around the patient, or the healer may work with hand-held crystals (see pages 134–135)

Some healers work in near silence or with gentle background music. Others ask for feedback to establish how the patient is feeling, whether there are any changes in perceptions or body sensations. These are simple signs that the crystals are beginning to regulate and balance energies; it will not necessarily mean anything in terms of assessment.

Crystal healing is primarily focused on removing the underlying stresses from the subtle energy systems of the body. If the healer locates an area that needs a lot of work, the patient might be asked whether any physical symptoms have been noticed there, but the imbalance may never have reached a physical level. Most healers will appreciate the patient relating experiences of sensations, memory, or visual impressions received while stones are in place but will also understand if the patient is so deeply relaxed that communication is reduced to a simple yes or no. Any feelings of discomfort or disorientation should be mentioned to the healer, as he or she can usually modify or ease them.

BELOW Discuss any recent emotional upsets so that the healer sees a complete health picture.

VISITING A CRYSTAL HEALER

LEFT *The healer may suggest a particular stone to hold during the initial discussion before a healing session.*

INTRODUCTORY DISCUSSION

The first step in the crystal healing session will be some recording of case history; the healer will review the patient's current state of health and his or her past experiences. Sometimes, particularly where the patient is distressed, the healer might suggest that one or more crystals are held in the hand during the introductory conversation to bring calm and create an initial balance.

THE HEALING SESSION

During the first session and subsequent sessions, the healer will use specific crystals to balance the patient's chakras, energy centers, and other subtle systems in order to allow the experience of increased harmony to be programed into the body.

LEFT *Several techniques may be used in one session, or a single placement may be enough.*

AFTER THE HEALING SESSION

The healing might end with a brief discussion of what has been addressed. Further visits may be considered worthwhile, as crystal healing works best as a cumulative process. A crystal balance once a month for three or four visits will really help to maximize the benefits in many cases. The healer might suggest a stone to carry or use at home, a gem essence to take, or may run through some simple exercises or meditations to help maintain energy balance between sessions.

RIGHT *The healing might end with a brief discussion of the energy work and any sensations the patient has experienced during the session.*

Grounding and Centering

Of all the qualities needed to be an effective healer, perhaps the most important is that degree of focus and awareness which has become generally known as being centered and grounded. Both states are intimately related. It is not possible to remain grounded without being centered, and vice versa. In all crystal healing, we ourselves are the machines that assess and calibrate. Grounding is making sure we are plugged into the correct power source, while centering is making sure we start with the dials at neutral so all readings are as accurate as possible. While grounding ensures that we do not accumulate excess energy, centering enables us to start any crystal work from a stable, clear base.

Grounding means being completely focused and present at all times. Subjectively this is experienced as a feeling of solidity and security. There is a quality of mental focus and stillness, and of having self control in any situation. A lack of being grounded is experienced as nervousness, an inability to focus on the present or to concentrate because of a wandering mind, or feelings of instability. When we are not grounded, energy either dissipates immediately or builds up to intolerable levels that may express itself as a loss of temper or restless discomfort. Being grounded means that all energy that passes through the body can remain in balance, with any excess flowing into the earth where it is safely dissipated. This helps to prevent us from being overwhelmed or feeling dazed or disoriented, which is essential when using crystals as part of the healing process. Habitual lack of grounding leads to a chronic imbalance of subtle energy, particularly in the chakra system, which can lead to burnout or health problems.

We are centered when all physical, mental, and emotional energies are integrated and balanced. It is similar to a state of physical balance where the body is relaxed but able to make adjustments to keep in position. To remain centered, there must be awareness of personal boundaries and the flow of energy. Being centered allows us to experience a state of calm receptivity in which it is possible to recognize intuitive thoughts and feelings.

Methods for grounding tend to reinforce our connection downward to the earth, and counteract any feelings we may have of floating off into space. Methods for centering tend to focus on awareness of the body's center of gravity. There are many ways of centering and grounding, some of which work better in certain situations than in others.

Before and after every healing exercise, a healer should carry out a grounding procedure. The more they are practiced, the quicker the body recognizes when it is out of balance and the more effective any correction becomes. The process of healing requires working within someone else's states of imbalance. If healers fail to ensure their own balanced equilibrium, they risk creating greater imbalance by inappropriate actions or taking risks and absorbing the imbalances of their patients.

Being grounded means having a sound connection to planet Earth, and this creates a circuit of flowing energy and protection. Being fully aware within the body is one of the best protections from imbalanced energy of any kind. There are some people who habitually live in an ungrounded state, frequently equating their lack of focus with spirituality. It is useful in these instances to think of the analogy of the tree that can only send its branches up and out if its roots are secure in the ground. No roots equals no growth, no tree.

LEFT *Being centered is like achieving a perfect balance through awareness of the body's center of gravity.*

ABOVE *Before beginning a healing session, a competent healer should feel focused and balanced. An effective grounding and centering technique involves visualizing a tree: imagine strong branches reaching upward, balanced by firm, healthy roots.*

BASIC GROUNDING SET

TIGER'S EYE
May have an attractive banded appearance.

SCHORL
Identified by its clearly striated sides.

SMOKY QUARTZ
Varies in color from smoky yellow to brown and black.

JASPER
An opaque, usually red, yellow, or brown stone.

HEMATITE
A dark, shiny mineral containing about 70 percent iron.

PASSIVE GROUNDING TECHNIQUES

Little or no thought is required for passive grounding techniques, which makes them ideal when there is such a loss of balance that it is impossible to focus attention. There are several stones that can be used to ground one's energies effectively. Those included here work for most people, but there are always exceptions. Get to know which are most effective for you personally. In general, deep red, dark, and earthy colored stones will help to focus energy within the physical body and reconnect it to the earth.

Black tourmaline, sometimes called schorl, is a very good grounding stone and will also help protect from negativity. Smoky or black quartz can also work well. Minerals of iron, such as lodestone (magnetic iron ore) and hematite (iron oxide), are equally effective. Often more gentle in their action are stones like tiger's eye, iron pyrites (fool's gold), dark citrine quartz, and the dark red stones like garnet and jasper (red quartz) that will help to ground by increasing physical energy.

The effect of grounding stones can be felt if they are held in the hands, worn, or placed near the body. If the stones have natural points, known as terminations, the technique is usually more effective if the points are facing down toward the ground. This encourages the grounding of energy. Likewise, putting the stone between the feet if seated, or below the feet, between the legs, or close to the base of the spine if lying down, encourages the base chakra and those grounding centers near the feet to balance body energies. Jewelry made with grounding stones will help keep a person grounded and protected, though ideally other more permanent methods should also be learned.

Most forms of crystal healing will benefit from the addition of one or more grounding stones placed near the base of the spine or near the feet. These allow for the stabilization of any healing work carried out, so that changes can be more easily integrated permanently into the subtle energy systems of the human body. Without grounding stones, disorientation can occur and corrections may not last when the stones are finally removed.

LEFT *Place smoky quartz crystals at the base of the throat and spine in order to collect thoughts and energies.*

GROUNDING LAYOUT

This will ground and center in a couple of minutes:

◆ Place a smoky quartz crystal point downward at the base of the throat.

◆ Place a second smoky quartz crystal at the base of the spine between the legs, with the point facing toward the feet.

ADDITIONAL EXERCISES

Focusing attention on the physical body can be a useful way of becoming grounded. Any moderate activity or exercise, particularly if it is in contact with the earth, will help.

◆ Walking, running, gardening, stamping your feet, dancing.

◆ Eat or drink a little. Once the digestive system is occupied, a feeling of solidity returns.

◆ Sip a little cool water. Water helps to speed up healing corrections by balancing the electrochemical systems of the body.

◆ Hot, sweet tea or a piece of chocolate are also effective.

ATTENTION EXERCISE

Breathe through a slightly opened mouth. Focusing on the roof of the mouth, notice that you feel the cool air as you inhale, but no sensation when you exhale. Focusing on this for a moment or two helps to calm the mind, centering awareness, into the meridians of the body.

ABOVE *Exercise can be used for grounding and improves all body systems.*

COOK'S HOOKUP

Kinesiology uses body movement and touch to rebalance energy. There is a useful technique derived from this called Cook's Hookup that will help both to ground and center when energies are scattered.

Because it integrates the left and right sides of the brain, this exercise reduces confusion and lack of co-ordination as well as easing stress and upset. It is best to perform the exercise while sitting in a chair.

1 Cross your ankles, right over left. If you are left-handed, reverse all procedures so it will be left over right.

2 Cross your wrists in front of you, right over left.

3 Now roll your hands so the palms are facing each other.

4 Interlace your fingers and then lay your hands on your lap.

Palms facing

Interlaced fingers

5 Relax, close your eyes, and breathe easily. As you settle, your feelings or emotions may seem to intensify. This is part of the stress-releasing process, so simply let the feelings come and they will subside.

6 When you feel calm and restored to normal balance, unclasp your hands and uncross your ankles.

7 Now place your feet flat on the floor.

8 Rest your hands in your lap with just the fingertips touching each other as if you were holding a small ball between your palms. If you keep this position for half a minute, the benefits will last longer.

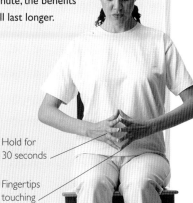

Hold for 30 seconds

Fingertips touching

ACTIVE GROUNDING TECHNIQUES

These grounding exercises are very effective so long as you are able to do them without getting distracted. If you don't have enough focus, return to one of the more physical passive grounding techniques mentioned on page 43.

When your energies feel scattered and have no direction and the mind is cluttered or racing – try any of the following imaging techniques.

WATER IMAGING TECHNIQUE

Imagine yourself immersed under a waterfall or fountain. Completely surround yourself with the descending streams and imagine them also washing through you and then sinking deep into the earth.

A more domestic image would be to imagine water faucets at the ends of your toes that you can turn on to drain away any excess energy, emotion, or tension into the earth.

BREATH IMAGING TECHNIQUE

Imagine that your breath is entering and leaving your body through the feet. When you inhale, simply draw the air up through the soles of your feet and send the exhalation out the same way. This will very quickly steady you as breathing deeper and more slowly than usual has a calming effect.

RIGHT *Picture a waterfall cascading through you and washing away tension.*

TREE MEDITATION

There are many types of Tree Meditations. They are easy to visualize and work quickly. Once you have become familiar with the imagery, a simple reminder will be all that is necessary to re-establish the grounding.

❖ Sit comfortably in a chair with your feet placed flat on the ground.

❖ Relax your arms and shoulders with hands in your lap.

❖ Breathe deeply a couple of times and feel yourself sinking comfortably into your chair.

❖ Start by imagining that roots are growing from your feet, spreading out and down into the earth.

❖ Continue seeing the roots spread, and become aware of the increased sense of security and solidity you feel.

❖ When the roots have reached as far as they can, feel the earth feeding you nourishing, life-supporting energy that flows back through the roots and begins to fill your body.

❖ Feel the earth's energy filling your lower body and gradually flowing upward. As the energy reaches your arms and chest, let it to spread out over your head.

❖ As it flows outward, the energy forms branches, twigs, and leaves. Feel the sunlight warming every part as energy flows back into your body.

❖ The energy is now flowing upward from the earth through your body, while the sun's energy is flowing down into you. Maintain this deep connection with the sun and earth for a few moments.

❖ Turn your attention to the heart where these two great flows merge. Feel the stability and sense of security.

❖ End by turning your attention to the area of the heart once more, then to your breath and finally become aware of the whole of your body, especially the feet.

❖ Sit for a moment or two and gently bring yourself back to reality.

ABOVE *Visualize the sturdy structure of a tree supported by spreading roots.*

CENTERLINE BREATHING

This visualization helps to focus attention on the central axis of the body using the breath to draw up energy along the mid-line.

Stand in a relaxed position, with your feet slightly apart, shoulders back and arms hanging loosely. Remember to keep relaxed and don't strain to visualize – this will come with practice.

9 When you have finished, relax, take a moment or two to resume normal activity. With practice you will be able to summon up this visualization whether you are seated, standing, or walking.

1 Imagine a line extending through your body from below your feet to the top of your head, positioned just in front of your backbone.

8 You may find that your breathing automatically settles into a slightly different pattern. Don't worry if this happens.

2 In your mind's eye, extend that line of energy down into the earth as deep as you can go.

7 Continue this new cycle for a few minutes by repeating steps 5 and 6 so that you are alternately breathing in from the earth and out into the universe, then in from the universe and out into the earth.

3 With each breath imagine pulling energy up the line and into your body.

4 As you exhale, let your breath pass down into the earth, each time you exhale pushing the line a little deeper toward the center of the earth.

6 With your next breath, draw universal energy into the lungs and breathe it out into the earth.

5 After a minute or two, move your attention to the top end of the line. Now, after you have drawn in breath from the earth, breathe it out into the universe through the top of your head.

CENTERING TECHNIQUES

Many traditional forms of meditation can be used for centering ourselves, although it is useful to discover those methods that create the desired result in only a few minutes. Focusing the attention on the breath can be very effective. Any simple yoga pranayama technique can be used.

BREATHING FOCUS

Sit comfortably with your back upright. If support is needed, a firm cushion near your lower back will give great stability without restricting your breathing. Close your eyes and let your attention focus on the center of your chest. Take long, deep breaths through the nose. Continue for at least three minutes.

SOUND FOCUS

Making use of sound can be a very quick way to return your body to a centered state. After settling

down a little, by closing the eyes and taking a few slow, deep breaths, strike a tuning fork, bell, singing bowl, gong, or wind chime – anything that reverberates and gives a sustained, clear and piercing sound when it is struck. Simply listen to the sound until it fades right away and is no longer perceptible. Continue sounding the note until you feel relaxed and your mind has cleared.

ABOVE *The clear tone of a bell quietens the mind.*

SIGHT FOCUS

The nature of clear quartz makes it an ideal tool for centering and focusing. To get the best results, use a large, self-standing clear quartz crystal or a shaped stone such as an egg or sphere. Place the crystal at a comfortable distance from you so your eyes can rest without straining as you gaze into the center of the quartz crystal. After a few moments gently close your eyes and rest. If there is still some agitation, repeat the process.

VOICE FOCUS

Making an open "AAAH" sound for as long as is comfortable causes the bones and soft tissues of the body to resonate gently and relaxes tension that has accumulated in muscles, particularly the chest, head, and throat. AAH is the simplest sound that can be made. It doesn't involve any tension in the vocal cords or mouth. Simply breathe out through the mouth and begin the sound. The volume or tone of the sound isn't important. Focus your attention on the quality of the vibration for as long as it can be sustained. Repeat the

Clear Quartz

ABOVE *Place a large crystal in front of you and focus on it for a few moments.*

process as many times as you like. Some people may be familiar with chanting other sounds such as "OM" or "Aum." This, too, can be a useful centering device, but it requires more vocal control and a little more effort.

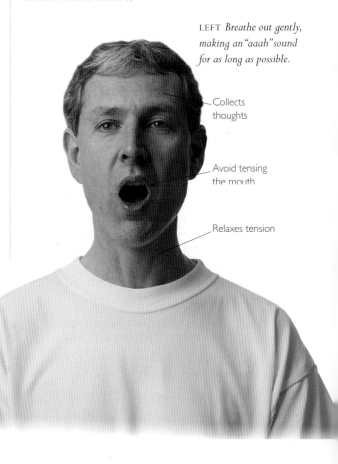

LEFT *Breathe out gently, making an "aaah" sound for as long as possible.*

Collects thoughts

Avoid tensing the mouth

Relaxes tension

TAPPING IN

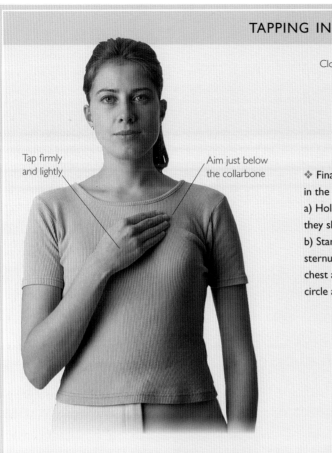

Tap firmly and lightly

Aim just below the collarbone

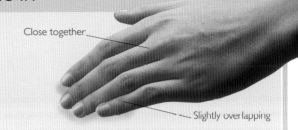

Close together

Slightly overlapping

❖ Finally, the thymus and navel tap can be combined in the following way:

a) Hold the fingertips of one hand close together so that they slightly overlap each other.

b) Start off halfway down the center of the chest on the sternum, tapping the fingers onto the rib cage and upper chest at small 1-inch intervals in a counterclockwise circle about 4–6 inches (10–15 centimeters) in diameter.

Focus on center of chest

Tap in a circle

Tapping in brings into balance all the major energy meridians of the body for about 20 minutes. It is also one of the simplest and most effective techniques for making sure that a stable, centered energy is kept in place. Following are a couple of variations.

❖ The simplest procedure is a firm, light tapping with the fingertips on the area of the upper chest just below where the collarbone, (clavicle) meets the breast bone (sternum). This is the approximate placement of the thymus gland, which is important for maintenance of the subtle energy balance in the body. If, while the thymus is being tapped, your other hand is placed palm open, over your navel, the balancing effect tends to last longer.

❖ Another variation of tapping in is to tap counterclockwise as you are looking down on your chest, in a circle about 3–6 inches (7–15 centimeters) away from the thymus point. Each tap of the fingers should be about 1 inch apart. Repeat the circle about 20 times.

❖ Many important meridian channels pass close to the navel. Tapping around the navel about 3–4 inches (7–10 centimeters) away in a clockwise direction also has a balancing and centering effect.

c) When the starting point is reached again, continue tapping down onto the abdomen, this time creating a clockwise circle around the navel, then returning to the center of the chest. This creates a figure-eight pattern.

d) Repeat this 15–20 times.

Tapping in should become an almost automatic process. It's a first step to creating focus and accuracy before any other work with healing or crystals is to begin. The more the body systems become used to existing in a state of harmonious balance, the easier it is to maintain balance and the more apparent it becomes when we occasionally lose that balance, thus ensuring that we notice and correct imbalances sooner.

Protection and Support

There are times in healing where the healer uncovers issues that are deep-seated, stressful, and difficult to examine. Even with problems we long to be rid of, there can be a fear associated with losing something familiar in exchange for an unknown beginning. At other times, a problem appears in a patient that closely echoes a difficult personal experience for the healer. This can lead to a confusion of emotions and energy fluctuations in which balance can easily be lost. Grounding and remaining centered is the best method of coping in these circumstances, but sometimes a little extra help is needed. A simple procedure for checking whether both healer and patient are in need of protection and support can avoid unnecessary stress and can make a crystal healing session much more effective.

A healing session can be likened to a small boat dragging a pond to clear out old debris collected on the bottom. When a large object begins to move, it can create numerous ripples and waves that might seem likely to overturn the boat. Protection and support techniques act like a steady hand that stops the violent rocking of the boat.

Protection, in this context, is seen as something that helps a person to maintain his or her own energy integrity in a situation in which another strong energy source may interfere with or influence them unduly. If, for example, you are meeting someone who makes you feel threatened, a protection technique would allow you to deal with the situation free from fear. Similarly, if your working environment is full of different electromagnetic frequencies that prove to be tiring or enervating, protection may be appropriate.

ABOVE *A crystal healing session can act as a calming influence on the ripples that upset and disturb our lives.*

While protection offers a means to withstand strong external pressures, support strengthens us internally, neutralizing or removing some of our inner resistance to positive change. Support is like an encouraging word from a guide helping us through tricky terrain.

There are many factors in our lives – some seen, some unseen – that can temporarily reduce our effectiveness as a healer. The cause might be something mundane, such as a certain food disagreeing with us, or subtle, such as an astronomical alignment. It is not important to know the exact source of the difficulty so long as it can be rendered harmless.

After an initial centering and grounding exercise, it is a good idea to carry out a check by dowsing or muscle testing (see pages 96–105) in order to learn whether protection and support are needed before any crystal healing work is begun. Should the response be positive, it will then be necessary to find the solutions.

If you are working with another person, check for both of you. This is particularly important when you know that there are deep underlying stresses or very important issues to be explored during the crystal healing session.

PROCEDURE

Dowse or muscle-test using the question: "Do I, or does this person, need protection and support before continuing with this healing procedure?"

◆ If the answer is no, continue as normal, but if the situation becomes emotionally charged during the course of the session, check again.

◆ If the answer is yes, then determine which steps need to be taken.

PROTECTING AND SUPPORT CATEGORIES WITH EXERCISES

There are many ways of gaining the necessary support and protection. Choose the one that works best for you in a given situation.

Grounding: Try exercises such as tree meditation, breathing, centerline breathing, or food for grounding.

Nutrition: Food for extra energy, vitamin or mineral supplementation, or a drink of water.

ABOVE *Eat lots of fresh, unprocessed foods, preferably produced organically.*

Exercises: Cook's Hookup, meridian massage, tapping in, cross-crawl.

Sound: Mantra, affirmation, toning, chanting or singing, listening to music or sound, playing music or sound.

Smell: Essential oils to smell, essential oils to wear, any other fragrance.

LEFT *Evocative fragrances help to form a protective bubble.*

Sight: Visualizing a color; looking at a color or combinations of colors, patterns, symbols, mandalas, images (people, animals, a landscape, etc.).

Crystals: Wearing a crystal, carrying a crystal, meditating or attuning to a stone, looking at a stone.

Any activity, object, sense, or symbol may act as an energy support in different circumstances. It is fairly common to find one or two methods that work well for you in a wide range of instances. For example, you may always find that using one particular crystal or color is satisfactory.

Although the actions required in many cases may seem magically simple, it is worth remembering that every shape, sound, color, and object has its own characteristic energy pattern. When chosen with care and precision, these can act like keys to unlock the stubborn doors within us that prevent the development of our potential.

ABOVE *Certain symbols may assist with energy support, like this Buddhist "wheel of life" painting.*

LEFT *Wear a carefully selected piece of crystal.*

Exploring with Crystals

It is a good idea to begin by doing a few simple experiments just to see what differences you notice when using crystals and gemstones. In order to increase your awareness and sensitivity, get used to noticing the differences in how you feel before, during, and after each session. There are two basic methods of placement: one with the points of all the crystals facing inward, the other with all the points facing out from the body. Generally speaking, when the points are outward, they help to release imbalances, and when pointing inward, they infuse the body with energy.

Take time to note down your experiences. This will eventually speed up your growth in confidence and the ability to use your intuition.

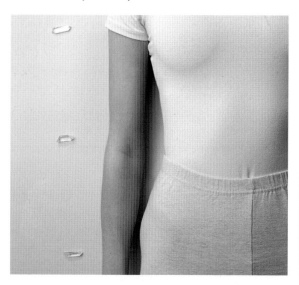

ABOVE *Begin with a simple crystal placement. Space the crystals out along one side of the body and then on the other.*

ANALYZING HOW YOU FEEL

1 Lie down comfortably for about 10 minutes. After this time, note how your body feels, what you were thinking about, and so on.
2 Continue your normal routine for half an hour at least.
3 Then lie down again for about 10 minutes. This time use a simple placement of stones, such as one of those suggested here, and again record how you feel, your thoughts, etc.

SIMPLE PLACEMENTS

Take three clear quartz crystals, preferably ones with naturally terminated points, and try each of the following in sequence, spending two or three minutes on each.

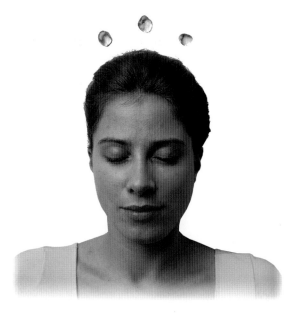

ABOVE *Lay the crystals around your head, first pointing them outward, then turn them inward.*

1 Place all three crystals, evenly spaced, next to the left side of the body. Start with all the crystals pointing in toward you, and after a minute or so turn their points away from your body.
2 Next put all three crystals next to the right side of your body. Again, begin with their points facing inward and then turn them outward.
3 Now try with all three stones placed around your head – points outward followed by points in.
4 Follow this by positioning the quartz crystals, points down, below the feet. You will probably notice a difference in sensations within your body. Perhaps your mind will become quieter or busier than usual, your breathing may alter. Make a note of your experiences, even if it's as vague as feeling comfortable or fidgety. When you have clear results, try with the same stones, but this time place them on your body and see how your experiences differ.

ABOVE *Clasp the crystal and imagine your breath passing to and from it.*

PRACTICAL EXERCISES

We all experience the energy of crystals in different ways. It is much easier to notice a contrasting feeling or sensation than an energy. The following exercises will help to identify in which ways a crystal may be acting upon our subtle energy systems and where we might be sensitive to its characteristics. Remember to cleanse the crystals carefully before beginning.

With every new stone that you use, it is helpful to repeat the following procedures.

1 Hold the stone in both hands close to the solar plexus. As you breathe out, imagine your breath passing over the top of the stone. When you breathe in, see your breath entering the crystal and being drawn into your body. The breath creates a cycle passing from you through the crystal and back into your body. Continue the breathing process for a while and then relax. This is an easy and effective way to integrate a crystal's energy into yourself.

2 Look closely at the crystal, examining it from as many different angles as possible. Close your eyes, imagine the shapes, and then look again. Then relax and hold the stone in both hands for a minute or two. Make a note of any thoughts or impressions.

ABOVE *Study the crystal from all angles; imagine it with your eyes shut.*

3 Take a good look at the crystal and then quickly draw it large on a sheet of paper. Don't worry about accuracy. Now, imagine and draw how energy seems to move in, through, and around

LEFT *Sketch the crystal, expressing your intuitive feelings about it.*

the crystal. Note down any words, thoughts, or images that occur during this time. It is important to relax and be playful here. Suspend any esthetic or analytical judgments you have if they interfere with your impressions.

RIGHT *Complete the sequence by meditating on the crystal for a short while.*

4 a) Place the crystal on a surface a comfortable distance in front of you. Sit quietly with your eyes closed for a moment.

b) Open your eyes and look at the crystal before you.

c) Close your eyes again and sit quietly.

d) Reach out and pick up the crystal and hold it in both hands for a little while with your eyes closed.

e) After a minute or two, place the stone back in front of you.

f) Repeat this picking up and putting down several times and notice any changes in how you feel.

VARIATIONS

▲ Pick up and hold the crystal alternately in your left and right hands. Notice any differences.

▲ Hold or place the stone for a couple of minutes on your main energy centers. The center of the forehead, the heart, and the solar plexus are very often the most sensitive.

▲ Try below the feet and above the head as well.

▲ Place the stone close to your body while lying down. Move it to different sides and distances from you.

Simple Healing Layouts

These simple healing layouts are intended to restore the body's natural balance of energies in a general way, and help to bring relaxation and a settled, receptive state of mind. If the stones are very small, smooth, or irregular, you may want to tape them in place.

Addresses crown chakra

Works on heart chakra

Anchors energy

LEFT *Clear quartz will clear and balance the mind and upper chakras.*

Clear Quartz

BALANCING AND CALMING

Place a clear quartz point outward at the crown of the head, a small rose quartz in the center of the chest, and a smoky quartz, point downward, close to the base of the spine, between the legs.

Rose Quartz

RIGHT *This layout energizes and balances the chakra energies; it also helps energy flow.*

Relaxes heart and throat

Smoky Quartz

Quiets unnecessary energy

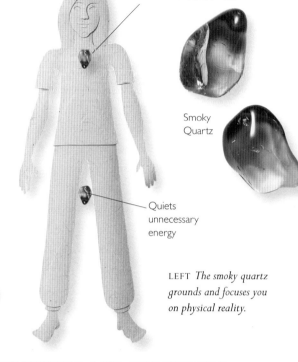

LEFT *The smoky quartz grounds and focuses you on physical reality.*

CENTERING AND GROUNDING

This is an excellent way to bring yourself back down to earth when your thoughts and energies are scattered, or when you feel confused. Two smoky quartz crystals are used; one is placed point down at the base of the throat, just above the collar bone, the second stone is placed, point down, at the base of the spine, between the legs.

Energizes chakras

Soothes and settles the mind

Balances chakras

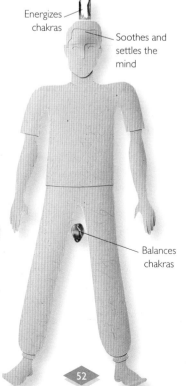

FEELING DISORIENTED

This layout is for when you are feeling not quite right but can't figure out why or what to do. Clear quartz is placed at the crown of the head and smoky quartz between the legs, close to the spine. The third stone is placed in the middle of the forehead and can be either a turquoise or a piece of lapis lazuli. If you have both, you might feel more comfortable with one more than the other.

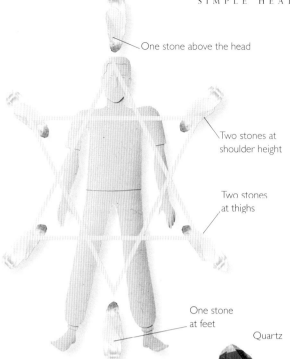

One stone above the head

Two stones at shoulder height

Two stones at thighs

One stone at feet

Quartz

ABOVE *Stones on the body can be held in place by tape*

THE SEAL OF SOLOMON

Also called the Star of David, this layout uses six quartz crystals and forms a six-pointed star. As a healing layout, it is effective and versatile in a wide range of situations.

Begin by placing the stones, points outward, to release any imbalances and tensions. After three or four minutes, reverse the crystals so the points face inward, to recharge your energy fields. Be aware of how you feel during this process. If you find that you feel uncomfortable, try changing the direction of the crystals. It is fairly common to find that the charging process needs less time than the cleansing.

The Seal of Solomon can also be used on and around smaller parts of the body to help reduce pain or to give some extra healing energy. Tape stones onto the body. To enhance or direct the healing, put a stone in the center of the star. For example, copper, malachite, or turquoise can reduce swelling; rose quartz or carnelian will calm and heal.

LEFT *The star represents the elements and the connection between heaven and earth.*

RECHARGING BODY AND SPIRIT

There is a very simple way to re-energize the body and mind by placing a quartz crystal on a pulse point or by using several crystals on different pulses. If you are using a single quartz, hold its largest facet gently to the skin. Imagine drawing the sun's rays into your body through the crystal. Doing this in direct sunlight enhances the process.

BELOW *Place crystals on both wrists to regulate body energies.*

CRYSTALS AND BREATHING

1. Inhale to bring energy into your aura
2. Hold your breath for 3-6 seconds and focus your awareness into a crystal in your hand.
3. With a forceful, rapid breathing out, the accumulated energy is projected out through the top of the crystal with intensified force.
4. Point to a specific area that needs healing and use several cycles of the sequence.

Quartz Crystal

LEFT *Hold the stone in both hands and draw energy through it.*

SELF-HEALING

1. Place a crystal over a chakra area (see pages 70–92).
2. While inhaling, place both hands on top of the stone and draw energy through it into the chakra.
3. Hold your breath for 3-6 seconds and concentrate the energy in that area.
4. Exhale forcefully and throw hands out to each side of the body, dispersing negative energy.
5. With the next slow inhalation, bring your hands back to the chakra.
6. Repeat several times.

PART THREE

CRYSTALS AND COLOR

Of all the qualities that attract us to crystals, it is very often the color that we notice first. Many crystals originally got their names from their color; and before the invention of more precise measuring devices, color was one of the main ways a stone was identified.

Color is how the human eye and brain interpret different parts of the energy we call light. Each color has specific effects on the human system, physically, emotionally, and mentally. White light, which reflects all energies, is made up of all the colors in the light spectrum. By learning the main properties of each of these colors, we are able to identify some of the characteristic healing qualities of any crystal — simply from the color that it displays.

ABOVE *The color of a crystal is an inherent part of its appeal.*

Color and Light

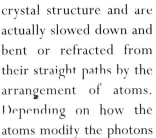

CLEAR CRYSTAL
Light rays are bent by the crystal's atom arrangement.

The coloration of a crystal results from how it interacts with light, and this is dependent upon the atomic structure of the mineral. There are two main types of mineral colors. Idcochromatic minerals are those whose chemical composition directly affects their color. Thus minerals based on copper all tend to be different shades of blue or green, and minerals of chromium are always red or orange. Allochromatic minerals, on the other hand, are colored by small amounts of impurities, usually no more than a few atoms of some other element, that create anomalies within the crystal lattice. These minerals can vary a lot in color, depending on what other atoms are present. So crystals like quartz, fluorite and corundum have many varieties of color and may be given different names: corundum, when pure, is colorless; when red it is called ruby; when blue, it is called sapphire. Likewise, violet quartz is called amethyst, yellow quartz is citrine, and so on.

In opaque stones the colors we see are those frequencies of light that are not absorbed into the crystal lattice. Where a stone absorbs all frequencies of light, it appears black; and where absorption is uniform across the spectrum, the stone looks gray. White stones reflect the full color spectrum without absorbing any light at all.

With a crystal that is transparent or translucent, light rays enter the crystal structure and are actually slowed down and bent or refracted from their straight paths by the arrangement of atoms. Depending on how the atoms modify the photons of light, the crystal will shift a full sunlight spectrum toward the slower frequencies, thus appearing red, or toward the faster frequencies of blue and violet. With allochromatic stones, the minute anomalies in the crystal structure carry different energy charges that capture proton particles and form centers of coloration.

In some crystals the color changes depend upon at what angle it is viewed. This is known as pleochromism and occurs when the internal structures and symmetry of the mineral break up separate rays of light in different ways depending on where the light enters the crystal. Diffraction is where the light becomes polarized, shifting its speed and frequency, and eventually emerges from the crystals at different angles. So not only does a crystal display its internal atomic structure in the ways the external angles and planes are arranged, but also in the way the complex lattice modifies light energy by reflection, refraction, and diffraction. Color plays a very important role that should not be underestimated in the process of crystal healing. Visible light is one small part of the vast electromagnetic spectrum of energy that bathes the physical universe. The human eye has evolved to recognize this part of the energy as sunlight and starlight. The characteristic energy vibration or light frequency of each part of the

TOURMALINE
This ideochromatic stone can be white, black, red, green, brown, blue, or varicolored.

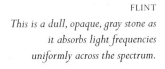

JET
An opaque black stone, which is a form of soft coal.

FLINT
This is a dull, opaque, gray stone as it absorbs light frequencies uniformly across the spectrum.

MALACHITE
An ideochromatic stone which was once ground to make a bright green dye.

REFRACTION AND DIFFRACTION

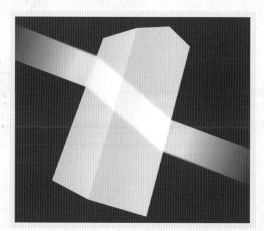

When a ray of light passes through a crystal, it is either refracted (bent) or diffracted (diffused) by the arrangement of atoms within the crystal. The color of a crystal depends on whether the light-absorbing atoms shift the light toward the shorter (violet/blue), medium (yellow/green), or longer (orange/red) wavelengths of the light spectrum. White stones reflect the full spectrum, whereas black ones absorb it.

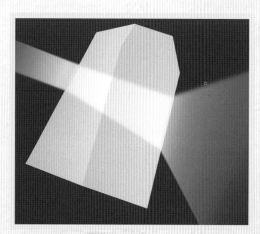

ABOVE *Refraction is when a ray of light is bent as it enters and leaves the crystal.*

RIGHT *Diffraction is when light is bent off course in various directions.*

spectrum affects us at every level – physical, emotional, mental, and spiritual. Learning the key processes and states that each color promotes within us can become a useful foundation both for identifying the general healing effects of a gemstone and for guiding the healer's assessment of what imbalances are present, the possible roots and their correction.

Minerals have been used for centuries as a source of colored pigments for dyes and paints. Their strong colors are stable, not fading in sunlight like vegetable dyes, although over long periods of time the original colors can change through oxidation. Not all minerals will produce the same color once ground up into powder. Hematite usually is silver/black, but, when ground, it makes a deep red powder known from ancient times as red ocher. This quality is often used to help identify minerals. A streak test involves rubbing a rock sample on a piece of unglazed tile, which leaves behind a powder that shows the true color of the mineral.

MINERAL DYES

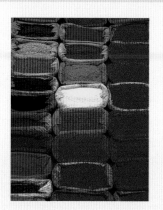

ABOVE *Colored dyes. Ground hematite is a deep red color, and forms the basis for the red ocher dye used since ancient times.*

Many dyes are ground from toxic minerals and have now been largely replaced by man-made aniline dyes.

Red: derived from proustite; cinnabar (mercury oxide); realgar (arsenic oxide)

Orange: crocoite; wulfenite; vanadinite (toxic)

Yellow: orpiment (arsenic); sulfur

Yellow-green: autunite; uranium minerals

Bright green: dioptase; emerald; malachite

Blue: lapis lazuli; vivianite; azurite

Violet: amethyst; fluorite; kammerite

Red

Vibration of energy

Red is associated with heat and dynamism, practical survival drives, lust, energy, and passion. At the physical level, red is associated with activity in general such as movement, energy, and survival. The ability to succeed in any endeavor, the skill and manipulation of physical things, being down-to-earth and businesslike are all manifestations of red energy.

Red is the primary color of the base chakra, or energy center, that connects us to the earth and our physical reality. The physical relationship with the color red connects us with the legs, feet, hips, and base of spine. Red is, of course, associated with the circulation system and blood, and on a mineral level, with the iron content of blood.

Enthusiasm and drive require red energy. The dynamic, explosive qualities of red energy mean that when it is suppressed or blocked, it can become violent when it finally escapes. The best way to balance red energy is to allow it to flow. Red is the color that is associated with pain, swelling, and inflammation, all heat sensations. Lust for life, a strong sexual drive, and a positive sense of the physical self (libido) are also characteristic qualities.

On a mental level, red energy shows as assertiveness and self-confidence and, when out of balance, aggression and arrogance.

ABOVE *Red light energizes many chemical reactions.*

Red energy is always needed at the start of any creative venture. Being grounded, focused, realistic, and in contact with the earth and the physical body shows a balance of red within an individual.

In its essence red energy is the passion to be. It is our strength and zest for life.

Red stones include garnet, ruby, spinel, zircon, jasper, iron, red quartz, red tourmaline, hematite, and granite.

ABOVE *Red energy is always directed toward practical creative expression.*

RED ENERGY IMBALANCES

Indications of a lack of red energy include:
▲ Cold, inactive, congested conditions
▲ Difficulty with physical movement, coordination, or circulation problems
▲ Inability to sustain energy levels, physical weakness, and exhaustion
▲ Being emotionally and mentally unable to experience life as it is, lacking in drive and enthusiasm, uncomfortable with physical activity
▲ Feelings of vulnerability and alienation, inability to maintain personal boundaries, easily drained by company

An excess of red energy might manifest as: hyperactivity, inflammation, physical tension, inability to relax, anger, fear, mental and emotional confusion, rapid mood swings, impatience, fidgeting, intolerance, exasperation, violent outbursts, and exhaustion through continually overextending one's abilities.

Zircon

Granite

Ruby

Jasper

Garnet

Hematite

Orange
Vibration of creativity

Orange is the energy of red modified by yellow. It takes the raw power of red and channels it in those directions where it is most needed. Red is like the power of a burst dam, while orange is the channel through which that force of water can be harnessed for the benefit of all. Any injury, shock, or trauma, whether life-threatening or transitory, whether physical, emotional, or mental, whether in the distant past or the present, can be dissolved and healed with the help of orange.

Orange vibration stimulates creativity on all levels for the same reasons that it is effective in healing, because it helps to remove any blockage in the way of growth. Orange energy appears in the world as all forms of creative endeavor, including art, music, and healing. It is related to the energy and functions of the second sacral chakra.

The organs within the lower abdomen, especially the large intestine and the reproductive organs, as well as the kidneys higher in the abdominal cavity, all carry out orange-type activities. The kidneys and large intestine are primarily concerned with detoxification and elimination of waste or excess material from the body. These cleansing processes are essential if a buildup of toxins is to be avoided.

Orange at the emotional level works positively with creativity and negatively with stress. With the cleansing and correcting of subtle energy bodies, healing on the physical level speeds up considerably. Because there are fewer

ABOVE *Orange energy encourages creativity in all its aspects, inspiring us to continually expand and experience.*

disturbances in the flow of energy, conscious awareness can become broader and more receptive. This leads to a clearer understanding at intuitive levels, and a flowering of wisdom.

Orange stones include tiger's eye, citrine quartz, copper, sunstone, topaz, orange calcite, carnelian, amber, agate, and some garnets. As detoxifiers, Herkimer diamond and selenite also have orange characteristics.

ORANGE ENERGY IMBALANCES

A lack of orange energy might manifest itself as:
▲ Physical rigidity
▲ Restricted feelings
▲ Digestive disorders
▲ Lack of focus
▲ Lack of vitality
▲ Being stuck in the past, holding on to memories
The nature of the orange vibration means that it is unusual to find a buildup of excess energy.

Amber

Orange Calcite

Citrine

Topaz

Copper

Carnelian

Yellow

Vibration of information

Yellow is the color of the sun, and like the sun, yellow energy tends to make us feel happy and in harmony with our surroundings. At a physical level, the yellow vibration is associated with the solar plexus chakra and with the upper abdomen. The digestive system identifies and selects useful energy sources from the food that we eat and absorbs and assimilates nutrients. Discrimination is a key function of the yellow vibration. Being able to recognize what is useful from what is harmful, the yellow energy expresses intelligence and clarity. Many other physical systems rely heavily on the yellow vibration, like the immune system – the body's natural defense against harmful organisms. Recognition of significant danger is what the immune system requires.

The skin and the nervous system, too, are also yellow in function. Both transmit information and

ABOVE *Like all colors, the exact shade of yellow will alter our response. A warm golden yellow elicits comfort and happiness, while lemon yellow is mentally stimulating.*

help to define where and what we are in relation to our surroundings. Yellow energy in the world expresses itself as all those organizations and activities that use information, organize, and lay down rules and regulations to maintain orderliness. Law, education, and information technology all function by defining and creating boundaries. Emotionally, yellow energy positively translates as joy, happiness, and contentment. Negatively, it becomes fear, worry, anxiety, and panic. The source of these negative emotions is usually confusion and lack of knowledge. We panic because we lack the right information to know what to do next. Once there is a clear idea of what we can do, confusion vanishes and choices become clear. Yellow emotional states are thus a response to our mental state. Where yellow energy is strong, there is clear knowledge of who one is and how to interact with the world.

Yellow stones are not the most common of minerals, though many do sometimes display this color. Iron pyrites (fool's gold), gold, amber, light citrine quartz, lemon quartz, yellow sapphire, yellow jasper, agate, heliodor (yellow beryl), and fluorite are all in the yellow family.

YELLOW ENERGY IMBALANCES

Physical imbalances of yellow energy might manifest as:
▲ Stress-related ailments such as indigestion, insomnia, panic attacks, headaches, muscle tension
▲ Skin complaints such as eczema and psoriasis
▲ Nervous disorders
▲ Allergic reactions, food intolerance, or arthritis
▲ Tension, worry, and confusion

An excess of yellow mental energy could be exhibited as:
▲ Overanalytical, fussy behavior
▲ Narrow conceptual categorizations, prejudices, and lack of tolerance

Lemon Quartz

Heliodor

Citrine

Agate

Fluorite

Green

Vibration of balance

Green is the primary color of vegetation and has associations with life, growth, and the world of nature. Green is the color of harmonious balance, a calming, restful energy that is linked with the central chakra, the heart.

Physically, green is associated with the heart, lungs, diaphragm, and the arms and hands. The functions of respiration, growth, and the ability to change and adapt are closely linked with this color.

Green is associated with our personal space and a sense of freedom with the ability, or lack of ability, to express ourselves from the heart.

The basis of green energy is the need to grow, expand, and increase our influence and power. It is able to achieve this only by balancing polarities. At a physical level, green links all the systems and organs that maintain balance. At an emotional level, green reflects the balance within the heart. Loving, caring, and sharing are the expansive, inclusive qualities of this color, expanding the self by establishing relationships with others. Relationships also require balance and an interplay of opposites such as freedom and restraint, independence and dependence, sharing and privacy.

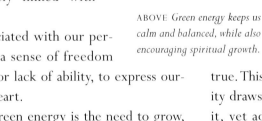

ABOVE *Green energy keeps us calm and balanced, while also encouraging spiritual growth.*

Mentally, green energy gives structure to our existence. Routine and discipline may seem to be restrictions to some, but they do create a framework within which freedom can be experienced in a positive way. Green energy expands from the level of the heart where something is felt to be true. This level of intuitive activity draws on what has gone before it, yet adds a new dimension of personal interpretation. Expansion of knowledge, invention, and innovation are all green mental qualities.

Spiritually, the green vibration relates to all aspects of personal growth and the ability to discern and travel our own personal road.

Green stones include aventurine, jade, peridot, malachite, tourmaline, calcite, moss agate, emerald, garnet, and dioptase.

ABOVE *Green is the color of the vibrant world of nature and our need to experience it.*

GREEN ENERGY IMBALANCES

Green imbalances include anything that intrudes into or restricts personal boundaries and equilibrium, e.g:

▲ Invasive illness
▲ Abnormal growths
▲ Lack of control at any level
▲ Sense of claustrophobia, being trapped, unfulfilled, restricted, dominated
▲ A need to be in control or to be controlled
▲ Lack of self-discipline
▲ Confusion as to who one is and what direction should be taken, and isolation

Aventurine

Peridot

Dioptase

Calcite

Jade

Blue and Indigo

Vibrations of communication

Like its complementary color orange, blue is about flow and communication on all levels from the interstellar to the cellular. Whenever there is a buildup of tension, a sensation of friction or frustration, a blocking of energies, blue light will restore the flow. Blue light has been used for years in orthodox medicine as a quick way to reduce inflammation and other hot conditions like burns and arthritic pain. Blue is the antidote to any over-concentration of energy and is the opposite to red light in this respect.

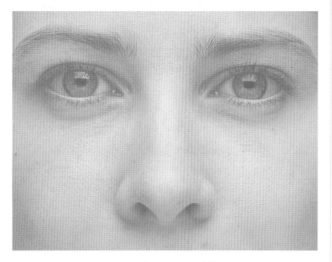

ABOVE *Calming, tranquil blue is linked to communication, information, and understanding.*

The coolness of blue is the depth and silence of the sky, both the bright blue of early morning and the midnight blue of night. Blue is presence with absence; the sky is there above us but there is no object on which to focus. Effortlessly staring at the sky tends to empty our mind of thoughts yet leaves us fully aware. It is like water, hypnotic and entrancing. The energy of blue also works in a similar way to water in that it always finds a common level for itself. Where there is an imbalance, a gradient of some sort between greater and lesser, blue helps their inequality to disappear by speeding the natural direction of flow. In

this way pressure is released safely and constructively. Physically, the color blue connects with the throat and brow chakras. It covers the neck, throat, face, ears, eyes, nose, mouth, and forehead. All forms of communication, expression, and learning are blue in quality. Communication of any sort is a flow of information from a position of greater knowledge to a position of lesser knowledge, from a quality of fullness to a quality of emptiness. This is true whether it is the level of a teacher and pupil or on a level of gossiping neighbors.

Every system, to be effective, requires the best available communication between its parts. Without a constant flow of information and energy, without an awareness of what is going on elsewhere, every organization collapses into ineffectual isolation. It is somewhat paradoxical that a hot red state of activity and energy, in order to maintain itself, needs the blue cool vibration to keep it coherent and functional. This is a reminder that no one vibration, energy, or color can exist in isolation without the support of all the others, and that imbalance in one area almost inevitably leads to an increase in disorderliness within the whole organism. When the blue flow of energy creates stability, there is a state of peace in which no tension or pressure exists. As a temporary state, it is restful and relaxing; but if it becomes too entrenched, it can lead to detachment and depression.

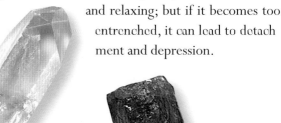

Celestite

Sapphire

Calcite

Aquamarine

LEFT *If there is an excess of blue energy, it results in emotional detachment.*

Communication and self-expression are basic human requirements. We need to see a response from others; we need some form of acknowledgment. The punishment of ignoring and excluding someone from the personal community is emotionally and psychologically damaging. When there is an excess of blue energy, its coolness becomes all-enveloping. Emotional detachment and mental aloofness are the result. Blue is not a color to use in cases of depression, nor is it wise to use blue for extended periods without the balancing effect of more activating colors.

The spaciousness and flow of blue energy encourage the mind to explore subtleties and nuances of thought. Blue is a color that can increase our ability to contact the deep areas of the mind where inspiration and imagination reside. It also allows intuition to flourish, and at the same time its cool quality means that information coming from the finer levels of the mind can be looked at and assessed clearly without interference from any inappropriate responses. Seeing clearly, perception, and understanding sum up the effects of blue energy.

Blue stones and crystals range from the light blue of celestite, blue topaz, aquamarine, blue lace agate, and blue calcite to the dark blues of lapis lazuli, blue quartz, indicolite or blue tourmaline, kyanite, sapphire, and azurite.

At an emotional level, the color blue can create a flow that helps understanding, appreciation, empathy, and acceptance. It is a color that can reduce the irritation we feel when something jars against our own preferences or beliefs. By increasing our ability to communicate with others and express ourselves effectively, the blue energy can prevent the buildup of friction that would otherwise develop into a red condition of anger.

Azurite

BELOW *Light blue stones work well with the throat chakra, while darker blue stones energize the brow chakra.*

Lapis Lazuli

Kyanite

BLUE ENERGY IMBALANCES

Indicators of blue imbalances are

▲ Throat problems, laryngitis, sore throats, and tonsillitis (these all suggest difficulties within the sphere of personal communication either at an everyday level, or sometimes simply the need to become involved in some artistic activity)

▲ Blocks to creativity and inspiration

▲ Cold, congested states show excess of blue

Extreme agitated states can be helped with blue initially, although the calming qualities of green are more suitable in the long term.

Violet
Vibration of integration

The key to understanding violet energy is in the combination of its constituent colors blue and red. The energy of violet is a synthesis of the hot, activating, dynamic, manifesting quality of red with the cooling, sedating, pacifying, dematerializing quality of blue. The tones of violet are thus a spiritualization of matter and an energizing of spirit, a union of apparent opposites.

Physically, the violet vibration relates to the crown chakra and the head generally, but specifically the cranium or the skull, the functions of the brain, and the pituitary and pineal glands.

ABOVE *Related to the crown chakra, violet is associated with conscious awareness and reflective thinking.*

Within the physical body, violet energy works to create coordination and integration between systems. Physical coordination problems and learning difficulties in children often arise from an imbalance between the left and right hemispheres of the brain.

The tendency to switch off, or not recognize, what is going on at some level is a very violet characteristic of imbalance on any level.

Violet energy provides the flow of information via the blue qualities, together with the activating energy of the life force via the red. Together they serve as a switch to turn on those mechanisms that will help the body to recognize and deal with situations of imbalance and illness. This makes violet one of the most useful, generally applicable, healing energies in crystal work.

Violet energy at an emotional level tends to foster understanding and sympathy for others, and at a mental level opens the awareness to imagination and inspiration. Violet encourages all aspects of artistic expression and practical problem solving. The expansive nature of the vibration also helps to enter and maintain meditative states.

Violet and purple stones are not frequently found and can be rare and expensive. The most common and most broadly effective is amethyst quartz. Others include fluorite, sugilite, charoite, tanzanite, iolite or water sapphire, lepidolite, and kunzite.

VIOLET ENERGY IMBALANCES

Violet imbalance can become extreme, expressing itself as.
▲ An exaggerated need to sacrifice for others, that often disguises guilt or poor self-worth
▲ A tendency to live in a world of illusory value judgments or to escape into fantasy and day dreaming
▲ Delusional states and reinterpretation of reality based on personal fanaticism
The following can be helped by violet energy:
▲ Headaches
▲ Problems with eyes and ears
▲ Deep-seated glandular imbalances and other chronic imbalances of the whole system
▲ Lack of focus mentally and spiritually, inability to concentrate, failure to understand what is happening in life or to integrate change

Fluorite

Iolite

Charoite

Sugilite

Pink

Vibration of connectedness

Pink is a combination of white and red and so tends to be dynamic, expressing the energy and activation of red with the all-encompassing, cleansing qualities of white. Jealousies, aggression, and misunderstandings all fade away when illuminated by the pink vibration. Whenever there is a violent or negative situation, the use of pink light for short periods of time quickly reestablishes calm.

Visualizing a pale or pure pink light emanating from one's heart dispels negativity, and projecting pink around or at someone who is aggressive toward you or who is annoying you, will help to calm the situation before it gets out of hand.

ABOVE *Pink is a unifier, reinforcing the link that all things have to each other and quickly neutralizes all false divisions.*

In crystal therapy, pink is found with green at the heart center, where it is used to help release emotional stress. All issues to do with self image can be greatly helped by pink light. Pink energy increases levels of tolerance and sympathy, and the effectiveness of healing. It works well as first-aid and in the release of long-term trauma.

Pink colored stones include rose quartz, rubellite (pink tourmaline), rhodonite, rhodocrosite, kunzite, cherry opal, coral, and thulite.

Rhodocrosite

Rhodonite

Rubellite

Turquoise

Vibration of individuality

Turquoise comes in a variety of shades between green and blue. The heart center, represented by green energy, is linked together with the throat chakra, the light blue energy, indicating that turquoise helps to articulate and express the true wishes of the heart. Expression of the uniqueness of each individual is a powerful and essential part of everyone's life. Turquoise reaffirms our sense of value and purpose, and significantly increases the life energy available to each of us.

ABOVE *The light-blue energy of turquoise is the means by which our desire for growth is communicated.*

Consider using turquoise in any situation where stress and illness are clearly draining the individual.

Turquoise-colored stones include aquamarine, turquoise, chrysocolla, larimar, gem silica, and amazonite.

Turquoise
Amazonite
Chrysocolla

White

Vibration of purification

White light is the complete, unseparated spectrum and reflects all energies out from itself. It is the union of all colors, so essentially it has the potential to become any color. When talking about crystals and color, white includes those crystals that are clear, which allow light to pass through them unaltered. Stones that appear white in color are reflecting all frequencies of light from their surfaces. White has no clear connection to the physical body, although it is often associated with the area just above the top of the head, at or above the crown chakra. White is the vibration of pure potential. Everything exists within it and anything might manifest from it, yet white itself displays no characteristics. In practical terms this means white will supply whatever energy is needed, or, when combined with another color, will amplify and augment that color.

ABOVE *Culturally, white has diverse meanings: in the modern West, white relates to cleanliness, purity, and the spirit, while in China white is the color of death.*

At an emotional level white feels cold and undefined. Since it cannot absorb anything, it remains somewhat remote and inviolable, hence its ties to purity. The purification that white light brings is rapid and unequivocal, and as such it can be a harsh experience. But if the more temperate color of orange doesn't free up blockages, then white light might be successful.

With white light, all shadows and distinctions dissolve. It can be utterly cleansing, stripping away all masks and pretensions, and destroying everything that is not part of your true nature, so it should always be used with caution. White is the brand-new start, the blank page. The projection of emptiness can seem remote and unsympathetic until the time comes when it is absolutely necessary to use its powerful frequency.

Clear stones that reflect the purifying force of white light are clear quartz, Herkimer diamond, diamond, Iceland spa (a variety of calcite), and gypsum, selenite, and apophyllite.

White stones include milky quartz, moonstone, opal, and chalk.

ABOVE *In Native American tradition, white is assigned to the north, from which comes snow and ice.*

Iceland Spa

Moonstone

Opal

Chalk

Black

Vibration of potential

Black contains all colors within itself and absorbs all the energies into itself so that no light at all can be seen. A black hole exists because its immense gravity draws all matter, time, and light into itself. Black, in the same way, is the ultimate expression of gravity, pulling everything inward to experience its core, central nature.

Blackness as an experience can be frightening because of its lack of definition. Anything or everything may be out there in the dark. But everything may be all the good, beneficial experiences as well as terrors and fears. In this way, the lesson of black is the same as white. It contains within itself all potential, but where white will create the energy for a rapid, immediate change of state, black will allow a rest period, a dormancy within which growth and change can begin to take shape.

All aspects of the hidden – the concealed factors, the subconscious and unconscious, and everything that is not in the present moment of conscious awareness, can be represented by the color black.

Black can be a good grounding color because it contacts the deepest, most solid foundations of any situation. Black can also be the means by which the underlying, hidden factors can be brought to the surface and examined.

ABOVE *The rainbow swirl of colors is pulled in and absorbed by a black hole in deep space. Black indicates rest and dormancy.*

As an energy of meditation, the color black can be extremely useful as a restful silence in which to explore deep levels.

Black is also a very protective color, not only because it hides but also because it absorbs all energy, no matter what the source. The combination of black and white can produce an extremely powerful blending of protective and cleansing qualities.

Black stones include schorl or black tourmaline, smoky quartz, obsidian, jet, and onyx.

ABOVE *Black is a protective color, with the power to absorb all energy. It also represents the hidden aspects of the self.*

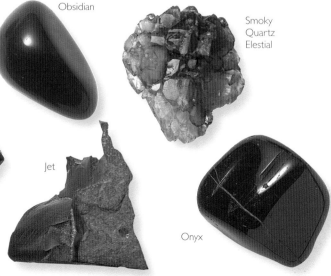

Obsidian

Smoky Quartz Elestial

Jet

Schorl

Onyx

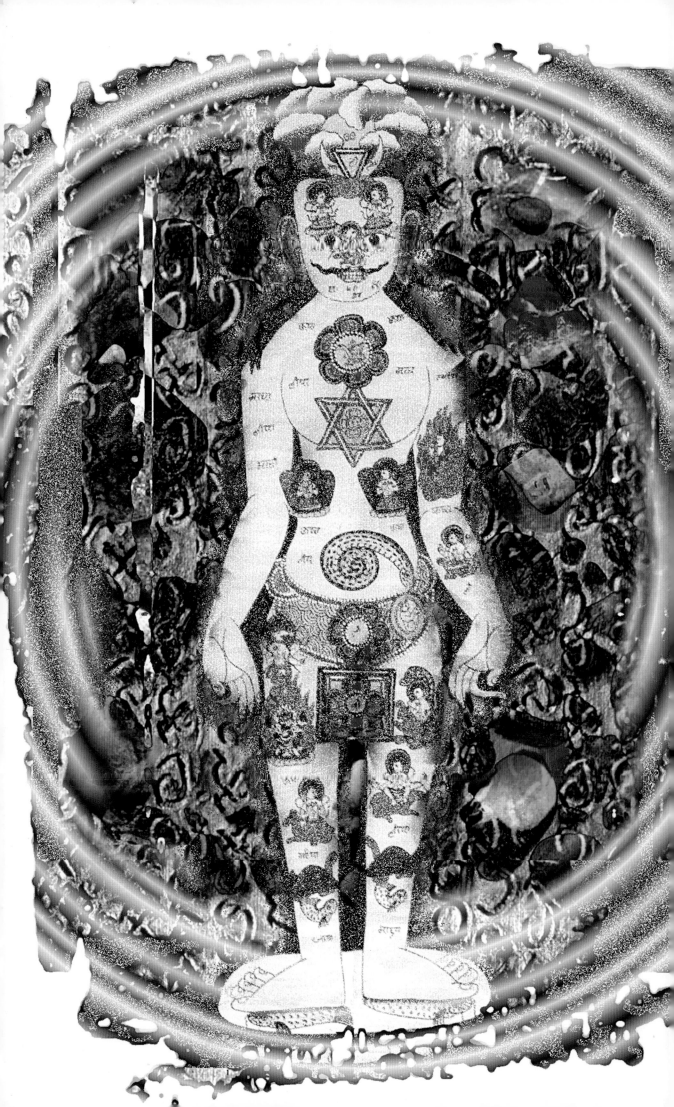

PART FOUR

CHAKRAS

Most crystal healers work with a holistic model of the human being. Physical health is seen as part of a larger picture that includes emotions, mental state, lifestyle, and aspirations. Crystal therapy has taken its perception of the human being largely from traditions that describe other more subtle, nonphysical systems that are thought to affect well-being.

Ancient texts from northern India describe a system of subtle channels that run through the body. Arising from the central channel, along the spinal cord, are seven main energy centers, called chakras (which means "wheel" in Sanskrit).

The classical chakra system is a complex set of associated symbols using sound, color, shape, animal and god forms, and the senses.

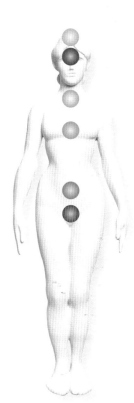

ABOVE *The seven chakras are linked to the seven colors of the spectrum.*

The Chakra System

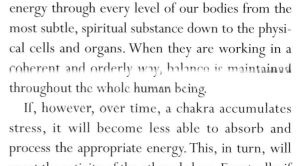

The seven main chakras include the base, the sacral, the solar plexus, heart, throat, brow, and crown. Many crystal healers work exclusively with the main chakra system, learning how to correct imbalances that appear as physical symptoms, emotional problems, or mental distress. The seven main chakras are located close to concentrations of nerves and lymphatic tissues. Aligned, too, are some of the main endocrine glands in the physical body. Although there is no evidence of a direct connection between the body's different systems, it may help to explain why the placement of crystals around those areas have such a noticeable effect.

Each chakra can be visualized as a complex meeting point of many different streams of energy that form a vortex of spinning energy. So a chakra is the location where a multitude of different influences interact with the human being. Each chakra, although physically separated along the spine, has complex interactions with every other center so that every change in one will affect the functioning of the others. The chakras transmit life-sustaining energy into the body not only from our immediate environment but also from multidimensional and universal sources. From each chakra point, this energy is distributed into the rest of the body through a number of very subtle channels or nerves known as "nadis".

The chakras can be seen as a series of elevators that have particular activities that can move

RIGHT *Chakras are like elevators that move energy through the body, supplying spiritual and physical nourishment.*

energy through every level of our bodies from the most subtle, spiritual substance down to the physical cells and organs. When they are working in a coherent and orderly way, balance is maintained throughout the whole human being.

If, however, over time, a chakra accumulates stress, it will become less able to absorb and process the appropriate energy. This, in turn, will upset the activity of the other chakras. Eventually, if not corrected, this may contribute to physical illness or mental and emotional upset.

In the original Indian descriptions of their functions, the chakras were intended to direct the aspirant to meditations that would help them to achieve spiritual growth and so they emphasized the qualities of the chakras above the heart center. But in order to function properly in the everyday world of work, relationships, and practical living, it is essential that all seven main chakras are given equal attention. Perhaps the original writers assumed that in the well-balanced society of the time the three lower chakras — base, sacral, and solar plexus — were already fully functioning and required little clearing.

The goal of a chakra balance in crystal healing should be to return each chakra to its optimal working state in harmonious relationship with the other energy systems. There is always a certain degree of natural flexibility in each system to take account of individual life patterns and differing requirements, and this awareness in a crystal healer will help to achieve maximum benefit from a healing session.

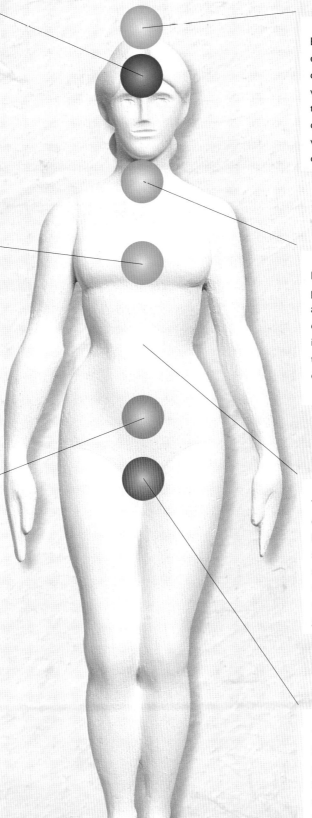

BROW

The eyes and brain are linked to this chakra. Its associated color is dark blue or indigo, including stones such as lapis lazuli, sapphire, sodalite, blue tourmaline, and kyanite, which quieten mental noise, enabling finer levels of perception.

CROWN

Expressing its potential in expansion and fulfillment, the crown chakra is partnered with the pituitary gland and the cerebrum. Its attendant colors are violet, gold, and white; stones include amethyst, quartz, and opal.

HEART

The center of emotion; also of the mind and soul. Although green is the main color associated with this chakra, a combination of green and pink stones, such as jade and rose quartz, ensures a balanced release of emotional stress.

THROAT

Related to the thyroid and parathyroid glands, and associated with creativity. Its color is light- to mid-blue, including blue lace agate, blue tourmaline, blue topaz, blue calcite, turquoise, and fluorite.

SACRAL

The second chakra's purpose is enjoyment. Its designated color is orange, encompassing stones such as carnelian, orange citrine, calcite, and dark topaz, which work well with issues of self and painful conditions, both emotional and physical.

SOLAR PLEXUS

This is the powerhouse where energy is transformed for use by the body. This chakra is synonymous with yellow, so shades of that color will resonate well with its energies. Stones include fool's gold, tiger's eye, and heliodor.

BASE

The foundation system of the body. Linked to the adrenal glands. Associated with red, the color of energy and activity, useful to it are stones such as ruby, jasper, garnet, hematite, and obsidian.

RIGHT *The chakra system clearly defines different functions and uses of energy in the human body. Because of its simplicity and flexibility, working with the chakras has become one of the main techniques in crystal healing.*

The Base Chakra

The first chakra, called the base, is found at the lower end of the spine. It is often represented as a downward pointing vortex. For crystal work, the whole area around the base of the spine can be used for stone placements: the groin points on each side, where the legs meet the torso, are useful placements on the body; otherwise, the stones can be placed between the legs from the knees to the thighs.

Its traditional Sanskrit name is muladhara, which means root or support, and sums up the important functions of this chakra. The base chakra is the foundation upon which every other body system relies for stability, and it is the primary source of usable energy.

A link is often made with the functions of the adrenal glands even though these are much higher in the physical body, because both adrenals and the base chakra focus on the survival of the individual. Both are drawn upon in times of danger and threat to supply extra energy and practical, physical solutions to life-threatening problems.

The base chakra roots the rest of our complex energies into physical existence. It is the plug that links us to our mains supply, the earth itself. Although there are important smaller chakras in the legs, feet, and the area below the feet that have to do with grounding, the base chakra is vital if we are to keep a practical grip on reality. A block or stress within the base chakra can lead to feelings of unreality, of not belonging, or of not being able to cope. There may be a sense of pointlessness and an

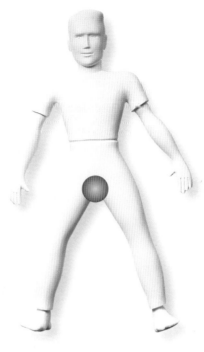

ABOVE *The base chakra, or muladhara, is situated at the bottom of the spine.*

inability to achieve goals. Even if all other chakras are working well, without the base chakra there will be no anchor to make manifest our desires and wishes.

Centering and grounding are key attributes of the base chakra, establishing us firmly within our physical system, alerting us to the world around us and protecting our energies from depletion.

At a physical level, the base chakra can increase our energy levels and improve circulation of the blood. Problems with the feet and legs and anything to do with movement and coordination indicate some need to work with this center. Working with the base chakra in conjunction with the sacral chakra above it can prove useful with arthritis and lower gastrointestinal disorders.

Since the base chakra deals with our energy levels, it can be useful in controlling the amount of built-up stress. A great deal of stress is created through worry about events over which we may have only limited control. The base chakra works with the practicalities of the present and so helps to give us a real sense of perspective. This chakra's ability to ground excess energy as well as assimilate it means that when it is stimulated by appropriate crystal placements it can help to release stress from all areas of the individual, creating a greater ability to relax physically, to let go of emotional tensions and worries, and to focus on the enjoyment of the present moment, returning us to our natural sense of vitality and optimism.

Jasper

Hematite

Ruby

Jasper

BASE CHAKRA LAYOUT

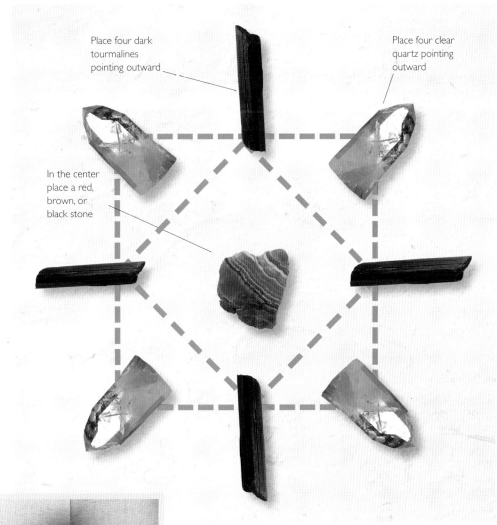

Place four dark tourmalines pointing outward

Place four clear quartz pointing outward

In the center place a red, brown, or black stone

ABOVE *To boost the base chakra, place the stones next to, or on, the body.*

There are many ways to place crystals that will strengthen the activities of the base chakra. Here is a layout that can support and enhance the natural functioning of this center. It is designed to help the release of stress and encourage healing. The position of the stones is not important; some can be on the body, others next to it. Stones can be close together in a small area or spread out to cover the whole area of the hips and base of spine. Place four clear quartz crystals diagonally in a square, pointing outward. Between these stones put four dark tourmalines, also with points outward if they have any. In the center place a red, brown, or black stone.

Garnet   Obsidian   Schorl   Zircon

The Sacral Chakra

The second chakra is associated with the qualities of movement and flow of energy. It is usually known as the sacral or sexual chakra, and is placed near the sacrum on the spine. On the front of the body, it is on the lower abdomen between the navel and the pubic bone at the center of the pelvis. This chakra's Sanskrit name is svadhisthana, which means sweetness. Essentially, the purpose of this center is to allow us to explore and enjoy our existence. It is connected to the sensuality of touch and the innocent desire for pleasure as seen in babies who reach for everything in sight. By this exploration we learn who we are in relation to other things, and we develop emotions and attachments.

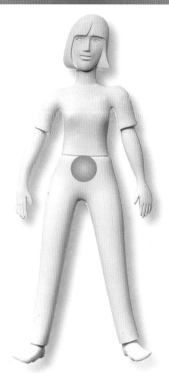

ABOVE *The sacral (or sexual) chakra, or svadhisthana, is between the navel and pubic bone.*

The sacral chakra is all about nonjudgmental, spontaneous enjoyment, something adults usually find difficult to experience. This chakra is often under stress from its negative characteristics of rigidity and restriction. The rigidity can be at a physical level with tension and pain in the lower back, digestive problems of the lower intestine, bladder or kidney trouble. It may manifest as sexual tension, either emotionally triggered or with physical symptoms that can cause impotence or frigidity. Menstrual pain and irregular periods will also have sacral chakra involvement in many cases. The pelvic girdle is a complex area where deep muscles can become strained or overtense, and it is often difficult to massage and relax them. Many physical problems in the pelvic area begin with tension restricting blood flow and nerves. Balancing the

sacral chakra energies releases built-up toxins and can ease problems.

The sacral chakra is also where our deep emotional responses are registered. We have learned to disguise or hide our negative emotions. They tend to get locked into our muscle structures and also in our subtle energy systems, especially those linked with the second or sacral chakra. The more emotion is suppressed, the greater the energy required to keep it hidden and the less energy we have available to carry on our lives and fulfill our goals. Crystal healing is one of the most effective tools for gradually releasing this stored-up emotional energy, making it available for creative uses.

The buildup of rigidity deprives us of the enjoyment of playfulness and creativity. It can burst out as anger, frustration, and aggression. It can create anxiety about who we are and our self-worth and self-image. Stiffness in the physical system, such as arthritis, can be eased by stimulating the flowing relaxation of the sacral chakra.

The taste for life is driven by desire and motivation. If this is restricted or suppressed, creativity cannot grow and boredom sets in. Fear of change starts to grow even when change is the one thing that will stimulate us to find that "sweetness" in life. Tension and fear can alienate us from ourselves and our surroundings. Blocked energy disrupts normal function and can lead to illness. Working on the sacral chakra can help us keep the freshness and enjoyment in our lives. It will release blocks, stress, and trauma, and detoxify the whole system.

Tiger's Eye   Orange Calcite   Topaz   Citrine

SACRAL CHAKRA LAYOUT

A downward-pointing triangle of three clear crystals

An arc of three stones

ABOVE *Working on this area will release blocks, stress, and trauma, and detoxify the whole system.*

A layout to stimulate the second chakra can be put on the lower abdomen. A downward-pointing triangle is made using three clear crystals. The crystals can be three clear quartz, or rutilated quartz, Herkimer diamond, or even diamond. Below this triangle, make an arc of a further three stones, again all of the same kind, choosing from moonstone, rose quartz, lapis lazuli, aquamarine, sugilite, amethyst, charoite, or blue quartz. The stones you decide to use will depend upon what is available and most appropriate.

Carnelian   Copper   Moonstone   Herkimer diamond

The Solar Plexus Chakra

The third, or solar plexus, chakra motivates us to bring about change. Its traditional name is manipura, or lustrous gem. This fiery chakra deals with our use of energy and ability to transform it from a raw state into usable forms. With this transformed energy, the solar plexus chakra creates change both in the self and in the outside world. It is an organizing control center that gives us the will and ability to mold our lives in a powerful, effective way.

At a physical level, the solar plexus chakra works with many different systems of the body. Located between the base of the rib cage and the navel, it covers

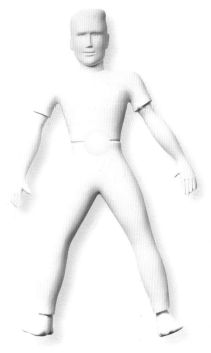

ABOVE *The solar plexus chakra, manipura, sits between the rib cage and the navel.*

the major areas of digestion such as the stomach, small intestine, liver, and pancreas. All these organs work to absorb and transform the external matter of food, identifying what is of use to the body as nutrients. In the same region is located the spleen, one of the most important organs of the immune system, which relies on its ability to recognize what is useful and to identify and destroy harmful organisms. The solar plexus chakra also plays a part in the proper functioning of the nervous system and the skin, systems that also depend on communication and identification of outside messages.

Indications that the solar plexus needs support can be overacidity, ulcers, digestive problems (particularly the inability to absorb nutrients), misidentification of harmless or useful substances as harmful, leading to allergies and intolerance, and difficulties with immune system function from

constant colds and persistent viral infections. More serious problems may include autoimmune disorders, chronic fatigue, burnout, or hypertension. On an emotional level, look for anxiety, stress, lack of confidence, insecurity, or nervous disorders.

The solar plexus chakra integrates us actively into the world. The "on top of the world" feeling is a reflection of this chakra's characteristics. Optimism, self-confidence, spontaneity, flexibility, a sense of humor, joy, and laughter are the natural balanced expression of the solar plexus.

Since the solar plexus chakra tends to assimilate everyday levels of stress, working in this area can be important for stress reduction and relaxation. This chakra is close to the diaphragm, which is linked to our breathing patterns. Under stress there is a tendency to restrict the depth of breathing, which can lead to habitual shallow breathing or tension in the solar plexus area. When crystals begin to release this tension, there may be an increase in deep, full breaths or yawning and sighing for no apparent reason. This is a sign that stress is being released and should be encouraged. Crying and sobbing are also good signs of release. If at any stage the release becomes too overwhelming or emotionally draining, remove all stones from the solar plexus and gently rest a hand there until calm returns. Increasing the number of grounding stones at the legs and feet helps to stabilize the new balance of emotions.

Agate

Amber

Citrine

Heliodor

SOLAR PLEXUS LAYOUT

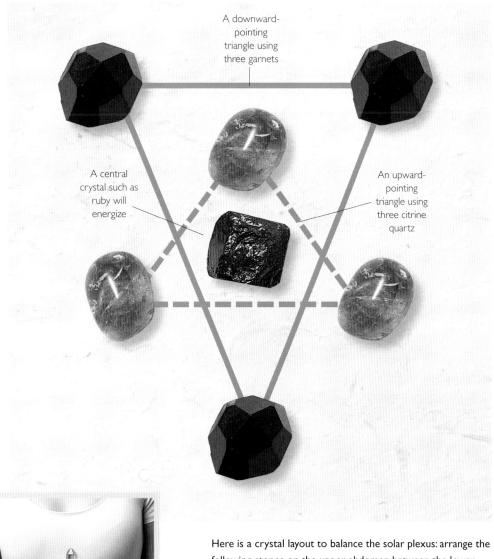

A downward-pointing triangle using three garnets

A central crystal such as ruby will energize

An upward-pointing triangle using three citrine quartz

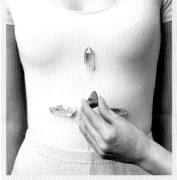

ABOVE *When crystals begin to release tension, there may be an increase in deep, full breaths, sighs, or yawning.*

Here is a crystal layout to balance the solar plexus: arrange the following stones on the upper abdomen between the lower edge of the rib cage near the diaphragm and the navel. Make an upward-pointing triangle of three citrine quartz crystals with points facing outward. In the center of this triangle, place one of the following: tiger's eye, ruby, garnet, jasper, or iron pyrite. The stone you place here will determine the quality of energy being balanced. For example, the red stones ruby and garnet will energize, jasper and pyrites will gently ground and stimulate digestion. Tiger's eye will ground and encourage practical social skills. Surrounding these four stones, make another triangle, this time with three garnets pointing downward.

Fluorite

Lemon Quartz

Pyrite

Tiger's Eye

The Heart Chakra

At the center of the chest is the heart chakra. This is the midpoint of the entire chakra system, with three above and three below. Balance and equilibrium are the keys to understanding heart chakra energies. In Sanskrit texts, the heart is known as anahata, the unstruck [sound], referring to the underlying vibration at the heart of all creation. Complete wellness begins and ends with the balance within the heart. The heart chakra is concerned with the balancing act of relationship in all its aspects.

ABOVE *The heart chakra, anahata, lies at the center of the chest. It is the midpoint of the chakra system.*

If the physical systems related to the heart chakra are examined, there appears to be this give-and-take quality in common. The heart works by alternately contracting and expanding, taking blood into itself and then pumping it around the body. The lungs inhale air by expanding and exhale on contraction. Both these systems only work when a balance is maintained. Too much contraction or too much expansion destroys the balanced rhythm, and the entire system suffers. This equilibrium of opposite actions is what maintains the friction and flow of life energy moving through the universe.

When the heart chakra is balanced, there is a sense of calm, clear-sightedness, friendliness, and tolerance of others. We are comfortable with our own space and can accept the personal space of others. There is clarity in decision-making and an ability to grow in a sustainable way. It is possible to understand the needs of others without feeling our own needs have to be ignored or suppressed. We know where we want to go, and we can hold our own ground as well.

When the heart chakra is out of balance, it is easy to lose our own emotional perspective. Becoming possessive or obsessive, constantly seeking reassurance, experiencing self-doubt, and lack of self-worth are all signs of an insecurity brought about by incorrect understanding of our relationship with the world.

Heart chakra imbalances can lead to cold, emotionless power-seeking, where a lack of resonance with others creates intolerance, prejudice, and cruelty or power over other people. On the other hand, there can be an overwhelming sense of personal responsibility for other people's welfare, or even for the state of the whole world. This can lead to desperate self-sacrifice and guilt that undermines all sense of self-worth and can also lead to exploitation and manipulation by other people.

In many cases, chakra imbalances will exhibit elements of both under- and overactivity in different aspects of our lives. For example, a power-mongering manipulator may have learned to act this way because of an underlying sense of lack of self-worth or guilt.

The heart chakra is a vital healing location where the swings of polarized emotions, feelings, hopes, and wishes can be evened out and a positive calm can be restored in which to reestablish a life-supporting relationship with the world. In complex urban societies, individual freedom is often restricted by consensus views. Balancing the heart chakra releases these constrictions without the need to break away from society.

Jade

Malachite

Aventurine

Calcite

HEART LAYOUT

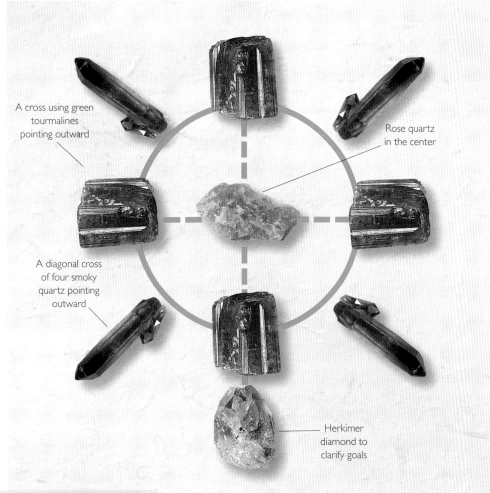

A cross using green tourmalines pointing outward

Rose quartz in the center

A diagonal cross of four smoky quartz pointing outward

Herkimer diamond to clarify goals

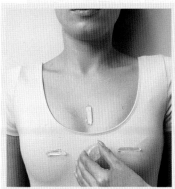

ABOVE *When the heart chakra is fully balanced, the entire chakra system works in harmony.*

Put a rose quartz at the center of the chest. Make a cross with points outward around this along the axes of the body. The cross can be made with green tourmaline crystals or, alternatively, clear quartz, rose quartz, or other pink crystal. If tumbled stones are used here, add clear quartz points to direct the energy out and away from the center stone. Midway in the first cross place another of four outward-pointing smoky quartz crystals. This layout balances and emotionally clears and unstresses the heart chakra.

Where there is a need to clarify goals or fulfill desires, a Herkimer diamond can be placed just below this arrangement. A small chakra, the Anandakanda Lotus, is located here, and that helps to access deep levels of our true nature.

Rhodonite

Rubellite

Rhodocrosite

Rose Quartz

The Throat Chakra

The throat chakra is found at the base of the throat around the sternal notch where the clavicle meets the sternum. Physically, this chakra is related to the thyroid and parathyroid glands, which sit on each side of the windpipe, and to the upper chest, neck, throat, mouth, nose, and ears. The shoulders, arms, and hands can be affected by both the heart and throat chakras.

ABOVE *The throat chakra, visuddha, is sited at the base of the throat, where the clavicle and sternum meet.*

The throat chakra is primarily concerned with communication – it allows us to transmit our thoughts, ideas, and desires so our relationship with the world can be maintained. Without language it is very difficult to make ourselves understood and receive cooperation from other people.

Both throat and sacral chakras are associated with creativity. The second chakra initiates the impulse to create, to explore possibilities. The expression of that desire can only materialize via the throat chakra because it can find a way in which to form and express the creative idea.

Sore throats and stiff necks can often be indications that there is a problem with some level of communication. Very often something is being held back by force of will that would be better verbalized in some way. It can also show that a desire to express individuality is being stifled. This can feel like a buildup of energy in the

LEFT *Restoring the balance of the throat chakra helps to ease postural problems.*

heart center that needs to expand, turning into a restrictive claustrophobia as it is blocked from manifesting by the activities of the throat chakra.

Without this natural flow of communicated energy traveling out into the world, other sorts of energies also slow down, and there is a danger of stagnation on many levels. At the physical level, thyroid activity may be disrupted, leading to states of either lethargy or hyperactivity. Muscle stiffness in the neck, shoulders, and jaw results from a lack of energy flow in those areas. Chronic tension in the jaw can lead to headaches.

The arms and hands are a physical extension of our expressive ability. They carry out on a physical level what our words do at a verbal level. They enable us to interact, to make things happen, to express ourselves as creators.

On an emotional level, throat chakra problems can lead to an inability to express and feel emotions at a deeper level. This dissociation can lead to withdrawal and isolation or, alternatively, can create a chatterbox who doesn't feel comfortable unless talking, but doesn't communicate any true feeling.

The Sanskrit name for this chakra is visuddha, meaning pure or purification, because the throat chakra focuses on refining thoughts and desires. Mentally, this chakra is closely connected to all aspects of knowledge. It deals specifically with the use of symbols, images, and concepts that can crystallize and encompass complex ideas. All three upper chakras deal with aspects of the mind and perception, but the throat chakra is primarily concerned with establishing clear understanding.

Aquamarine

Celestite

Blue Calcite

THROAT CHAKRA LAYOUT

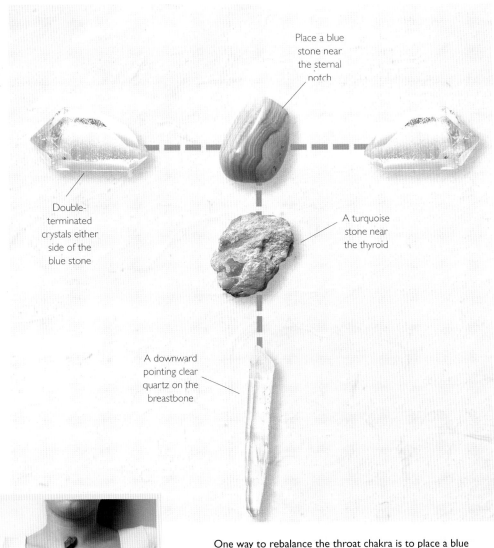

Place a blue stone near the sternal notch

Double-terminated crystals either side of the blue stone

A turquoise stone near the thyroid

A downward pointing clear quartz on the breastbone

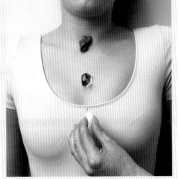

ABOVE *The throat chakra is closely connected to the mind and all aspects of education, learning, and knowledge.*

One way to rebalance the throat chakra is to place a blue stone near the sternal notch. Close beneath this near the thymus gland, put a turquoise-colored stone. Below this on the breastbone, set a downward-pointing clear quartz crystal. Finally on each side of the uppermost blue stone, place a crystal with double terminations or points at each end. These two crystals can be of any sort so long as they are the same stone. Probably small quartz crystals with natural double terminations will be easiest to find.

Turquoise

Amazonite

Blue Lace Agate

The Brow Chakra

The sixth, or brow, chakra is perhaps the best-known of the subtle energy centers, for this is the fabled "third eye" that aspiring clairvoyants strive to open and activate to enhance their subtle visionary skills. Its name is ajna, meaning to perceive, command, or know. Its primary function is concerned with the understanding and analysis of reality. It differs from the throat chakra in that it has a more passive quality; the brow chakra is inward-looking rather than expressive in its nature.

ABOVE *The brow chakra, ajna, is located at the center of the forehead, between the eyebrows.*

Physically it is in the area of the center of the forehead that is sometimes defined as between the eyebrows. The eyes and the conscious workings of the brain are directly related to the brow chakra, whose main function is to make sense of the raw information received from the sense organs. It also works with memory and planning, so it is able to extend itself beyond the everyday experience of time and space by receiving and analyzing information from the remembered past and the projected future. The brow chakra is the center where our personality is focused, for our view of reality is an expression of who we are and how we see ourselves in relation to the universe.

ABOVE *This chakra is also known as the "third eye," and is used for clairvoyance.*

One of the main functions of the brow chakra is to leave behind the constraints of time and space, because it gives us greater insight. But, when this chakra loses its balance with the system as a whole, the mind has a tendency to retreat from reality into the self-constructed realms of fantasy and delusion. More than most chakras, the brow needs integrated balance and a firm grounded energy if it is to be of real use to us.

As the brow increases its range, moving from making sense of sight and sounds to increased subtle levels of perception and intuition, imagination is needed in order to process the new information to make sense of it in terms of personal experience.

With an active but imbalanced brow chakra, it is possible to see visions, receive messages from the subtle senses (like clairvoyance and clairaudience), and be bombarded by intriguing psychic information. But unless there is a balanced and equal emphasis on the energies of the base, sacral, and solar plexus chakras, it is almost impossible to determine what is valid and useful to our lives and what is simply wishful thinking and delusion. Imagination, the ability to form a mental image of something never perceived before in reality and to project future possibilities, can benefit us when we try to bring those ideas down to a practical level. Otherwise, they tend to clutter the mind.

When the brow is stressed, the mind becomes clouded, and thought patterns run in chaotic circles, making practical activity and taking decisions very difficult. But this energy center is extremely sensitive, so placing an appropriate crystal on the forehead for a few moments can really have a profound balancing effect.

Blue Quartz

Indicolite

Azurite

Lapis Lazuli

BROW CHAKRA LAYOUT

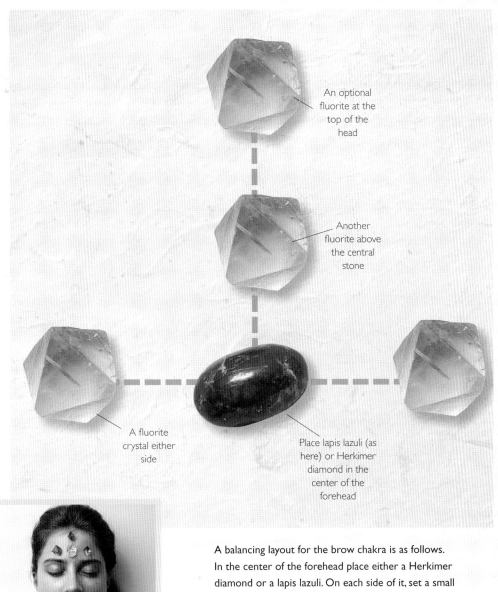

An optional fluorite at the top of the head

Another fluorite above the central stone

A fluorite crystal either side

Place lapis lazuli (as here) or Herkimer diamond in the center of the forehead

ABOVE *Crystals can bring out the best qualities of the brow chakra — including an expansive intuition focused sharply by a clear, perceptive mind.*

A balancing layout for the brow chakra is as follows. In the center of the forehead place either a Herkimer diamond or a lapis lazuli. On each side of it, set a small fluorite crystal of any color. These should be positioned approximately at the center of the eyebrows. Another fluorite goes right above the first central stone. An optional blue or violet fluorite can be added near the top of the head, by the crown.

Kyanite

Sapphire

Fluorite

The Crown Chakra

The seventh, or crown, chakra is called sahasrara, "thousand", referring to the image of the thousand petaled lotus that represents it in classical Indian texts. It is said to be located a distance of four-finger breadths above the top of the head, although in practical terms the whole area of the crown and above can be used.

A replica of all of the other chakras and the total energy signature of each individual is said to exist within the crown chakra. Here, our unique pattern of consciousness is kept in constant touch with all sorts of information from the outer universe and the subtle dimensions of spiritual energy.

The crown chakra is our connection to the whole of creation. Aspects of this wholeness are filtered, transformed, and utilized by the rest of the chakra system, like transformers taking high currents of electricity down to a level where they can be used to run different machines coming from one powerful generator.

As the base chakra connects us safely and firmly to the earth, so the crown chakra opens us to universal energy. We certainly are not able to exist in physical form without both these centers working together in harmony. In some ways, imbalances in either have similar symptom pictures.

ABOVE *The crown chakra, sahasrara, is located just above the head. It links us to the rest of the universe.*

ABOVE *In ancient Indian manuscripts, the lotus flower symbolizes the crown chakra.*

In general, the crown chakra, which is more universal in character, is more robust than the clearly defined base chakra.

When the crown chakra loses its balance, a shadow is cast over the whole system. There is a feeling that something is not right, although it can be difficult to describe clearly what is the matter. Feelings of alienation and depression, and of a weight descending that makes one listless, exhausted, and prone to boredom, all signal a possible crown chakra imbalance.

Physically, apart from its links with the pituitary gland which it may subtly energize, the crown chakra directly affects the functions of the higher brain. The cerebrum, consisting of the two hemispheres of the brain, is the seat of higher consciousness. A lack of balance between the left and right hemispheres can cause confusion and coordination difficulties both physically and mentally. When balanced, the crown chakra increases the ability to understand things in a wider context. This allows the individual to become more intuitive and more likely to act appropriately, and thus success in action increases with the expenditure of less effort.

Working with greater efficiency, the mind becomes quieter and is able to focus on its tasks. This smooth flow of energy makes meditative practices more fulfilling and allows the experience of bliss – the joy felt in every system, organ, and cell when everything suddenly slips into perfect working order. In these circumstances, the healing potential within the body is at its greatest, stress can be released, and tissue repair quickened dramatically.

Amethyst

Sugilite

Fluorite

Iolite

CROWN CHAKRA LAYOUT

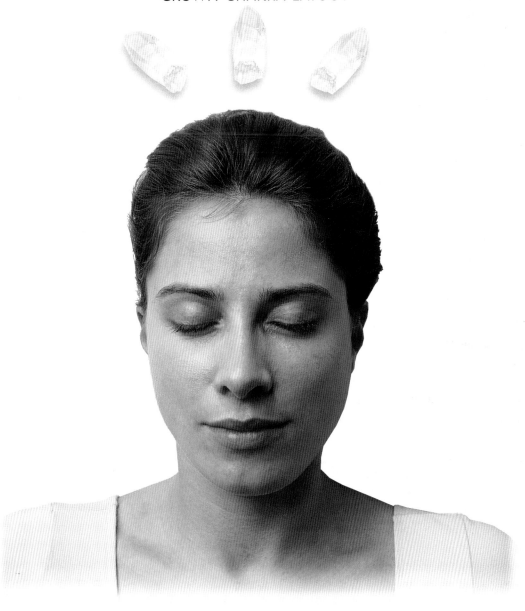

During crystal healing sessions, it is a common practice to place a clear quartz crystal close to the top of the head in the same way that a grounding stone is automatically placed near the feet. Clear quartz will add an extra dimension of order and brightness to the energy passing through the crown. With both these channels open and balanced, the body is free to absorb those qualities of energy most suited to its healing at that time.

Because of its holistic character, stones of other sorts may be discovered to balance the crown chakra, although the following suggestion will provide a good basis for individual needs. Use three clear quartz crystals and place one centrally at the top of the head and one on each side. If the stones have points, direct them outward. Other stones can be added to this layout if necessary.

Milky Quartz   Opal   Moonstone   Chalk

Minor Chakras

In addition to the seven main chakras aligned along the spinal column, there are numerous other energy centers that are located within and around the body. These are only minor in the respect that their functions are very specific. However, if a serious imbalance occurs in some of these energy centers, the effect on the whole system can be significant. Quite often stones will intuitively be placed to balance these points, and intuition is probably the best guide, as different authorities and systems suggest many different locations and functions.

ABOVE *Minor chakra points can be located with a pendulum.*

There is a series of chakra points continuing along the body midline both above and below the physical points. The five chakras located above the head, numbered from 8 to 12, are related to universal and multidimensional vibrations that are held within our finer subtle bodies. It is quite easy to locate these centers by using a sensitized hand or a pendulum (see pages 96–97). Occasionally it is necessary to work with crystals on some of these upper five chakras. It normally signifies that some help is needed with subtle information input into the conscious levels of the self.

ABOVE *Use intuition when choosing stones to balance minor chakras.*

The chakras located below the base of the spine – both midline and on the body at the knees, ankles, and feet – all work with aspects of physical existence such as practical support, flexibility, and the relationship of self to surroundings. All of these chakra points can all be used as alternative grounding positions. The chakra located just below the feet – the earth star chakra – is an especially powerful anchor point into this reality.

There are as many chakras to be found outside the physical body within the aura as there are on the body. Do not be disconcerted if you find that you are wanting to put one or more crystals some distance from the body. Stones that are placed a considerable way from the body can have a profound effect and are often clearly felt by the patient to be very powerful. The type and color of stone that you choose will suggest the energy required at each place in order to restore balance.

BELOW *The earth-star chakra lies below the feet. Placing a stone here is energizing, stabilizing, and helps you to bond with the planet.*

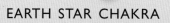

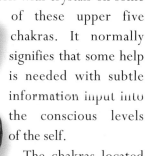

EARTH STAR CHAKRA

There is an important chakra – known as the earth star chakra – located about 3ft (1m) below the soles of the feet, which, when activated, can really lock the individual's energies into a harmonious relationship with the planet and the solidity of the present. It can be visualized by first imagining a triangle between the base chakra and the soles of the feet. This triangle is then reflected down into the ground, forming a diamond with the base chakra at the top point and the earth star chakra at the lowest point. Holding this image can be a powerful meditation, thoroughly linking and rooting energy firmly in the present. It can be deeply energizing and stabilizing. Placing a stone here helps to focus attention on the larger self.

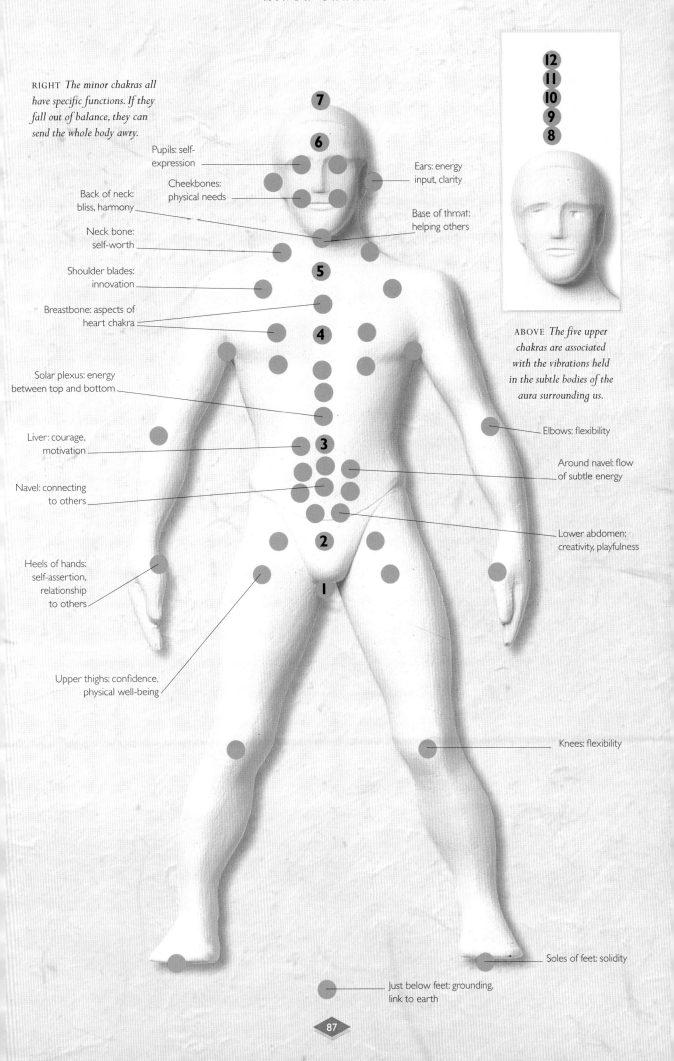

RIGHT *The minor chakras all have specific functions. If they fall out of balance, they can send the whole body awry.*

Pupils: self-expression

Ears: energy input, clarity

Cheekbones: physical needs

Back of neck: bliss, harmony

Base of throat: helping others

Neck bone: self-worth

Shoulder blades: innovation

Breastbone: aspects of heart chakra

ABOVE *The five upper chakras are associated with the vibrations held in the subtle bodies of the aura surrounding us.*

Solar plexus: energy between top and bottom

Elbows: flexibility

Liver: courage, motivation

Around navel: flow of subtle energy

Navel: connecting to others

Lower abdomen: creativity, playfulness

Heels of hands: self-assertion, relationship to others

Upper thighs: confidence, physical well-being

Knees: flexibility

Soles of feet: solidity

Just below feet: grounding, link to earth

Simple Chakra Balances

Becoming familiar with the chakra positions and their primary associated colors and functions is best learned by starting off with simple healing exercises using a few crystals. Remember that the purpose of all chakra healing techniques is to restore a normal functioning balance to the system as a whole.

Haphazard activation or focus on any one chakra can lead to serious imbalance on many levels – physical, emotional, mental, and spiritual. Learning and practicing spiritual exercises regularly, using crystals and other methods to alleviate stress and promote health, will naturally and safely enhance the quality of experience and the energy available within the body's chakras and other subtle systems.

ABOVE *Practicing spiritual exercises regularly will help to balance the chakras naturally.*

CHAKRA BALANCE 1

Use clear quartz crystals, either natural or tumbled stones, of roughly the same size and weight. Place one on each chakra point and leave them for three or four minutes. After this time, remove all stones and simply lie relaxed for a few moments more. You may feel there is a need for a grounding stone placed between the feet. When you are doing these exercises by yourself, it is helpful to lay the stones out next to where you will be lying down. It is then much easier to place each stone without the others falling off.

Sometimes a stone will continually slip out of place. If this happens more than a couple of times, leave it where it has come to rest. Often the body has recognized a more appropriate placement for the stone and has made small movements to relocate it.

Some stones will feel extremely heavy, almost sinking into the body, while others will feel so light they won't be noticed. Some stones may feel very cold, others burning hot, or itchy or even electric. You may also feel as if you are floating above the ground, or there may be a sensation of energy moving through the body or visual impressions of colors or patterns. All of these are natural as the body systems find their new equilibrium or release long-held stress and tensions with the help of the crystals.

Very often a crystal healing session is the first opportunity a person has had to relax completely while they are still awake. Gentle feedback is useful, allowing the healer to give reassurance.

CHAKRA BALANCE 2

Place clear quartz crystals, points inward, next to each side of the body at the level of each chakra. Here all stones are off the body, confirming that the sensations and experiences have been caused by a change in the energy flow rather than the weight or temperature of the stones.

A variation on this balance is to first place the crystals with their points facing outward, releasing stress and tension. After three or four minutes, reverse the direction, so the points are now inward-facing to recharge and energize the centers. After a few minutes, move the stones away from the body and rest a while. Use a grounding stone if necessary.

CAUTION

It is not appropriate to work on chakras in order to encourage spiritual growth. An analogy would be allowing a child to drive a turbocharged motorbike as soon as she can ride a bicycle. Without practice and experience, it would be too much power for her to control and would end in disaster.

RAINBOW STONE SEQUENCE

Begin with a red stone, such as garnet or jasper, for the base chakra, placed either between the legs or two similar stones on the groin points.

The sacral chakra is balanced by an orange stone like carnelian, orange calcite, or a dark citrine quartz.

The third chakra, the solar plexus, has a yellow stone such as citrine quartz, tiger's eye, pyrites, amber, or topaz.

The heart chakra is in the center of the chest where a green stone like jade, aventurine, bloodstone, or malachite is placed. A small pink stone could also be added.

At the throat chakra just above the sternal notch, place a light blue stone such as blue lace agate, turquoise, or aquamarine.

In the center of the forehead at the brow chakra, use a dark blue or violet stone: lapis lazuli, sodalite, fluorite, or amethyst.

At the crown chakra, a white or clear stone like clear quartz would be best. Golden or violet stones could also be used such as amethyst, gold, or lemon quartz.

Place a dark citrine, smoky quartz, hematite, or black tourmaline by the feet to stabilize and ground all the energies.

ABOVE *Chakra balance 3: the rainbow stone sequence. A stone of the main chakra color is placed on each energy point.*

These are some techniques to practice on another person. They will encourage reliance on intuitive decisions as well as familiarity with the sequence of color and chakra (see also page 110).

TECHNIQUE I: CHOOSING THE MOST APPROPRIATE STONES

Placing a stone of the related color onto a chakra point, i.e. a light blue stone onto the throat center, has the effect of reinforcing the general qualities present there. This helps to stimulate and balance the overall functions of each chakra, but does not necessarily directly remove imbalances. In order to focus healing energy specifically on the areas needing attention, it may be that a crystal of another color is the best choice. A good assessment technique or well-tuned intuition is needed to work in this way.

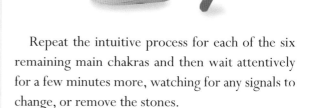

BELOW *Select a stone of related color and place it on the chakra point you are going to work on.*

RIGHT *Dowse over the chakra to see which stone is appropriate for balancing the area.*

Using intuition alone, move to each chakra center and, with the palm of the hand or a crystal held in the hand, open your awareness to the energies present and clearly intend that you will recognize any imbalances that are ready, willing, and able to be released safely and effectively. It is not necessary to be aware of this information at a conscious level. When you feel ready, move over to your healing crystals and pick up the first one that attracts your attention. Whatever the mineral or color, this will be the stone that will balance that chakra.

Repeat the intuitive process for each of the six remaining main chakras and then wait attentively for a few minutes more, watching for any signals to change, or remove the stones.

When the stones are all removed, settle the aura – sweep your hands slowly from head to feet with the clear intention to settle all energies to a normal functioning level, protecting and securing chakras and subtle bodies.

TECHNIQUE II: ASSESSED BALANCE

Dowsing (see pages 96–98) or muscle-testing (see pages 102–105) can be used in a similar way. Begin as always by centering and grounding your energies.

Dowse over each chakra center to determine what stone will best balance each area. Use color categories to narrow down the identification in the first instance. First, ask if it is a warm-colored stone (red, pink, orange, yellow) or a cool-colored stone (green, turquoise, blue, indigo, violet). If your testing indicates neither of these categories, ask about white, clear, gray, black, or multicolored. The second question will identify the exact color of the stone needed, for example, pink.

The third question will identify which one of the pink minerals you have is the most appropriate to use. If you have more than one example of the crystal, a fourth question may identify one particular stone as being more effective than another of the same variety. This is not always necessary, but some bodies can be very fussy!

This way of working is much faster to do than to describe once the above pattern of questions is clear in your mind.

When all stones are in place, dowse for the length of time they need to remain on the body. Remove the stones and settle the aura as before.

TECHNIQUE III: SINGLE SPECTRUM

As a variation to this balance, begin by placing a single color stone on each chakra: red at base, orange at sacral, yellow at solar plexus, and so on. This will settle down the energy system and begin the healing process of the body. Once this is done, go back to the base chakra and check whether another stone will be of use to further increase the effectiveness of the balance. Proceed as with I or II. Particularly when you are learning crystal healing, it can take a while to work out which stones go where. For example, beginning with a basic chakra spectrum layout, or another simple calming and balancing layout (see pages 52–53), while you are finding out what is required, increases the efficiency of the session and allows more profound healing to take place.

TECHNIQUE IV: BALANCING CHAKRAS FOR OVER- AND UNDER-ENERGY

We have seen how an intuitive approach can identify and balance any chakras that are over-energized or lacking in energy. Exactly the same procedure can be adapted to the use of assessment by pendulum or muscle-testing.

STRUCTURE AND INTUITION

▲ In a learning situation, it is vital to begin with a clearly discernible working structure within which personal experiences can be firmly set or measured. Time and again I have watched very adequate trainee healers flounder simply because they "don't feel anything" or place no confidence in their own intuitive abilities. Intuition flourishes when there is stability and confidence. It withers away when there is any doubt about ability. Structure provides the relaxation within which personal skills can begin to mature.

Check if it is appropriate to balance the body for over- and under-energies with the following steps:
1 Move to each chakra in turn. Ask the question: Is this chakra balanced?
2 If the answer is yes, ask whether it requires a stone to maintain its balance while you are working on the remaining chakras.
3 If the chakra is out of balance, the next questions will be: Is this chakra under-energized? Is this chakra over-energized?
4 Next, identify, using color and type categories, which crystal will restore the chakra to normal, balanced function.
5 Check whether additional crystals are needed, in the case of under-energy, to direct energy toward the chakra or, for over-energy, to lead it away from the area. Use quartz points or other crystals with strong direction to help to restore a balance of energy. Tourmalines, topaz, kyanite, kunzite, selenite, and all stones with parallel striations tend to be good energy shifters.
6 Remove the stones. Dowse first in order to find out whether the order of the stones' removal is important. Sometimes extra or directional stones are best removed first, before the main chakra stones are taken away. This makes the whole process a smoother experience.

LEFT *A pendulum can also be used to check out whether a chakra is out of balance.*

Color Meditation for Assessing Chakras

The imaginative skills of the mind can provide the crystal healer with many ways to recognize and assess energy patterns within the subtle anatomy. The art of using these methods requires a degree of careful attention to notice what comes into the mind. Unexpected images and feelings are an indication that your mind has gone beyond the stage of guided visualization and is really perceiving with some accuracy what is actually present on subtle levels. Often the awareness initially needs to be pointed in the right direction. Guided visualization, imagining or "pretending", sets the scene and helps to establish a state of passive attentiveness in which the everyday conscious mind drops some of its analytical hold on what is perceived.

THE USES OF GUIDED VISUALIZATION

Often your awareness initially needs to be pointed in the right direction. The more familiar your mind becomes with a repeated sequence of images, or instruction, the easier it is to slip into a receptive frame of mind where intuition can arise, and the visualization takes on a life of its own.

BODY VIEWING/BODY OVERVIEW

This exercise in visualization allows someone to scan their body in a way that may suggest which areas are in need of balancing and healing.

1 After grounding and centering your energies, and totally relaxing your physical body, imagine that you are looking at an image of yourself. It might be a mirror image or a picture, or you might see if you can move away from where you are lying and then turn around to look at yourself. Or you may visualize yourself floating upward and then looking down on your resting body. The image does not need to be photographically clear; a faint impression will do to start.

ABOVE *The key to using guided visualization and body overview methods is to be attentive and receptive to what comes into your mind.*

2 Now take a look over, in, and around your body image. There may be areas of color, or light and shade, or you may find it difficult to see some parts.
3 Wherever there is a darker area, or turbulence of some kind, or a lack of definition, gently focus on that with your subtle senses. Be aware of any emotional content or any thoughts that arise. These may indicate the causes of disturbance and the crystals that will help to rebalance the body.
4 It is not necessary to become intensely attached to what you see. This is simply a quick glance using fine levels of the sense perceptions to identify and deal with areas of imbalance. Unless you have already set mental parameters, your vision will include all energy levels, from the physical to the highest spiritual body, so avoid analysis and the temptation to diagnose.

The technique opposite will give you an indication of the state of your chakras, while at the same time strengthening the energy of each with the appropriate color. Any area that seems more difficult to imagine with clarity may indicate some lack of energy there, so spend a little more time focusing color into that spot.

DRAWING DOWN COLORS

This meditation can be fully visualized and elaborate, or carried out very quickly, drawing colors one after the other to the chakras and down to the ground. The exercise strengthens each chakra center with its balancing color vibration. You will probably notice that some parts seem easier to imagine than others. Some chakras might seem never to get filled, for example. This will give some indication which energy centers may need more attention at the moment. Any area difficult to visualize needs more work to integrate it fully into the whole system. This technique can be a useful diagnostic tool.

1. Make sure you are seated comfortably. Center and ground yourself and then imagine a large bright sphere of white light suspended above your head.

2. From this sphere you will be able to draw down any color at will.

3. Imagine a good, strong red light in the sphere. Pull it down into your body and down the spine to fill up the base chakra with deep, red energy. Allow the color to completely fill the chakra and let any overflow simply pass down into the earth.

4. Next, take orange from the sphere. Let it sink down to your lower abdomen, to the sacral chakra, the hara, the center of gravity between the pelvic bones. Let the orange completely fill the area and allow any excess to drain away into the earth.

5. Now return to the white light sphere and let yellow stream down to your solar plexus. Let it gather there until it becomes like a bright sun that illuminates the whole of your body. Take time to make sure there are no areas left in shadow or lacking this warm golden light. Allow any excess to flow into the earth.

6. Now take a rich, vibrant green and fill the heart center with green light. Feel it balancing and calming the emotions. Allow as much green as you need to be soaked up, and any extra can flow into the earth.

7. Take a sky blue light from the sphere above you and flood the throat center with cool blue radiance. See the blue flow in and all around you, forging links of information and understanding with the world. Let the extra energy sweep right through you into the earth.

8. Now find a deep midnight blue and bring it to completely fill the brow chakra. Feel the soothing, quiet calm descend on you as the depths of space rests your inner sight and dissolves away tension. Let any extra indigo energy spread into the universe.

9. Finally, return to the sphere and draw down a subtly shining violet that pours over your crown chakra and infuses the whole of your aura in a continual stream, protecting and balancing all aspects of the self.

10. After a minute or two, let the images fade and bring your attention back to your body. Take a couple of deep breaths, feel your fingers and toes, and when you are ready, slowly open your eyes.

PART FIVE

ASSESSMENT TOOLS

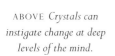

ABOVE *Crystals can instigate change at deep levels of the mind.*

Crystal healing is primarily concerned with creating positive changes at subtle levels of awareness that are not usually accessible to the conscious mind. It can be useful to have one or two ways in which to check what is going on, and how effective any healing has been. The only machine capable of recognizing these nonphysical energies is the human body itself.

Developing intuitive skills is vital to any healer, as is learning to recognize the intuitive information always available to us. In the West there is a tendency to emphasize conscious, rational thinking processes and the outer senses rather than what are considered nonverifiable sensations and feelings. This means great care must be taken to build up confidence in our intuitive assessment. Doubts and insecurity obscure our intuitive processes and push us out of a grounded and centered state of mind. Having physically verifiable methods to clarify and back up intuitive skills means we can be more effective healers.

Pendulum Dowsing

A pendulum is any balanced weight suspended by a chain or thread and is simply a means of visibly checking what the unconscious mind already knows. The pendulum represents an extension of the inner senses and creates a visual representation of inner energy changes. The pendulum amplifies small muscle movements that result from changes in subtle energy flow through the physical body. The conscious mind, emotions, and physical tension can all affect the pendulum. When there is an emotional investment in the answer, dowsing will nearly always produce an unreliable result. The skill in effective pendulum dowsing is to remain in a relaxed, neutral frame of mind and to have a good system of questioning. When dowsing, it is a good idea to check your positive and negative responses each time the pendulum is used. It is also a good idea to check any new pendulum you might use. Occasionally the natural swings change because of the weight, shape, or material of the pendulum. A pendulum that is used only for assessment work needs to be cleaned occasionally, but not as regularly as healing crystals or jewelry.

Carnelian
pendulum

Blue
Quartz
pendulum

Amethyst
pendulum

Aventurine
pendulum

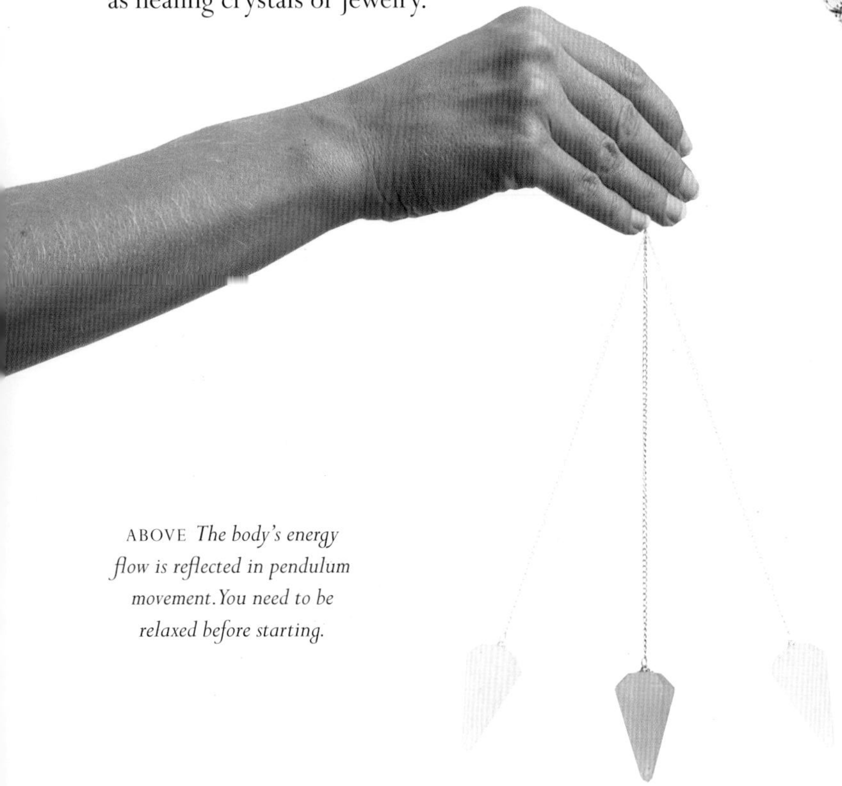

ABOVE *The body's energy flow is reflected in pendulum movement. You need to be relaxed before starting.*

LEFT A pendulum is a tool for revealing inner energies: by watching it swing you get an indication of changes in subtle energy flow.

Amethyst pendulum

Clear Quartz pendulum

PENDULUM PROCEDURE

1 Choose a pendulum with which you feel comfortable. It should be well balanced and feel neither too heavy nor too light. You can use either your left or your right hand.

2 Keeping the string, chain, or thread about 4 or 5 inches (10 or 12 centimeters) long, hold the pendulum between your thumb and index finger. Make sure your forearm is held parallel to the ground, with your wrist relaxed.

3 Set the pendulum in a gentle, neutral swing, moving in a straight line away from you. Let it swing about 8 times to get the feel of it. Bring it to a halt either by stopping it with your other hand or by using a small upward jerk of the pendulum hand.

4 Repeat the neutral swing to begin, and after a short time mentally ask the pendulum to begin to develop into a clockwise, circular, or elliptical motion for another 6 to 8 rotations. Stop the pendulum again.

5 Repeat the exercise; this time intend a counterclockwise movement.

6 When you are confident with these exercises, use your intention to stop the pendulum swing.

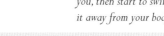

RIGHT Hold the pendulum in front of you, then start to swing it away from your body.

PENDULUM RESPONSES

Before you start, use a grounding and centering technique (see pages 40–47). It is good practice to get into the habit of automatically balancing your energies before beginning any sort of assessment to ensure the most accurate results possible at that time. The next step is to find out in which direction the pendulum will move in a response to yes and no answers.

Yes and no responses are entirely individual. Some people have circular swings, some elliptical, some directional straight lines. In all, there may be several hundred different swings a pendulum is capable of making. The important point is to be able to easily recognize what the pendulum is indicating.

RESPONSE PROCEDURE

1 Hold your free hand over your solar plexus between the bottom of your rib cage and navel, and set the pendulum into a neutral swing. This position effectively taps you into your own energy systems directly.

2 Without focusing on the movement of the pendulum, ask for it to move in a direction that indicates a "yes" response.

3 Once a strong swing becomes clear make a note of the type of swing and its direction.

4 Stop the pendulum.

5 Repeat the procedure, and ask to be shown a "no" response. Again, once a clear swing has developed, make a note of the direction.

6 This process may need to be repeated several times until you feel you have confidence in the responses. Where there is only a small distinction in the response it is possible to instruct the pendulum that a swing one way is yes, and the opposite is no.

Techniques for Pendulum Dowsing

Pendulum assessment is only as accurate as the questioning techniques used. A line of inquiry can easily be diverted from its correct path by the careless framing of a question or the misinterpretation of the answer. Dowsing can be tedious and confusing without set procedures to follow. Although it seems very easy to watch a pendulum swing to and fro, the movement is simply the physical confirmation of activity within your unconscious and subtle levels of awareness. Effective dowsing requires entering an altered state of awareness slightly removed from everyday processes. This is quite hard to describe, but with practice it can be recognized by its feel and quality of focus. It is a delicate state to maintain, and the following guidelines may be helpful.

1 Center and ground your energies before you begin dowsing assessments.

2 Check the yes or no swings of your pendulum.

3 Confirm that you are ready, willing, and able to carry out the assessment work at this

BELOW *Pendulum dowsing can be a useful method of confirming the effectiveness of healing techniques.*

time. If there is a negative response here, check whether you need to do something else first (see Protection and Support, pages 48–49).

Always ask questions or make statements in the simplest language and make sure that they can be answered with a yes or no. For example, frame the question "When will this healing be complete?" as "This healing will be complete in … minutes." The pendulum can then respond with a movement that indicates either "Yes, this is a true statement" or "No, this is not accurate."

Where there is a question with significant emotional loading for the questioner, that is, there is an obvious preferred outcome, neutrality can be slightly enhanced by clearly stating "Yes or no" after the question. On the whole, it is much better to avoid ALL questions where there is a serious personal involvement. Anything as important as "Do I have a life-threatening disease?" will throw all energy systems into an unbalanced panic state where all responses will be inaccurate or random.

DOWSING WITH LISTS AND ARCS

Mental and emotional neutrality can be easier to maintain if dowsing is done with lists, arcs, or with your free hand touching or pointing to stones. Lists can be made of anything useful to the healer. They can be specific, such as chakras, meridians, types of stone, or general, such as colors or numbers. A number list, for example, can be used to find out how long a stone needs to be in place, how often a stone needs cleansing, and so on.

All questioning should start off with big categories and work down to small areas. For example, "Does this chakra require a warm-colored stone?" The response immediately narrows the search to either red-orange-yellow or green-blue-violet areas. The next stage is isolating the color and then running through the individual crystals you have.

It works similarly with timing or amounts. Use the phrase "more than…" i.e. "Does this correction need more than five stones?" or "Does this stone need to be in position more than ten minutes?"

The less the conscious mind needs to be used, the easier it is to remain neutral. Using lists and arcs means being able to determine answers quickly without having to consciously frame questions.

Use lists in the same way, beginning with large categories, such as: "Is this list appropriate?," "Is this column?," "Is what is needed between here and here…?," "Is this what is needed?" With your free hand, touch or define what you are asking about. It is not necessary to focus on your lists, just keep your eyes relaxed so that you can see, but not read, the words. When making your own lists, keep them random and out of alphabetical order.

Dowsing arcs are even easier to use than lists. Arcs are used instead of circles because any pendulum swing on a circle will pick out two sections at the top and bottom of the swing, but only one possible section is indicated on an arc.

DOWSING WITH ARCS

❖ Ground and center yourself (see pages 40–47).

❖ Place the dowsing arc in front of you on a flat surface.

❖ Touch the arc and ask if this arc is appropriate. If it is, ask the pendulum to swing in a line to indicate the appropriate answer. Keep the pendulum fairly close to the flat surface so that it is easier to identify the correct section.

❖ Let the pendulum move in a straight swing from the central point where you are keeping it. When the pendulum settles to a new angle of swing, check the response by placing a finger of your free hand on the segment, and use the yes or no procedure. It is wise to avoid focusing on the pendulum until its angle has stabilized. The eye can hold back the movement by its concentration at an inappropriate location.

❖ Always get into the habit of asking: "Is there anything else?" You should not assume you have all the answers when more information might be available.

RIGHT AND BELOW *Dowsing arcs can be made simply using a compass and protractor. Dowsing lists can be specific or general.*

- Amethyst
- Carnelian
- Lapis lazuli
- Clear quartz
- Rose quartz

- Sacral chakra
- Crown chakra
- Throat chakra
- Base chakra
- Heart chakra
- Solar Plexus
- Brow chakra

ABOVE *Dowsing arcs can be divided into several sections. For example, an arc divided into color sections can help the healer decide which colored stone is most appropriate to use.*

ABOVE *Dowsing arcs divided into numbers will help answer any questions regarding timing and quantity. A list of numbers can be just as effective, too.*

Assessment Using Kinesiology

Kinesiology, commonly known as muscle testing, is perhaps one of the most useful assessment tools any healer can learn. When used properly, it opens huge areas of possibility, both for learning more about subtle functioning and for resolving problems at every level. Kinesiology appears to be a simple process to learn and apply, but in order to use it judiciously and accurately, it is necessary to follow the correct procedures carefully. Essentially, muscle testing is an extension of the same processes that allow pendulum dowsing to work. That is, the physical body responds clearly to very small changes of energy flow within its subtle systems. Every stimulus, whether it comes from the sense organs, from a verbal cue, from a thought or emotion, affects the quality of life energy, either enhancing or depleting it. Like a light bulb dimming and brightening with a change of current, the body systems reflect variations in energy flow. So there is potential here for an on-off switch, or a yes or no, response.

Kinesiology testing arose when chiropractors noticed that a muscle would tend to have less tone when held in certain positions or when other points on the body were touched. This observation was developed into a coherent assessment and healing system by applying muscle groups to the main energy meridians identified in traditional Chinese medicine. Responses in certain muscles would indicate that a particular meridian was either strong or weak.

Kinesiology testing does not use the mechanical strength of a muscle since it is not a test of strength. The testing is of muscle tone. Muscle tone is the ability of a muscle to respond smoothly and with equal resistance to a gentle pressure placed on it in a certain direction. Where subtle energy flows are healthy, the muscle is able to respond well to the applied pressure, but when there is some reduction

MUSCLE TESTING

▲ Also known as kinesiology, muscle testing is used to test muscle tone. This gives the healer an indication of the strength or weakness of particular energy flows in a patient's body.

▲ This technique links each muscle group to the main energy meridians that are used in Traditional Chinese Medicine. A weak muscle tone usually indicates that there is a blockage in energy flow from meridian to muscle.

▲ Crystal healers use muscle testing techniques to determine which crystals are the most effective for improving energy flow in a patient's body.

ABOVE *The strength of the body's energy flow can flicker from time to time, and kinesiology is able to detect this.*

or blockage in energy flow to it, it becomes unable to resist steady pressure of energy in the muscle.

Working with the basic observations of muscle testing, numerous types of kinesiology have developed. All use muscle testing as an indicator of energy status, but the key differences are in what questions are put to the body and how the information is gathered and applied.

In crystal healing, the most useful techniques deal mainly with a yes or no response. The advantage of using accurate muscle testing in crystal work is that it actively involves the patient. It is their own body that responds to questions about what methods of healing would be the most useful. It is very apparent when a muscle tests strong and when it tests weak. It can be a clear demonstration, for example, that a certain crystal dramatically increases the available life energy, or that a weak test before crystal healing becomes strong when retested at the end of a session. A healer using a pendulum may obtain the same degree of accuracy as from muscle testing, and in some circumstances dowsing will be more appropriate, but having a choice of tools increases a healer's flexibility.

THE MERIDIAN SYSTEM

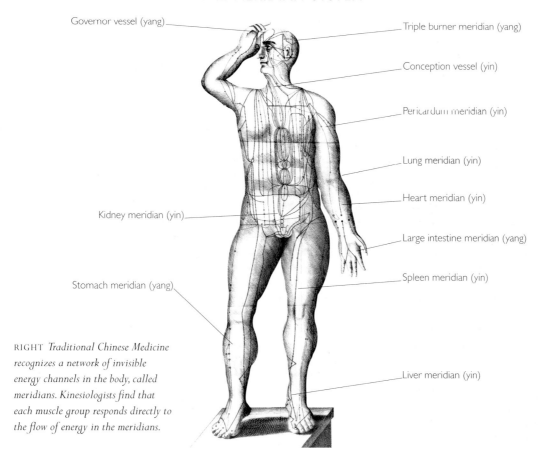

Governor vessel (yang)

Triple burner meridian (yang)

Conception vessel (yin)

Pericardium meridian (yin)

Lung meridian (yin)

Heart meridian (yin)

Kidney meridian (yin)

Large intestine meridian (yang)

Spleen meridian (yin)

Stomach meridian (yang)

Liver meridian (yin)

RIGHT *Traditional Chinese Medicine recognizes a network of invisible energy channels in the body, called meridians. Kinesiologists find that each muscle group responds directly to the flow of energy in the meridians.*

Muscle testing directly stimulates the feedback systems of the body. The process automatically allows the finer levels of awareness to become available to the conscious mind, which in turn gives more confidence to intuitive information.

Like pendulum dowsing, the accuracy of muscle testing depends upon a baseline of grounded and centered energy where there is stability and focus, free from expectation of results, and a carefully maintained mental neutrality. As with dowsing, any stress factors are likely to disrupt temporarily the baseline energy of either healer or the patient. This is known as switching, where responses to questions become random and inaccurate. The greatest fault in muscle-testing procedures is failure to take account of the switching phenomenon.

Always begin all testing by tapping in or using other grounding and centering exercises (see pages 40–47). Where switching is suspected, repeat these procedures. The therapeutic advantage of muscle testing is that every stage of corrective work can be checked for its effectiveness.

Although it uses the physical body — testing muscles and holding energy points — kinesiology is a subtle energy technique, and, as such, it is prone to being influenced by the belief patterns and mental constructs of the tester. This is to some extent unavoidable in any healing modality, but many kinesiologists seem to think that the techniques are always completely accurate and foolproof. Healing is always a joining and an understanding between healer and patient. Belief systems and preconceived ideas become part of a circuit of merged energies, and there is no way to avoid this. Correct attitude, humor, self-awareness, humility, and confidence all reduce the possibility of deception. Ultimately, every practicing healer and therapist needs to remind themselves constantly that they are merely catalysts in the healing process. They are not the cause or the creators of health.

Muscle-testing Procedures

Muscle testing is a simple procedure, but it needs the correct mental attitude, the right approach, and plenty of practice. The accuracy of the testing is the responsibility of the tester.

Make sure you are centered and grounded. Begin by using the tapping in procedure on you and your partner. Bring your fingers together so the fingertips are overlapping. Tap around the thymus gland near the top of the sternum in a counter-clockwise direction 10 to 15 times.

GENERAL MUSCLE TESTING

The key with muscle testing is to feel the response in the muscles on which you are working. Every person is different, so you will need to practice to find the appropriate level of testing for an individual. Both people should be relaxed

ABOVE *Before muscle testing can begin, it is essential to feel focused. Ground and center yourself by using the tapping in technique.*

before you begin. The amount of physical effort used needs to be minimal (see step 1, below).

Although kinesiology relates specific muscles in the body to the main energy meridians of Traditional Chinese Medicine, here we are simply concerned with using muscle testing as an indicator. Any muscle test can be used as an indicator, but some are easier to use, and less tiring.

Testing can be carried out standing, sitting, or lying down, but make sure the body is not lopsided, the hands are not touching the body, and the legs are uncrossed. Make sure other muscle groups are not being used to strengthen the test. If you make sure that both of you are not holding your breath when testing, or are both gently breathing out, this will help prevent tensing.

GENERAL MUSCLE TESTING

1 Stand a little way from a wall so that if you raise your arm, you will touch it. Feel your muscles activating as you push forward gently against the surface. This is all the pressure you should be using in testing others.

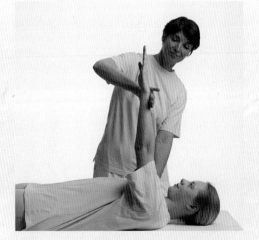

2 Demonstrate the movement of the limb with your partner. Move your partner's arm through the range of movements to show the direction and muscles being used. This picture shows the anterior serratus muscle being tested.

MUSCLES TO TEST:

◆ Anterior serratus

A stronger muscle test than the previous one but can be less tiring when lying down. The arm is held upright at 90 degrees to the body, palm facing down toward the feet. The movement is straight down along the line of the body.

◆ Brachioradialis

The upper arm is held close to the body, lower arm bent at an angle of about 35 degrees with palm toward the body. The movement is straight down. This is usually an easy test since it doesn't need much effort and isn't too tiring. (See below.)

◆ Anterior deltoid

The arm is held straight out at an angle of 35 degrees. The elbow is locked, palm down. The movement is straight down. The tester should use light downward pressure just above the wrist.

◆ Latissimus dorsi

This is a good muscle to test for those with very strong muscles or with little energy. It must be tested very lightly with two fingers only. The arm is held straight, elbow locked tight to the side with palm facing outward. The tester pulls gently away from the body just above the wrist.(See below.)

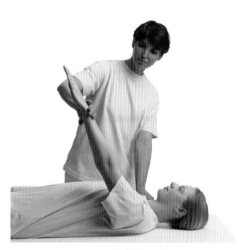

3 Put the limb into position and say "hold." When carrying out a test, stay away from pulse points and do not grip the arm. Use a flat palm or two or three fingers held straight.

4 Pause for a second, and then evenly and gradually apply enough pressure to see whether the muscle locks or feels weak and spongy. After a couple of seconds, gently and gradually release the pressure.

OTHER HINTS FOR MUSCLE TESTING

◆ Always support the arm once it has been tested. Leaving it in the air or letting it drop is very tiring.

◆ If all tests seem to be weak, have the person drink a little water, then retest.

◆ If a result is unclear, repeat the test. A weak muscle will become progressively weaker; a strong muscle will strengthen further.

◆ Ask the person how a test feels if you are not sure whether a muscle is strong or weak.

◆ There are degrees of weakness: no resistance at all, slow weakening, hesitant weakness, a spongy feeling. Many people's arms will move some distance before locking. This distance needs gauging in each person. In some, the difference between a strong and weak test is subtle. If you continue to be unsure of the responses, either use self-testing surrogate techniques or change to pendulum dowsing.

◆ Keep your tone of voice constant when making statements. Do not favor one possibility over any other.

◆ Don't stare or maintain long eye contact during testing, because this reduces the emotional and mental neutrality essential for good results.

◆ If muscles on one side of the body are weak or tired, try those on the other side. Muscles will eventually tire too much to continue testing.

◆ If responses become confused, or don't make sense, it is usually a sign of switching (see box). Tap in to restore balance. Important, traumatic, or emotional issues are likely to cause switching.

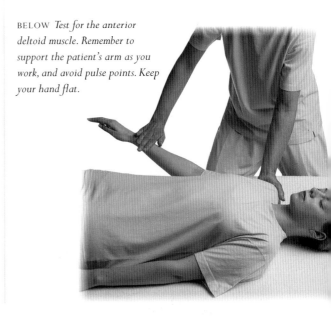

BELOW *Test for the anterior deltoid muscle. Remember to support the patient's arm as you work, and avoid pulse points. Keep your hand flat.*

TESTS FOR SWITCHING

Now that you have a strong indicator muscle, it is necessary to check whether the body is in sufficient balance to test accurately that it is not switched. Following are four quick pre-tests to carry out.

1 Ask your partner to place the palm of their free hand over their navel. Test the muscle again. If the muscle test remains strong, continue to 2.

2 Put the tip of one finger on any muscle and test. This time, the muscle test should be weak. Repeat the test with the tips of two adjacent fingers on any muscle. Now the muscle should test strong.

3 Now lightly pinch the center of any muscle. This should weaken your test muscle. Smooth over the muscle and the test should now be strong.

RIGHT *Test for switching by asking your partner to put their palm over their navel while you test the indicator muscle.*

4 Silently or out loud say "Yes" and test the muscle. It should stay strong. Then say "No" and test the muscle. It should be weak.

Now the muscle test has clearly indicated that the body can react to both positive and negative states. Continue with your assessment. If any test did not produce the correct response, tap in the body and repeat the tests. These switching tests are checking that the body is, first, in general balance with all its meridians, or energy pathways, and second, that it recognizes electromagnetic polarity.

Different areas of the body carry different electrical charges – some areas are positively and some negatively charged. The test means the body is recognizing these polarities accurately. Third, it checks that the nerve impulses to and from the brain are working correctly, and last, that the body recognizes the difference between positive and negative statements.

SELF TESTING AND SURROGATE TESTING

Self testing is a useful technique to muscle test yourself as an alternative to pendulum dowsing. It can also be used in surrogate testing. This is where the tester keeps in physical contact with the patient to ensure a flow of information and energy and asks questions of the patient via the tester's own energy system.

1 As with all forms of muscle testing begin the session by grounding, centering, and tapping in (see pages 40–47).

2 Let the tips of both thumb and little finger of the left hand touch together.

3 Now insert the thumb and index finger of the right hand with tips touching into the gap between the palm of the left hand and the thumb and little finger of the left hand.

4 By parting the thumb and index finger of the right hand sharply outward to contact the thumb and finger of the left hand. You are testing the muscles that are responsible for keeping the left-hand fingertips together.

5 If the fingertips of the left hand stay in contact or move only slightly apart and then lock, the energy is still flowing through the muscles, and for most people this indicates a "yes" response.

6 If the fingertips of the left hand part appreciably, the muscles have weakened, and for most people this is a "no" response.

Learning to Sense the Auric Field

Working with crystals naturally seems to increase the sensitivity to subtle energy fields, and there are many ways to explore and increase this ability. Everyone is familiar with receiving information from non-conscious levels of awareness. It is a normal part of functioning as a human being and such a natural skill that it is rarely given much thought.

We all have a sense of personal space, an area around us that we feel belongs to us. Intrusions into this space make us feel uncomfortable and threatened, although closeness with those we like does not present any problems at all. What is being experienced here may be some sort of disharmony between auric

ABOVE *An aura is an energy field, which everybody has. Every individual's aura is different. Some people find that they are able to see auras as a haze of colored light.*

fields. Similarly, many of us will notice a change of atmosphere when certain people enter a room, even when we are not aware of the fact because we are looking in another direction. Recent experimentation also clearly suggests that at some unconscious level, we are aware of being stared at by someone hidden from view. It is frequently the case that students of subtle energies become discouraged because they cannot see auras. Subtle sight is one of the last skills to develop and one that requires great skill to interpret correctly. At the level of feeling, with a mixture of intuition, emotion, and empathy, nearly everyone can achieve usable results with a little practice.

SENSITIVITY EXERCISE I

First it is necessary to turn our attention toward the energy feeling of our own bodies. One of the easiest methods is to rub the palms of the hands vigorously together. Separate your hands and then from a distance bring them toward each other.

At a certain point, there will be a sensation of pressure, a thickening of the air. There will be a feeling of pressure somewhere within the physical body, not necessarily in the hands, that could be described as heat, tickling, or itching, like static electricity. These differences of body sensation and emotional feeling are our responses to energy fields. Continue gently contracting and expanding the space between your hands. You may find that the force builds up and increases in size and that it becomes quite difficult to push your palms together. When you have experimented enough, relax and breathe the energy back into your body. The Chinese describe this chi energy as having the consistency of thick honey, so your receptivity will increase with slow, even movements.

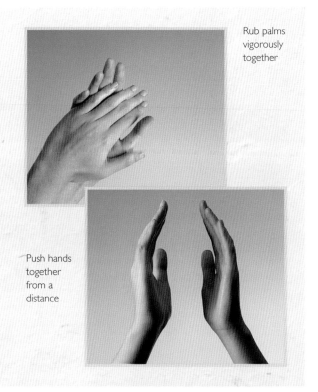

Rub palms vigorously together

Push hands together from a distance

SENSITIVITY EXERCISE 2

Try the same experiment with the hands after rubbing a crystal between your palms. What difference does this make to your sensitivity?

Use a small clear quartz crystal and then try out different sorts of stone, such as tumbled varieties of quartz: rose, rutilated, citrine, tiger's eye, aventurine. Make a note of any differences you notice between the different stones.

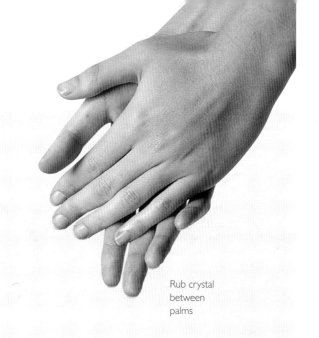

Rub crystal between palms

SENSITIVITY EXERCISE 3

Now, with sensitized hands, slowly approach other objects. See where you notice a change of feeling within your body. Try it with a plant, a book, a crystal, and another person. You should notice that the fields extend different distances away from animate and inanimate objects.

Always remember to center and ground yourself before starting so that you are clear about which sensations are yours and which you are picking up from the object.

See what you can sense from a book

What does a plant "say" to you?

Take time to experiment with hand dowsing. With practice, it is possible to receive other types of information when you link into these energy fields. Listening to your body in this way will greatly enhance your intuitive abilities at the same time as focusing away from the conscious, chattering, everyday mind.

Pay attention to any physical sensations as well as any changes in your emotions or thought patterns. If you are unsure of what you are feeling, move away and slowly back again. You should notice the same sorts of changes as the aura is encountered.

Working with Intuition

Working with intuition requires a light touch and a sense of play. Seriousness and the need to be right brings too much of the ego into the process. It is, to some extent, similar to turning over to automatic systems

Begin these procedures by grounding and centering your energies as usual. Working at this level of intuition can create a slightly more dissociative state than using other methods, so it is important that grounding is maintained throughout.

RANDOM INTUITIVE LAYOUT

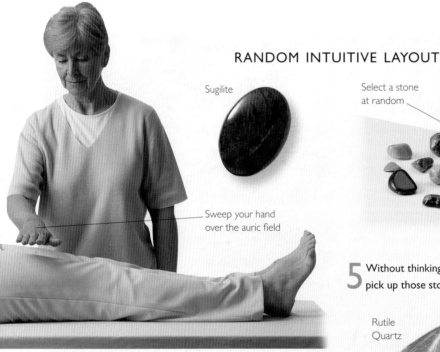

Sugilite

Sweep your hand over the auric field

Select a stone at random

5 Without thinking about their specific purpose, simply pick up those stones that attract your attention.

1 Start by framing a clear intention to balance the energies of this person.

2 Take time to sweep your hand over the auric field of your patient. Begin at the feet, and, holding your hand, palm down, a few inches above the body, slowly move upward.

3 Be aware of any changes you may feel. This is allowing information concerning the energy status of the patient to register in your own subtle awareness. If you scan the entire body up to the head without feeling any particular sensations, it doesn't matter. Trust your body awareness.

4 Having completed the scan, move quickly to where all your stones have been laid out so that you can see them all at once. Don't worry if your collection isn't very big; your intuitive skills will select the most appropriate stone.

Amber

Rutile Quartz

6 Return to the person's side and carefully place the stones anywhere on or around the body where it feels right.

Place stones on or around the body

INTUITIVE SELECTION

Be aware of what your body selects as the most appropriate crystals. It is helpful to know the areas of each crystal's use as suggested by its main color, but this is at best only a rough guideline. The same stone will bring about varying energy conditions as its vibratory pattern interfaces with those of different people.

7 Ignore any knowledge you might have about their health or about their chakra and subtle bodies. The aim here is to work without engaging the analytical brain.

Ametrine

8 Take no more than a minute to place all the stones.

Step back and study the stone placement

9 Step back a little so that you can see the whole body easily. If you now feel unhappy about some crystal placements, move them to a different place, or perhaps take them away completely.

10 Check how the person feels to make sure there is no discomfort anywhere.

11 Continue to gaze gently over the crystal placements. If you feel that any changes are needed, make them.

12 Stay relaxed and attentive, and you will probably have a clear sense of when the stones need to be removed, but remove them all within 10 minutes.

13 Repeat your hand scan and note any changes that have occurred.

14 Finish the scan with a couple of sweeps from head to feet, with the clear intention to normalize all functions and protect the aura integrity.

INTUITIVE CHAKRA BALANCE

1 After grounding and centering (see pages 40–47), frame the intent to balance the seven main chakras. Rub your hands together, or hold a crystal to stimulate sensitivity in your palms.

2 Make a quick upward sweep of the body, moving from the feet to the head.

3 Return to the base chakra. Hold your open palm over the area for a little while.

4 Move to where your stones are laid out and pick up the first one or two that draw your attention. Place them close to the base chakra.

5 Each time stones are placed, check the experiences of your patient.

6 Repeat this process for each of the main chakras. Do not be concerned about the color or type of stone. Your intention is to bring balance so that is what your intuition is helping to achieve.

7 When all chakras have one or more stones placed near them, stand back a little and look to see how it feels. Where the eyes settle repeatedly can often suggest that changes of some kind need to be made.

8 Leave the stones in place for about 10 minutes, or less time if you have a strong feeling that the balance is complete.

9 Remove all stones and then scan each chakra again, this time with the clear intention of protecting and restoring each to normal functioning.

10 Talk over any experiences with your patient, as feedback is always useful.

These are important exercises to practice. They can loosen up any tendencies to repeatedly use the same types of stones or corrections. Individual energy levels are unique, ever-changing, and far too complex for the conscious awareness of a healer to understand. Creating an intuitive link allows the precise needs of the body to be matched with the energy of a crystal.

BALANCING THE CHAKRAS FOR OVER-ENERGY AND UNDER-ENERGY

This method requires a slightly more detailed intuitive assessment of the state of each chakra. Here we want to establish if a chakra is under- or over-energized. This means identifying if the energy balance within each chakra is adequate to deal with all of its current energy requirements. If the chakra is unable to work at the optimum level for that individual at that time, it is under-energized. If the chakra is working above its appropriate energy level, it is over-energized. Both states will tend to create compensatory imbalances in other chakra centers in an effort to restore equilibrium.

Under-energy is often felt as coolness, hollowness, a dip in energy, a lack of some kind. Over-energy usually seems to be a pressure, turbulence, heat, a buildup, or excess of some sort. Where you come across stress or a need for healing energy, you may have a sense of discomfort or a feeling that something is out of place. This may be happening on many different levels – don't assume that it can be identified as a physical problem. Even if it is a very strong subjective experience, this doesn't necessarily mean the imbalance is large or significant. It may merely show that it is close to the surface or that you will be able to release it easily.

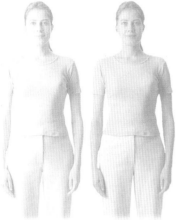

ABOVE *Under-energy is often experienced as coolness, whereas over-energy is heat. Both reflect imbalance in a chakra.*

You may wish to check whether any physical symptoms have occurred in the areas that feel disturbed, but it is important not to cause worry. Everyone has the tendency to want to know what's wrong, but crystal healing simply recognizes imbalances that can be dealt with safely at any one time.

Because crystal healing concerns the whole person from physical to spiritual levels, it isn't always possible to identify what is going on. The healer is simply helping the body to function more effectively and so more healthily.

INTUITIVE PROCEDURE

Depending on your lifestyle and level of activity, some chakras will sometimes need to be more active than others. Here we are helping to readjust inappropriate imbalances only.

1 Cleanse your stones, then ground and center yourself (see pages 24–25 and 40–47).

2 Frame the intent to help bring balance to any over- or under-active chakras, then scan the midline of the body from feet to head. This can be done just with the hand, but your sensitivity may increase if you hold a comfortably large clear quartz crystal in your hand. Hold the crystal's point almost parallel to the body lying down and move it slowly up toward the head.

3 When you come to the area of a main chakra, pay attention to how it feels.

4 You may want to repeat this scanning several times to allow you to gauge the difference between different chakras.

5 Those chakras in balance will often not give much response. Your intent is to look for imbalances, so that is what your subtle senses will notice most. Those out of balance will feel distinctly different, depending upon the way your own body translates the energy patterns into sensation. Only practice and experience will teach you exactly how your senses react.

6 Having identified any chakras that are under- or over-energized, return to each one in turn. Hold your hand or crystal above the chakra to refamiliarize yourself with its energy state, then quickly select stones that draw your attention. Three or four may come up.

Place the crystals facing inward to energize

7 Lay the stones on the chakra in a way that feels right or comfortable.

8 Where there is under-energy, use between two to four small clear quartz crystals and place them around that area with points inward. This will help to energize it.

9 Where there is over-energy, once the intuited stones are in place, use small clear quartz stones with their points facing outward to release any excess buildup of energy.

10 If, in adjacent chakras, one area is over-energized, and the other is under-energized, a clear quartz crystal can be placed with its point toward the under-energy, thus helping to balance out the centers.

11 It may feel appropriate to place one stone on each chakra, even those not out of balance. Within this procedural framework, follow your own intuitive feelings.

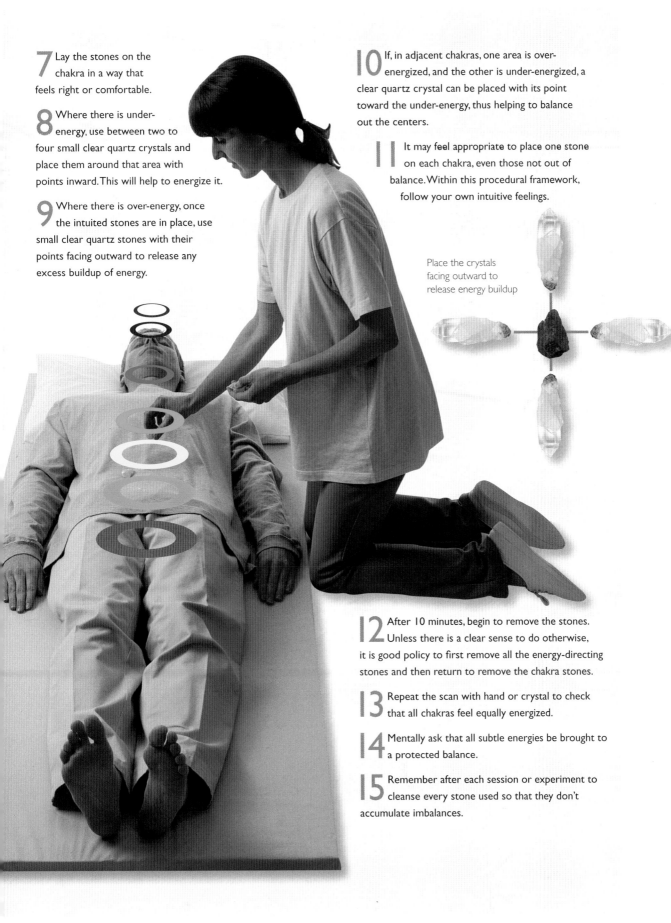

Place the crystals facing outward to release energy buildup

12 After 10 minutes, begin to remove the stones. Unless there is a clear sense to do otherwise, it is good policy to first remove all the energy-directing stones and then return to remove the chakra stones.

13 Repeat the scan with hand or crystal to check that all chakras feel equally energized.

14 Mentally ask that all subtle energies be brought to a protected balance.

15 Remember after each session or experiment to cleanse every stone used so that they don't accumulate imbalances.

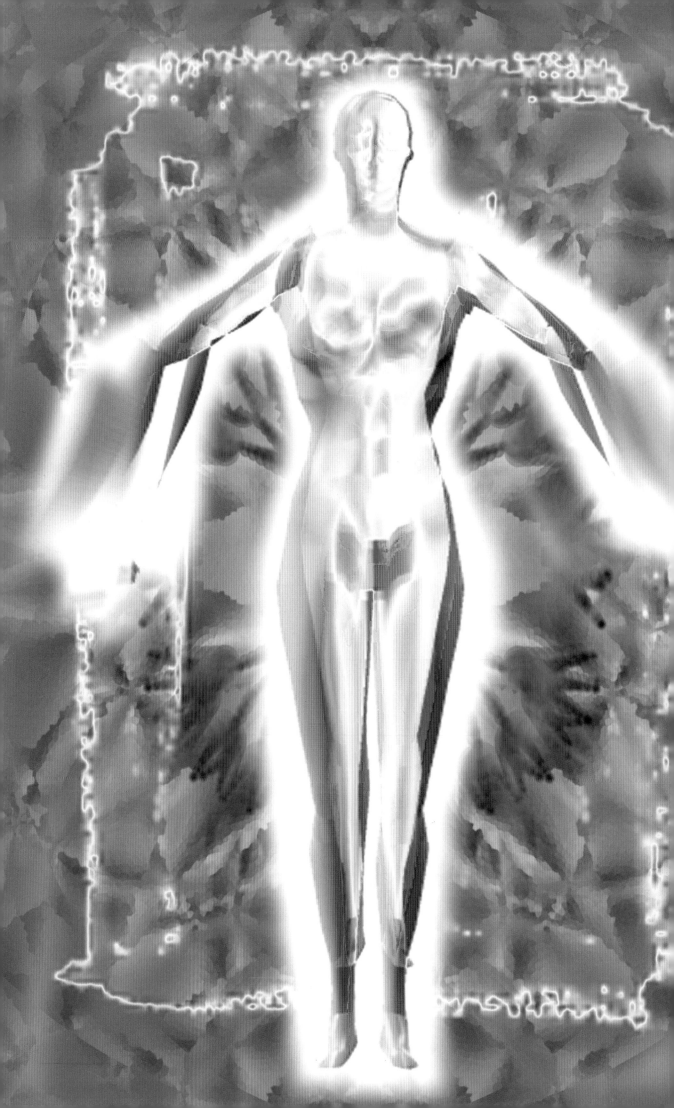

PART SIX

SUBTLE BODIES AND MERIDIANS

What is generally known as the human aura has been identified as a series of interrelated but discrete zones called the subtle bodies. For the crystal healer, these energy bodies present a powerful system that responds very well to crystal work.

Each subtle system, chakra, subtle body, meridian, or physical organ can be thought of as a different aspect of the individual as seen from particular viewpoints and at different frequencies. Every layer or level is as much "us" as our physical self but is not made up of solid matter. In much the same way as a normal photograph shows the external features of a person, an ultrasound scan shows the

ABOVE *Crystals work well on the subtle energy systems of the body — the finer and more subtle qualities of the self.*

internal organs and an X-ray photograph shows only solid and bony tissues of the body, the subtle bodies represent finer, deeper, and more subtle qualities of the self.

Seven Subtle Bodies

7 Described here is a model of seven subtle bodies, each level extending farther from the physical body and made of finer energy material. It is important to remember that each succeeding level interpenetrates all of the previous levels, including the physical, so that there is a continuous, dynamic, and complex interaction between them.

THE ETHERIC BODY

The etheric body is the closest to the physical, and it is considered to be the blueprint upon which the cells and organs are built. It contains an exact energetic replica of the body with the same organs and structures. When imbalance and weakness occur in the etheric area, they will eventually manifest themselves on the physical level. Clairvoyant sight describes a blue or blue-gray web of moving energy that extends a little way from the body. The meridian system is believed to be integrated with the etheric body and to act as the interface between etheric and physical.

THE EMOTIONAL BODY

The emotional body is the container of feelings. It roughly follows the body's outline but extends further than the etheric. It has no fixed structure and is composed of colored clouds of energy which are in continual flux, altering according to mood and emotional state. This field is often the aura of colors that sensitives are able to perceive around a person. The emotional body holds our emotional and psychological stability and our sensitivity to those around us.

THE MENTAL BODY

The mental body is associated with thoughts and mental processes. It is usually perceived as bright yellow, expanding around the head during mental concentration. Thought patterns exist here as bright shapes. It is in the mental body that we interpret information according to the belief structures that we have developed since birth.

THE ASTRAL BODY

The astral body is the fourth layer. Resembling the emotional body but with clouds of finer and more subtle coloring, this energy layer contains the essence of our personality. It is the boundary layer between the current individual personality and a more collective spiritual awareness, and is concerned with relationship, particularly in the sense of encompassing humanity.

ABOVE *Etheric body. Similar to the physical body, replicating organs and structures.*

ABOVE *Emotional body. Its color alters according to mood and emotions.*

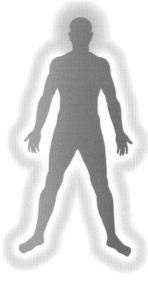

ABOVE *Mental body. Home of thought patterns and beliefs. Expands during concentration.*

ABOVE *Astral body. Links to relationships and spiritual awareness.*

THE CAUSAL, SOUL, AND SPIRITUAL BODIES

The three remaining subtle bodies are less often described, and their functions are not so clearly defined. They are composed of very fine energy.

The fifth layer is the causal body which links the personality to the collective unconscious and is the doorway to higher levels of consciousness.

The soul, or celestial, body is the sixth subtle level. It seems to focus fine levels of universal energy and is related to the idea of the Higher Self.

The spiritual body is the seventh subtle body. It is the container and integrator of all other subtle energies. It has access to all universal energies, but maintains the individuality of each being.

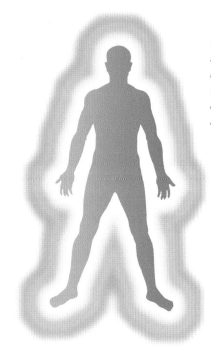

LEFT *The causal, soul, and spiritual bodies interweave with universal consciousness and energies.*

Crystal layouts

To work with particular subtle bodies, following are some specific layouts of crystals. These may be used in healing situations or to familiarize yourself with the qualities of each level of awareness. The more we understand of our own energy makeup, the less likely we are to misinterpret information from others or from the deeper levels of our own minds.

PHYSICAL BODY LAYOUT

Tourmaline is a crystal with many varied uses in healing. One of its most useful attributes is its ability to help repair the physical body, particularly structural problems in the bones or muscle tissue.

In this layout, black tourmaline is used. It grounds, protects, and integrates personal energy wherever we are on the planet. For this layout, use eight black tourmaline crystals; tumbled stones or fragments will work almost as well. If the

stones have natural terminations, they should be placed pointing toward the body. Create two intersecting rectangles. The first is made of four tourmalines: one above the head, one below the feet, one midway down the body next to each side. If you lie down with your head to north, the stones are aligned to the north, south, east and west.

The second rectangle is made with the remaining four crystals placed about 20–25 degrees clockwise to the first stones, making a slightly offset rectangle. A green background will enhance the effects of this layout. Initially there may be some increase in aches and pains, but these will diminish quite rapidly as the body gently realigns itself. If there are chronic skeletal problems, regular short exposure to this layout will prove most effective.

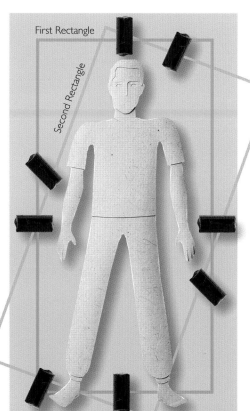

First Rectangle

Second Rectangle

LEFT *This layout uses tourmaline crystals which attune the physical body to the planetary energies as a whole.*

ETHERIC BODY LAYOUT

Giving healing energy to the etheric body will greatly accelerate the repair of physical tissues and may prevent other imbalances from gravitating into the physical body. The etheric levels are those that often tend to become misaligned from the physical body after shock and trauma. If this mismatch can't correct itself, the physical body loses some of its organizational flexibility, which can allow disease to take hold. Such etheric body dislocation may be the reason why in so many cases a serious period of illness follows a few months after significant shock. Any period of illness or recuperation would benefit from this layout.

Six carnelians are needed. One is placed at the throat and one above the top of the head. At the level of the sacral chakra, a carnelian is placed on each side of the body. The remaining two stones are put on the midline of the body, one between the legs at about mid-calf level and the last stone near the ankles. An orange-colored background to lie on will accentuate this layout's healing potential.

Orange, the color of the sacral chakra, is the ideal vibration for repairing shock to the system. Even the essential oils that have an orange-type vibration can help to restore the equilibrium. Sandalwood and cedar are soothing and warm oils. Those derived from the orange tree are especially useful, particularly neroli, made from orange blossom, and petitgrain made from the leaves and twigs of the same tree. A few drops of these oils placed in a warm bath can quickly reduce stress levels.

Signs that suggest the subtle bodies are out of synchronization with the physical body are: a lack or reduction of

Carnelian

emotional involvement with the surroundings, a feeling of being elsewhere or spaced out, poor physical coordination, inability to maintain personal boundaries and so an increased discomfort in crowds or situations where there is a lot of sensory input, a slowing down of healing processes, an increase in minor illness and infections, or the return of old symptoms or allergies.

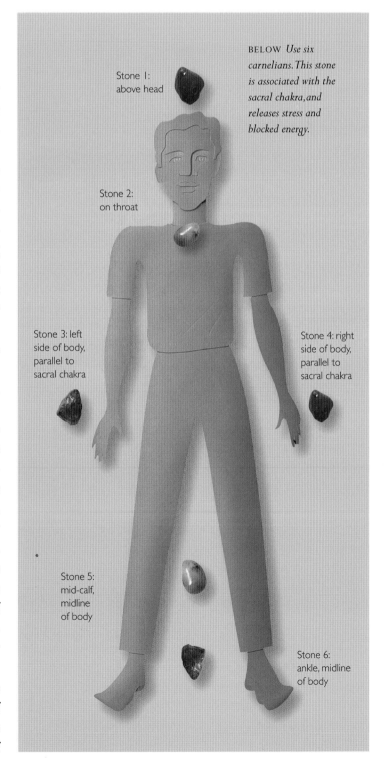

Stone 1: above head

Stone 2: on throat

BELOW *Use six carnelians. This stone is associated with the sacral chakra, and releases stress and blocked energy.*

Stone 3: left side of body, parallel to sacral chakra

Stone 4: right side of body, parallel to sacral chakra

Stone 5: mid-calf, midline of body

Stone 6: ankle, midline of body

EMOTIONAL BODY LAYOUT

The emotional body is the next vibratory level beyond the etheric. The etheric body holds the pattern for the physical body, the emotional body contains the volatile and changing energy of our moods.

Visiting somewhere beautiful can change how we feel quite dramatically, but the opposite is also true. A beautiful scene can mean nothing to us if we are in a bad mood. The same street can be threatening and dangerous if we have just lost our money or the happiest if we have fallen in love. Music can provoke the deepest-felt emotions almost against our will or better judgment. A color, scent or word can provoke intense irritation or melt our hearts. Emotion is the weather within us. It comes and goes, changes and flows continually. It hardly seems trustworthy or stable enough to base any decision on emotion, and yet, with most people, no matter how rationally important issues may be considered, the final choice is frequently an emotional preference.

Emotions can play a huge part in our health and well-being. Emotional balance is not an unfeeling, neutral state, but a center point to which the system can return between extremes of happiness and sorrow. Without this balance or axis as a natural resting place, the emotions can get stuck in a way that is inappropriate and deleterious to the whole body. Holding onto a particular sort of emotional energy disrupts the whole body weather system. Damaging emotional storms and unseasonable climate can create profoundly unhealthy conditions for the individual.

For balancing and healing the emotional body, 12 smoky quartz with their points directed outward are evenly spread around the body. The simplest way of doing this is to place one stone at the top of the head and one below the feet, then space five crystals evenly on each side of the body. An orange-colored background will accentuate the cleansing, flowing, and stabilizing qualities of the stones.

This emotional body layout is useful for increasing the healing potential of the body and will help to reduce the effects of trauma and stress.

Smoky Quartz

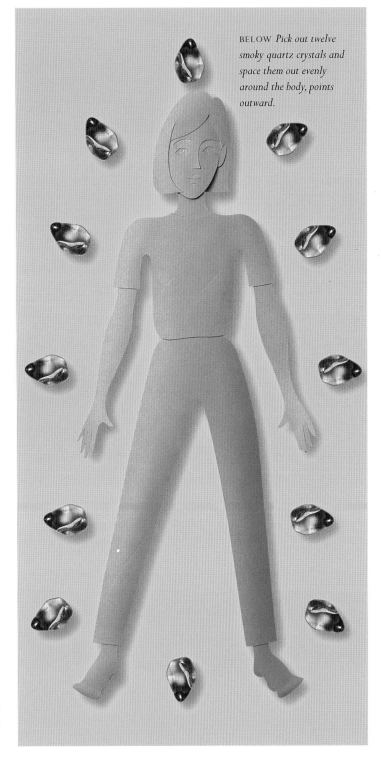

BELOW *Pick out twelve smoky quartz crystals and space them out evenly around the body, points outward.*

MENTAL BODY LAYOUT

Since our emotions are directly translated into thoughts and we seem to respond to most stimuli emotionally, it can be difficult to define the difference between the mind and the emotions. The mental body, however, does have distinct and discrete properties. The emotional body reacts; the mental body records, categorizes, and files these reactions. The mental body, from birth, constructs how we perceive the world and the way it seems to work. It uses all forms of information available to allow the individual to figure out what is going on. The mental body creates our core beliefs and then attaches all other experiences around these central truths. Our core structures are created very early in life when our tendency is to believe everything we hear, and so we often misinterpret events and the actions of others. Because these structures are so fundamental to our self image, they can be difficult for us to see.

Core beliefs can exist in complete contradiction to each other, so, when a certain issue arises in life, the opposite pictures of reality can create great stress. This stress very often translates into muscular tension and physical rigidity. Easing mental body issues can allow relaxation at many different levels, from posture to tolerance of others' beliefs, to flexibility in problem solving and finding positive options.

The layout that helps to balance the mental body will also tend to improve all types of communication skills. Speed of thought and clarity of mind also naturally improve as inaccurate mental structures are replaced by more useful ones. Left and right brain hemisphere activity is brought to a better balance, so coordination improves. A citrine quartz is held in each hand with its point facing down and away from the body. A third

citrine is placed at the solar plexus, also point down. This stone will help to activate the central nervous system, while the hand-held stones balance brain function. Clear quartz crystals are taped onto the top of each foot between the second and third toes, again pointing down, helping to anchor the mental energy into practical areas of life.

A clear quartz is placed on the forehead, pointing up toward the top of the head, energizing the brow chakra's perceptive abilities, enabling it to re-examine old truths in the light of greater understanding.

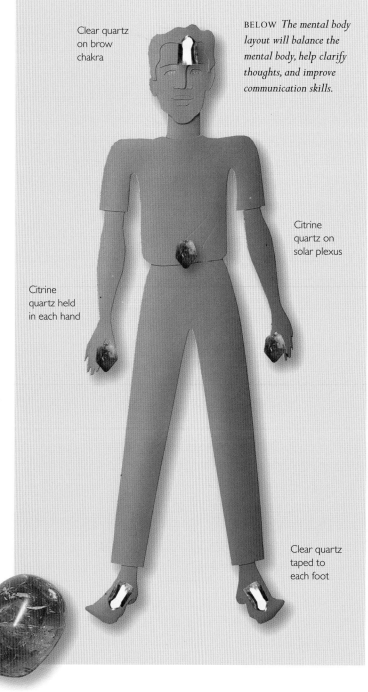

Clear quartz on brow chakra

BELOW *The mental body layout will balance the mental body, help clarify thoughts, and improve communication skills.*

Citrine quartz on solar plexus

Citrine quartz held in each hand

Citrine Quartz

Clear quartz taped to each foot

ASTRAL BODY LAYOUT

The fourth layer of subtle energy is called the astral body. Within it are all aspects of the individual personality. It is the container that allows us to recognize ourselves as unique beings. The astral body filters and tones down all other sources of energy and information so as not to overwhelm individual consciousness. It can act as a gateway on both the physical expanded, collective levels of awareness. Weakness at this level can create great confusion in our perception of reality as the normal constraints of physical reality break down. Too closed an astral body prevents useful information or other dimensions of energy from integrating into everyday consciousness, which can lead to feelings of isolation and loss of direction.

This layout is enhanced when laid out on a cloth of deep pink or magenta color. This helps to access the underlying universal flows of energy, the glue that holds everything together in a manner suited to the individual physical reality.

Twelve crystals are used in this layout – six tumbled pieces of milky quartz and six of black tourmaline. Milky quartz is a translucent white variety commonly found among river and seashore pebbles. It has a softer, warmer quality than clear quartz, and the pebble form accentuates the gentle expansive sphere of protective energy which emanates from this stone. The black tourmaline anchors the energy of the self, so that together these stones can balance the polarities implicit in the functions of the astral body. Put one tourmaline above the head, one below the feet, and alternate the remaining quartz and tourmalines evenly around the body.

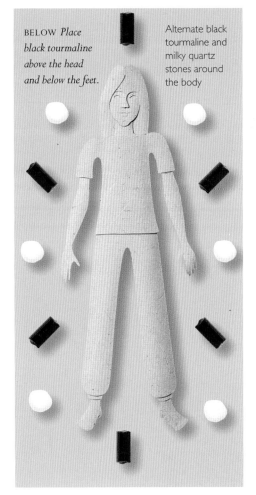

BELOW *Place black tourmaline above the head and below the feet.*

Alternate black tourmaline and milky quartz stones around the body

Finer levels of the subtle anatomy become more difficult to define or explore with the conscious mind, but they can still be accessed and positively altered with crystal healing techniques.

CAUSAL BODY LAYOUT

To balance the causal body, which can be seen by analogy as the projector that puts our image onto the screen of physical existence, just one stone is needed. Lie on a blue-colored cloth and then place a sodalite stone on the brow chakra at the center of your forehead.

Sodalite

BELOW *The causal body layout helps to focus the mind on higher levels of consciousness.*

Position sodalite on brow chakra

ilky Quartz

Schorl

SOUL BODY LAYOUT

The soul, or celestial body, the sixth subtle energy envelope that interpenetrates all the other levels, including the physical, can be brought into greater balance with seven small clusters of celestite. Celestite, or celestine, is a beautiful pale-blue mineral that forms clusters of soft heavy crystals. It is wonderful for lifting dark moods and bringing a subtle bliss to perceptions. Only small clusters of celestite crystals are needed, but it may take some hunting to find suitable pieces. Most people find this layout enjoyable, although it often requires considerable grounding afterward.

A white cloth amplifies the ethereal effects of the stones, which should be placed as follows: one cluster above the head, one beside each shoulder, one at the side of each thigh, one beside each ankle, if possible facing toward the body. With this layout it is easier to attune to fine levels of inspiration. There can be relief from worldly pressures and a sense of spiritual uplift-ment, fulfillment, and cleansing.

SPIRITUAL BODY LAYOUT

The finest level that we know, the spiritual body, encompasses our whole existence in and outside of time and space, so no single method is likely to bring balance to the whole. This layout helps to bring conscious awareness to the multidimensional reality and timeless nature of the Self. It can access information from the deepest levels of consciousness and from different parts of the universe, helping to integrate knowledge of our true direction, and increasing our sense of purpose. Often this information takes the form of dreams, ideas, or inspiration.

This layout is best done on a white cloth and needs three clear quartz, four amethyst, and five

BELOW Clusters of celestite bring relief from worldly concerns.

pieces of moldavite. Large pieces can be expensive, but small fragments are fine.

Moldavite is put in both hands, on the center of the forehead, and taped on top of each foot between the first and second toes. The clear quartz makes a triangle, one piece on each side of the body, about level with the solar plexus, and one below the feet, all with points inward. The four amethysts form a rectangle around the body: two above the head about shoulder width apart and one on each side of the legs just below the knees.

BELOW The spiritual body layout increases self-confidence and helps us focus our energies in a meaningful direction.

SUBTLE BODIES STONE PLACEMENT

Use an assessment technique, such as dowsing or muscle testing, to find out which subtle bodies could benefit from this process. Lists or arcs of the stones can be used to identify the most appropriate. Place the stones in their correct locations and check how long they need to remain in place.

After removing the stones, recheck the subtle bodies to see that all of them have been balanced. Certain stones seem to be especially balancing to each of the subtle bodies. The most appropriate of these stones is put precisely on or around the body at places that act as access points or sensitive points for each subtle layer.

Body	Point of focus/placement of stone	Balancing stones
Etheric body	No specified points of focus, since the etheric body is completely interconnected with the physical.	Abalone, azurite, amazonite, azurite, malachite, aventurine, aquamarine, bloodstone, chrysoprase, fluorite, clear quartz, galena, Herkimer diamond, garnet, picture jasper, jet, kunzite, jade, green jasper, lapis lazuli, lodestone, malachite, topaz.
Emotional body	Stomach.	Botswana agate, fire agate, moss agate, serpentine, aventurine, azurite, malachite, emerald, Herkimer diamond, jade, meteorite, sphene, green jasper, jet, moonstone, obsidian, opal, amethyst, smoky quartz, citrine, rose quartz, clear quartz, rhyolite, sapphire.
Mental body	Left hemisphere of the brain. Place the stone or stones around the left side of the head. Check the correct position for each.	Fire agate, moss agate, amazonite, amber, aquamarine, aventurine, azurite, green jasper, diamond, gold, lapis lazuli, meteorite, morganite, obsidian, dark opal, amethyst, smoky quartz, citrine, rose quartz, clear quartz, ruby, sphene.
Astral body	Kidneys. Check to see if different stones are needed near each kidney or whether the same one is needed on both sides of the body. Tuck the appropriate stones under the back at about the level of the elbow.	Copper, emerald, Herkimer diamond, jade, green jasper, meteorite, moonstone, peridot, iron pyrites, smoky quartz, citrine, rose quartz, rhodochrosite, sapphire, serpentine, silver.
Causal body	Medulla oblongata at the base of the skull.	No specific selection of stone is suggested. You will need to determine the most appropriate stone in each case.
Soul body	Pineal gland. The easiest placement here is at the center of the forehead.	Citrine quartz.
Spiritual body	Pituitary gland. Test for the best placement, which might be beside the head, level with the ears, behind the crown, or at the forehead.	Sphene, ruby, citrine, amethyst, lapis lazuli, gold, garnet, carnelian.

Cleansing the Aura

If the aura needs cleansing, this can be done by placing stones on appropriate spots or by sweeping stones through the aura, either held in the hand or on a pendulum.

THE CLEANSING PROCESS

Use an assessment method such as dowsing or muscle-testing to identify which subtle bodies would benefit from balance of the auric field.

Once the general picture is clear, identify the appropriate stones you are to use for each subtle body. Choose from sapphire, ruby, smoky quartz, lodestone, green jasper, or Herkimer diamond. But always check to see if something else is needed since there may be an ideal stone not listed here. Several stones may be needed for each placement. Remember that every crystal healing session deals with the unique energies of an individual. Techniques offer useful guidelines but are flexible. In your testing, always check to see whether there is anything else required, or anything else to do.

Ruby

Herkimer Diamond

Smoky Quartz

Sapphire

ABOVE *Together with lodestone and green jasper, these stones are ideal for aura cleansing. Draw each stone through the aura, or place them on or around the body.*

Place the stone or stones in the identified area, check that it is correct, and the length of time they are to be left in place. When checking how long the stones should be left, wait until all the stones are in position. It may have taken you several minutes to complete each layout so that some stones will have been in place quite a long time before the question is asked. The question can be framed, "How much longer do the stones…"

It may be that the stones will need to be removed in a particular order. Check before you start removing them. Remove all the stones and recheck the subtle bodies for balance.

Complete the balance by sweeping the aura with your hands, with the intention of normalizing the energy levels and stabilizing the correction.

ADDITIONAL PRACTICE

When you can quickly identify another person's auric field, see if you can isolate its different layers, mental, emotional, astral, and so on.

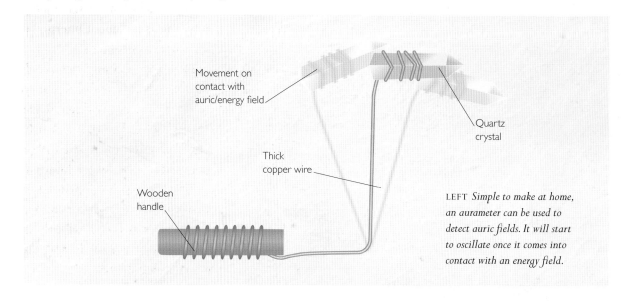

Movement on contact with auric/energy field

Quartz crystal

Thick copper wire

Wooden handle

LEFT *Simple to make at home, an aurameter can be used to detect auric fields. It will start to oscillate once it comes into contact with an energy field.*

Frame in your mind the clear intent to feel only one subtle body and then slowly, from some distance, approach the subject. Don't be surprised if the auric fields appear to extend much farther than you had expected.

This exercise can also be done using a pendulum or by self-testing (see pages 96–98). An aurameter is a specialized pendulum that is used to register auric fields. One can be made easily by wrapping thick copper wire around a quartz crystal and then attaching the free end to a handle of some kind. Put a right-angle bend in the wire and it will indicate by a clear horizontal oscillation when it encounters an energy field.

To appreciate how sensitive we really are to the energy fields of others, try the following exercise. Have someone you know stand up just a short distance from you, so that it is easy for you to scan the whole body. Now swiftly look to feel or sense their aura. If it helps, make a simple sketch and note down any areas that feel different. First, look or feel what the aura is like as a whole. Is it balanced? Or is it top or bottom heavy? Does it feel as though it extends evenly around the physical body, or are there variations? Is your attention drawn to particular areas, and, if so, how do they feel? Try to describe these sensations in sense words: tactile, aural, or visual. Do not draw any conclusions or value judgments. This is not about interpretation, simply recognition.

Practice this sensing with friends and strangers. Remember not to focus too hard, or to concentrate or intellectualize the process. A light touch of attention is all that is required to pick up the information. Once developed, this relaxed, neutral, aura scanning technique can prove valuable in healing situations for identifying areas needing attention.

ABOVE *Finish a cleansing session by sweeping the aura with your hands to balance energy levels.*

BELOW *Practice aura reading on a friend. It may help to sketch out what you sense in each area.*

The Meridian System

The meridian system of subtle energy is at the heart of Traditional Chinese Medicine. Knowledge of the meridians and the acupuncture points requires extensive in-depth study. Because of this, most crystal healers rarely work with the meridian system. There are, however, useful healing procedures that combine the energy of crystals with meridian energies in straightforward ways. Once there is confidence in an assessment technique, such as dowsing or muscle testing, the correct placement of a specific stone on a meridian point can make dramatic changes to a person's well-being.

RIGHT *Roll a clear quartz crystal between each finger and the thumb in turn. This balances the meridians.*

The meridian system, as conceived by the Chinese, has 12 main energy channels that follow recognized pathways near the surface of the skin. Although it is one integrated system, each meridian has a starting point and an end point, which indicates direction of flow and function. Each meridian is named after an organ or function, such as the liver or stomach, but this can be misleading in the West, as the physical organ is only a small aspect of the type of energy with which a meridian deals. The functions ascribed to physical organs by the Chinese rarely have any recognizable Western correlations, and it is important not to confuse these two different models of the human body.

ABOVE *Yin and Yang represent opposing, yet interdependent, energies in all things.*

It has been generally thought that the meridians are nonphysical, or etheric, vessels providing the physical body with the subtle nutrition of chi or life energy. Recent research suggests that meridians are, at least at some levels, superfine physical structures. The acupuncture points along each meridian, often visualized as access points or energy vortices like small chakra centers, have been clearly identified as having a different electrical potential to nonacupuncture points. Injecting minute amounts of a marker substance has demonstrated that it migrates rapidly out from the acupressure point along very specific pathways distinct from any nerve or blood vessels. Close examination of these pathways shows a system that parallels and interweaves with known physical organs and systems. It contains a fluid that has some similarities to blood and lymph, but in completely different proportions. When experimenters severed these channels around an organ, cellular disruption soon followed. The arrangement of this microscopic system suggests that it comes into being before any other cellular differentiation and may act as a template for the development of the body.

In addition to the twelve meridians that flow on each side of the body, making twenty-four channels in all, there are many other vessels that feed the chi energy into smaller channels for distribution. The most important extra channels are the Conception Vessel and Governing Vessel, both of which possess acupuncture points and flow up the midline of the body. These two channels help to maintain the flow of chi within the entire meridian system and directly affect vitality and health.

BALANCING WITH A QUARTZ

A double-terminated clear quartz can be used to balance meridian energy. Hold the center of the stone between the thumb and index finger and turn it around with the other hand for about a minute. This process is then repeated with all the other fingers, using the thumb as the balance point. Repeat the procedure with the other hand. A crystal of the correct length will need to be found – one that can be turned in the hand without catching the palm.

THE MERIDIANS AND THEIR EMOTIONAL CONNOTATIONS

One simple way of understanding some of the functions of the meridians is to associate them with emotional states. Thus, a positive emotion will energize or strengthen a meridian, while its corresponding negative emotional expression will tend to reduce the energy or weaken the meridian. In this way, it is possible to identify some of the underlying emotional energy causing disruption to the system. John Diamond, a pioneering kinesiologist, has discovered the attributes of the meridians and emotional states.

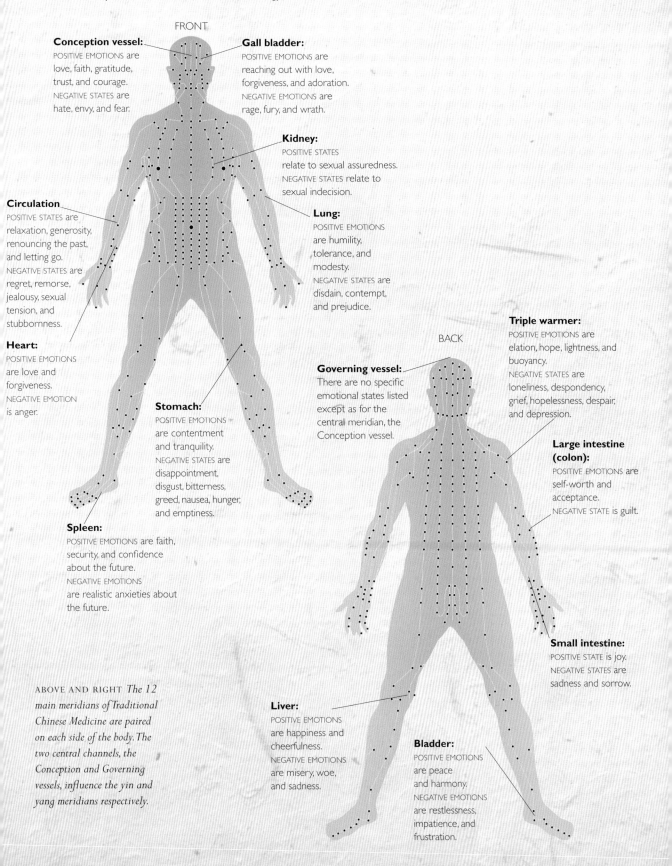

FRONT

Conception vessel:
POSITIVE EMOTIONS are love, faith, gratitude, trust, and courage. NEGATIVE STATES are hate, envy, and fear.

Gall bladder:
POSITIVE EMOTIONS are reaching out with love, forgiveness, and adoration. NEGATIVE EMOTIONS are rage, fury, and wrath.

Kidney:
POSITIVE STATES relate to sexual assuredness. NEGATIVE STATES relate to sexual indecision.

Circulation
POSITIVE STATES are relaxation, generosity, renouncing the past, and letting go. NEGATIVE STATES are regret, remorse, jealousy, sexual tension, and stubbornness.

Lung:
POSITIVE EMOTIONS are humility, tolerance, and modesty. NEGATIVE STATES are disdain, contempt, and prejudice.

Heart:
POSITIVE EMOTIONS are love and forgiveness. NEGATIVE EMOTION is anger.

Stomach:
POSITIVE EMOTIONS are contentment and tranquility. NEGATIVE STATES are disappointment, disgust, bitterness, greed, nausea, hunger, and emptiness.

Spleen:
POSITIVE EMOTIONS are faith, security, and confidence about the future. NEGATIVE EMOTIONS are realistic anxieties about the future.

BACK

Triple warmer:
POSITIVE EMOTIONS are elation, hope, lightness, and buoyancy. NEGATIVE STATES are loneliness, despondency, grief, hopelessness, despair, and depression.

Governing vessel:
There are no specific emotional states listed except as for the central meridian, the Conception vessel.

Large intestine (colon):
POSITIVE EMOTIONS are self-worth and acceptance. NEGATIVE STATE is guilt.

Small intestine:
POSITIVE STATE is joy. NEGATIVE STATES are sadness and sorrow.

Liver:
POSITIVE EMOTIONS are happiness and cheerfulness. NEGATIVE EMOTIONS are misery, woe, and sadness.

Bladder:
POSITIVE EMOTIONS are peace and harmony. NEGATIVE EMOTIONS are restlessness, impatience, and frustration.

ABOVE AND RIGHT *The 12 main meridians of Traditional Chinese Medicine are paired on each side of the body. The two central channels, the Conception and Governing vessels, influence the yin and yang meridians respectively.*

Meridian Massage

Meridian massage is a quick means to bring an overall balance back to the body, and meridian self-massage helps to ensure that you are in balance before and after working with crystals. Both methods can quickly restore energy levels, balance the aura and reduce a range of symptoms, emotional, mental, and physical.

Since you are moving crystals through the auric field as well as strengthening the flow within the meridian system, this will help to remove imbalances from the whole body. With self-massage, where your arms cannot reach, use intention to complete the circuit mentally as you do when massaging another person.

SELF-MASSAGE PROCEDURE

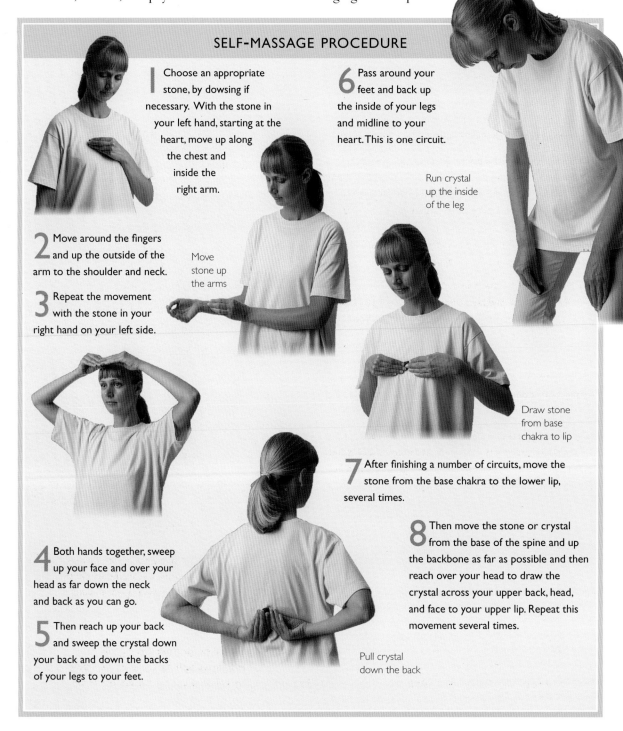

1 Choose an appropriate stone, by dowsing if necessary. With the stone in your left hand, starting at the heart, move up along the chest and inside the right arm.

2 Move around the fingers and up the outside of the arm to the shoulder and neck.

3 Repeat the movement with the stone in your right hand on your left side.

4 Both hands together, sweep up your face and over your head as far down the neck and back as you can go.

5 Then reach up your back and sweep the crystal down your back and down the backs of your legs to your feet.

6 Pass around your feet and back up the inside of your legs and midline to your heart. This is one circuit.

7 After finishing a number of circuits, move the stone from the base chakra to the lower lip, several times.

8 Then move the stone or crystal from the base of the spine and up the backbone as far as possible and then reach over your head to draw the crystal across your upper back, head, and face to your upper lip. Repeat this movement several times.

Move stone up the arms

Run crystal up the inside of the leg

Draw stone from base chakra to lip

Pull crystal down the back

GIVING A MASSAGE

Stand in front of the patient and keep your hands 1–2 inches (2–5 centimeters) away from the body throughout the massage.

1 Ask the person to stand comfortably with legs slightly apart and arms held away from the body, palms facing toward the body.

2 Choose two appropriate crystals or tumbled stones. Each stone should be large enough to cover the palm of your hand.

3 Holding a crystal in each hand, begin with both hands over the heart area.

4 Sweep up to the armpits and along the insides of the arms to the hands.

5 Pass over the fingers and return up the outsides of the arms to the shoulders, meeting again at the throat.

6 Sweep both crystals up the face and over the head, following as closely as possible down the midline of the back and then down the backs of the legs to the feet. You might not be able to fully reach around the person's back. This is not too important. Anywhere that you have to leave the exact line, simply use the intention of your mind to complete the sweep across the appropriate area.

7 Pass around the toes and up the inside of the legs and then on up the midline of the torso to the heart. This is one circuit. The number of circuits and the speed at which you move is up to you.

8 Move to one side and complete the sweep up the Conception and Governing Vessels by simultaneously passing both stones up the front and back midlines from the base to the lips.

9 Repeat several times. Sometimes it may be better to hold a different sort of stone in each hand. If this is the case, check to see if you need to swap them after a number of circuits to balance the stones' energies.

ABOVE *Sweep the crystals from the person's hands and up the arms to the shoulders and onto the throat.*

Front *Back* *Front*

LEFT *Complete a full circuit of the body according to the routes shown. Repeat the procedure as many times as you wish.*

Crystals and the Meridian System

A balanced meridian system usually means that there is neither a lack of energy nor an excess of energy in the system. Individual meridians or parts of meridians may be working outside their normal ranges, but in a balanced system the general equilibrium is kept by an excess in one area being balanced by a lack in another. Sometimes a localized imbalance needs to be corrected to bring about healing. This can be compared to fine-tuning a car for maximum efficiency.

REBALANCING A MERIDIAN

1 To determine which meridians need balancing, use an arc or list to dowse, or do a muscle test. Remember that apart, from the Conception and Governing Vessel, all meridians are in pairs.

2 Determine which side of the meridian pair needs balancing or whether both sides require attention.

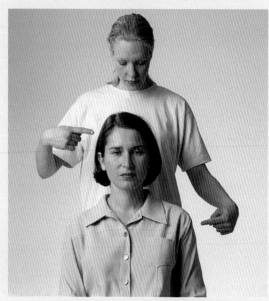

3 An effective demonstration of an imbalanced meridian can be to lightly touch one end-point with a couple of fingers. If that half of the meridian is out of balance, a previously strong muscle test will go weak. Muscle testing all meridians in this way, called "therapy localizing," will quickly show where work is needed.

4 In this method, it is not important which end point is touched, so choose whichever is most convenient. The point can be held by either the tester or the patient.

5 Once all meridians have been tested, find out which crystals will rebalance them. If you are dowsing, then work by color categories or lists. If you are muscle testing, start in the same way with color categories.

- Clear quartz
- Tourmaline
- Rose quartz
- Lapis lazuli
- Heliodor
- Amber

6 Once the stone is identified, ask on which end point it needs to be placed and for how long. You will probably need to tape the stone in place.

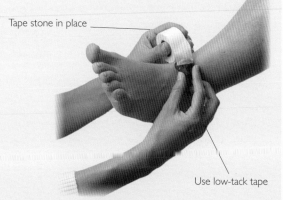

Tape stone in place

Use low-tack tape

7 Check to see if stones are needed at one end only or both ends of the meridian.

8 If stones are needed at both ends of the meridian, find whether different sorts of stones are necessary.

9 Once the process is completed and the stones removed, recheck all the meridians to make sure everything is in balance. If you are muscle testing, localize each point after the crystals have been removed to check on the efficacy of the rebalancing.

EFFECTS OF REBALANCING

▲ Like every other subtle system, and even the body's physical systems, a small change in one area may create a large effect overall. It is not possible to isolate one part from the whole. This means that care must always be taken to carry out only appropriate healing work.

▲ Sometimes the correction is at such a deep level that nothing much is experienced immediately. On the other hand, this technique can initiate some strange subjective feelings and emotions.

ACUPUNCTURE POINT CORRECTIONS

The meridian system may appear balanced even when individual acupuncture points may be seriously over- or under-energized, and occasionally it is necessary and appropriate to work with single points rather than end points. This is usually very powerful, and care needs to be taken to make sure the body has plenty of time to readjust and assimilate the changes. A rest period of several weeks, free of any other healing work, is usual.

ACUPRESSURE POINT PROCEDURE

1 Determine that it is appropriate and safe to work with an acupressure point by dowsing or muscle testing.

2 Find which meridian is involved, either by dowsing or muscle testing.

3 Find whether the left or right channels need work.

4 Find the exact spot to place the stone by lightly tracing the path of the meridian with your fingertips until your arm or pendulum indicates the correct spot. Always start from the beginning of the meridian and work toward the end. This way, you will be prevented from inadvertently weakening the meridian by moving against the flow.

5 Mark the correct spot with a piece of tape.

6 Work out the type of crystal needed and how long it needs to be in place. Don't put the stone on the point until you have all the information that you require.

ABOVE *Dowse the acupressure point to find out whether it is a suitable area in which to work.*

ABOVE *Run your fingers lightly along the meridian to determine where the stone should be placed.*

7 When placing the stone, double-check the exact location.

8 Monitor carefully how the patient feels during the period of placement.

9 When the correction is complete, remove the stone and retest to check that all is OK.

10 Make sure the patient is fully grounded and suggest they drink a little more water than usual for a few days to help the cleansing process.

Sometimes an exact stone is needed, so if you have several pieces of the indicated crystal, test each one to find the best one possible for your subject. It is not necessary to know the exact point required if the meridian is traced. If you have a diagram of the acupressure points, identify the necessary place and then check the exact location on the body. It may differ slightly from the diagram.

Figure-Eight Circuits

In Tibetan healing systems, there are a series of energy channels in the body that can be simplified as figure-eight patterns. Each of these circuits always flows in the same direction, but where there is stress or a blockage of energy, it may start moving in the opposite way, depriving the body of an important energy source.

THE CIRCUITS

One set of circuits is located on the front of the body and a corresponding set is on the back. Front and back, there are six figure-eights to check.

◆ **A lower circuit** moves between the hips and the feet.

◆ **A middle circuit** exists on the abdomen between the shoulders and the pelvis.

◆ **An upper circuit** can be found between the top of the head and the neck.

Where there is felt to be a significant area of unmoving or stagnant energy in the subtle systems, or when there is a need to shift a buildup of stress out of the aura, or when there seems to be a general lack of integration between the upper and lower halves of the body, perhaps manifesting as a lack of coordination or being grounded, it might be appropriate to create a figure-eight pattern around the whole body.

◆ First check the whole body circuit. If dowsing with a pendulum, ask if it is balanced and strong.

◆ If weak, check in which direction the flow needs to move to restrengthen it.

◆ Correct this circuit first, but if it tests OK, check the six smaller circuits for imbalances.

A circuit can be rebalanced by making a figure-eight with crystals of smoky quartz or black tourmaline, which are both ideal cleansers and removers of imbalance from many levels, physical and subtle. If your crystals have natural terminations, these should all be placed in the direction of flow. If you have no terminated stones or only tumbled stones, use a larger single quartz crystal like a wand and sweep it over the stones in the required direction several times.

If you are muscle testing for assessment, a downward pass from shoulder to opposite hip will weaken a strong indicator muscle if the circuit needs strengthening. In this case, the stones are pointed in the direction where a pass from shoulder to hip or hip to shoulder remains strong. The correction has been successful when, on retesting, passes in all directions stay strong.

The crystals can be placed on or off the body, and you might need some tape to keep some in place. The number of crystals you use is less important than their positions and direction, but it is a good idea to keep a balanced symmetrical placement.

Figure-eight energies can be corrected by using a single large crystal. Slowly and purposefully direct the crystal point down toward the body, along the path of the circuit. Repeat the loops until the energy returns to normal.

Sometimes there is a need to revitalize an area of the body to remove stress or tension. Here a figure-eight might be useful, especially if there appears to be a lack of integration with the body as a whole. This can often be the case with long-standing or particularly unpleasant ailments. In these situations, the figure-eights may be needed in a very particular part of the body different from the circuits already covered here. Many other smaller circuits also exist, for example, along the arms or in the feet, which may need stimulating.

Smoky Quartz

Schorl

Clear Quartz

ABOVE *Smoky quartz and schorl are the most fitting for this procedure; clear quartz is an alternative.*

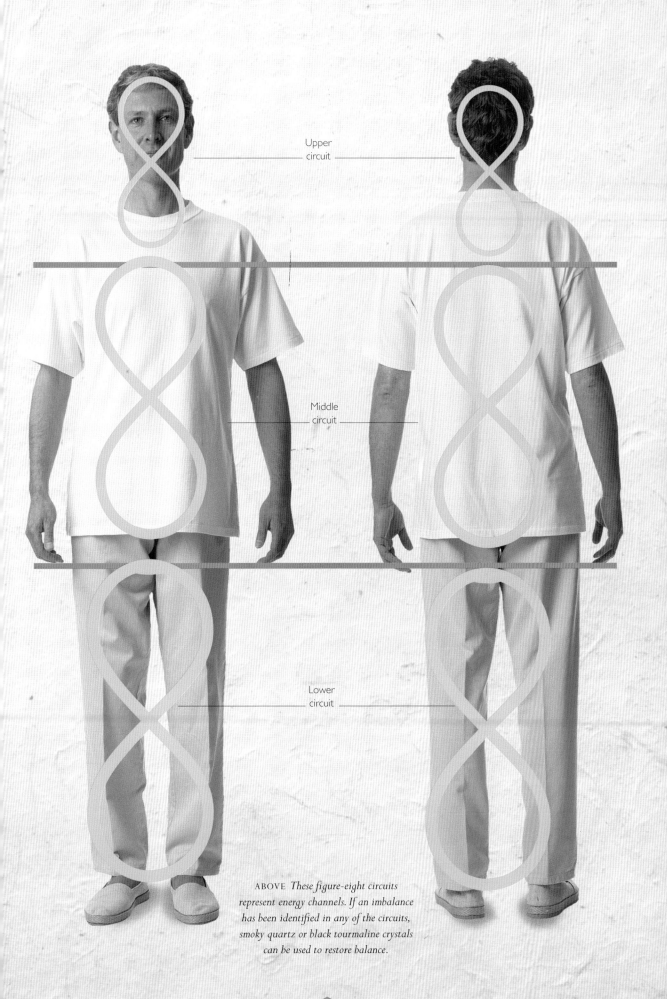

Upper
circuit

Middle
circuit

Lower
circuit

ABOVE *These figure-eight circuits
represent energy channels. If an imbalance
has been identified in any of the circuits,
smoky quartz or black tourmaline crystals
can be used to restore balance.*

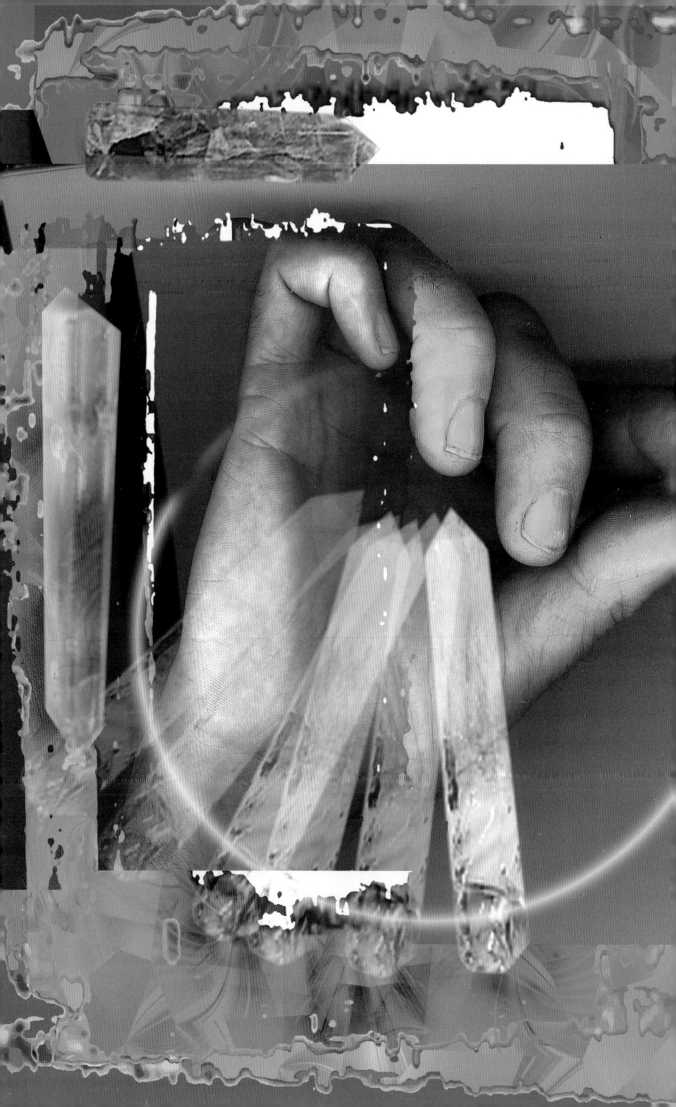

PART SEVEN

BALANCING TECHNIQUES

We have seen how crystal placements can be used to bring a new balance to the subtle systems of the body by working directly with chakras, subtle bodies, and meridians. There are other ways of working with crystals to bring about healing, many of which allow the crystal worker to develop and refine their own intuitive skills.

ABOVE *The combination of intuitive skills and crystals is a powerful one – there are many ways of using it.*

Hand-held crystals ensure the healer is more involved in the process. The healing can be further enhanced by working with two crystals, perhaps a wand or a smooth sphere. Sweeping a crystal pendulum through the aura has a powerful cleansing and balancing effect. It is also possible to program a crystal to focus its potential on a specific goal. Meditation, goal balancing, and emotional stress release can all be carried out using crystals with life-enhancing effects.

Hand-held Crystals

Many crystal healers use a single large clear quartz to energize or cleanse the auric field. Intention and visualization are an important part of the effectiveness of this method, and like all other processes in which the healer becomes actively involved, special care must be given to grounding and centering at all times – before, during, and after the session.

ABOVE *Holding a large, clear quartz crystal in your hand can either stimulate or cleanse the aura.*

Whenever we think of someone we know, a natural resonance is created. When we wish someone well, there is an automatic flow of healing energy, and this energy can easily be concentrated and enhanced with quartz crystals.

A stunning demonstration of how sensitive each of us is to the thoughts of others uses muscle testing. A strong muscle will dramatically weaken when the subject is the focus of a negative thought. Conversely, a weak muscle will strengthen with a positive, life-affirming thought. This is a clear illustration of the fact that those in healing situations need to cultivate positive values, not artificial moods, and should be personally committed to continuing self-development.

The first thing to establish is what methods feel right for you personally. If a recommended process doesn't feel comfortable, it will not be fully effective because, in these situations, it is the mind that directs and controls the flow of healing energy.

Working with hand-held crystals differs from the laying of stones in that the healer is more energetically involved in the healing process. Whatever the technique, even absent healing creates an immediate link between healer and patient. This cannot be avoided. There is however, a difference in degree of emotional and empathic response. To make sure that only appropriate work is done, it is necessary to remain truly grounded and centered, and be fully aware of how the patient is feeling during the process.

The body has a natural polarity, and various parts act like the north and south poles of a magnet. Usually, opposite sides of the body have opposite polarity. If opposite polarities are brought together, there tends to be a flow of life energy between them. Generally speaking, the right hand is positively charged in right-handed people, and the left hand is positively charged in left-handed people.

FINDING YOUR OWN ENERGY FLOW

The positively charged hand will always radiate or give out energy, while the negatively charged hand will tend to absorb and receive energy.

A simple exercise will help to establish your energizing hand and your receiving hand.

1 Hold a quartz crystal in your left hand pointed in and another crystal in your right hand, point out.

2 Imagine a flow of energy through your body between these points from the inward-pointing crystals to the outward-pointing crystal.

3 Now reverse the points of each stone and imagine the flow in the opposite direction.

LEFT *Use two quartz crystals to experience your energy field and to find out which way it flows.*

There will probably be quite a clear difference in the feel of each flow. The direction that feels the most comfortable is your natural flow from receiving (negative, yin) to energizing (positive, yang).

This natural flow of energy can be directed and amplified by holding a crystal in one or the other hand. A crystal tends to focus energy in the direction in which its point is facing. By changing the position of a crystal and the hand in which it is held, a crystal healer can easily learn to control flows of energy in the body. The two main processes of hand-held crystal healing are to release and clear areas of excess energy and to energize areas with a lack of energy, or under-energy.

RIGHT *To recharge energy, hold the quartz in your energizing hand and point it toward the body. Cup a small stone in your receiving hand.*

LEFT *Release destructive over-energy by channeling it through a downward-pointing quartz crystal.*

CLEARING OVER-ENERGY

Areas of over-energy are often indicated by feelings of tension, heat, pain, or congestion. Irritation, frustration, and anger may also be present. To clear this buildup of trapped energy, place your receiving hand palm down on the troubled area. In your energizing or directing hand, hold a clear quartz crystal with its point away from your body and facing down toward the ground.

Breathing deeply and evenly, imagine all the excess energy passing through your body via the receiving hand and out through the crystal in a more harmonious, balanced form and entering the earth where it can be put to good use.

ENERGIZING THE BODY

An area that is low in energy feels heavy, sluggish, cold, and dull. There may be a general lack of vitality and enthusiasm or simply a feeling of tiredness. An increase of energy needs to be directed into this area, so the quartz crystal is now held in the energizing, or charging hand, pointing toward the body. The receiving hand is held away from the body, palm upward, and is imagined absorbing life-energy from the universe, which passes into the crystal and then into the body.

Holding another stone, such as a small sphere or tumbled stone, in the receiving hand will help to transform all the moving energies to become more coherent and balanced.

This is a technique that you can use either by yourself or with other people. It is certainly simple enough to allow personal innovation and intuition to come to the fore.

Moving the crystal in a particular way may serve to speed up the healing process. Classically, a counterclockwise circle tends to draw out and remove imbalances, while a clockwise circle infuses energy into an area. Allow your intuition and your body's intelligence to direct you to move the crystal in an appropriate way.

Working with Two Crystals

Much useful healing can be achieved with different combinations of hand-held stones and the conscious directing of energy using the imaginative and visualizing mind of the healer.

USING TWO CRYSTAL POINTS

LEFT *The energy from two crystal points may help with nerve damage or scar tissue from bone breaks.*

◆ To increase the flow of energy through a blocked area, a crystal can be held on each side of the block with both points indicating the direction of flow. This works well where there is poor blood flow, nerve damage, or scar tissue from bone breaks. Repetitive stress injury, usually exacerbated by meridian breaks around the shoulders, can also be helped in this way. Tracing the line of the energy flow with one crystal point can also work well.

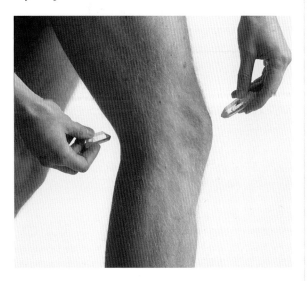

◆ Hold two points toward an area lacking in vitality and visualize a flow of life-supporting energy or light flowing down through the crystals.

◆ To clear a small area, or one perceived as deep within the body, a crystal point can be directed downward to feed in positive healing energy. The second crystal, in the other hand, can be held point outward to draw out and cleanse the released stress.

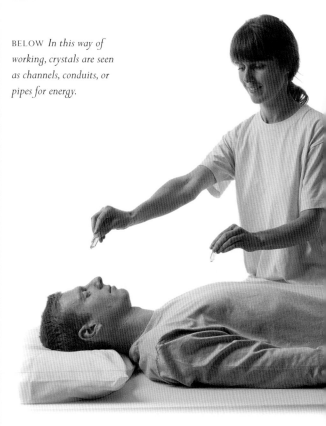

BELOW *In this way of working, crystals are seen as channels, conduits, or pipes for energy.*

The coherent organization of crystal lattices will always tend to increase the order of negatively perceived energies, thus significantly neutralizing their disruptive effects before they leave the crystal. If kept cleansed, a crystal will thus act as a transformer of disharmonious vibration.

Some people feel they need to avoid the disharmony or negative vibrations from the crystal so as not to receive the illness or disruption as it leaves the patient. Remember that imbalance, stress, and disease are simply the wrong sorts of energy in the wrong place. That energy, once removed from an aggravated situation, will not necessarily continue to cause a problem elsewhere. One person's inharmonious energy may be exactly what someone else lacks. It is good practice to avoid making any value judgments where subtle energy is concerned.

USING A CRYSTAL POINT AND SPHERE

BELOW *While a crystal point is used to heal a specific area, a sphere can be guided through the auric field to send a gentle diffusion of positive energy.*

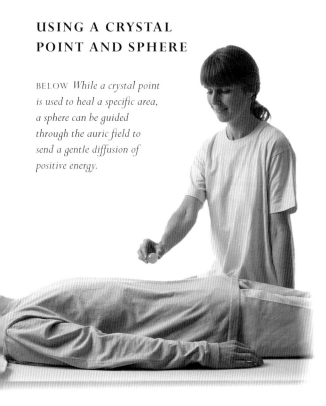

◆ Using the same types of pointed and smooth stones the other way around, it is possible to channel, focus, and draw the energy qualities of the sphere through a pointed crystal. A clear quartz can absorb and direct at an amplified vibrational rate the healing characteristics of another stone. Using a sequence of tumbled stones at the same point can feed a variety of energies into the aura.

◆ Where healing in an area is required, a sphere or

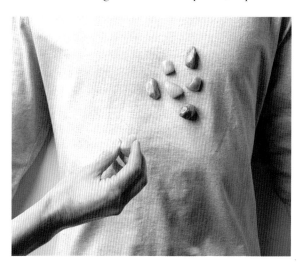

ABOVE *Using a selection of tumbled stones in front of a crystal point channels a variety of energies into the aura.*

◆ A crystal point naturally directs energy, and the mind of the healer adds to and accentuates this directional flow. Holding a smooth stone in front of the point diffuses the energy, allowing it to enter the aura in a gentler, smoother way. This same position can also be used to modify the quality of one crystal with another. For example, the frictionless clarity of selenite can be slowed and diffused by placing a moonstone sphere, egg, or tumbled stone in the path of its energy stream. The energies of one stone are focused through the lens of another and are gently diffused by the rounded shape into a patient's aura.

egg can be gently moved through the auric field sending a gentle diffusion of positive energy while the point can be directed to remove and transform any energy debris outward.

◆ The point can be used like a wand to cut or loosen blocks, followed by the sphere smoothing and resealing the healed areas.

LEFT *Two pendulums can be used to clear areas of blocked energy. Simply allow them to spin until they return to neutral.*

Programing Crystals

The process of programing a crystal focuses the activity and energy of the crystal toward specific desired goals. The process involves modifying the energy structures within the atomic lattice so that the memory of the intent remains for as long as required.

Before examining how this can be achieved, it is worth thinking about some of the ethical considerations in the process. The word "programing" has been borrowed from computer terminology. It is quite a useful word, and it is difficult to think of a substitute. However, it implies that a crystal is simply a natural computer waiting to be given instructions by its owner.

The fact is, there is really very little in common between a crystal and a computer. A computer is a man-made amalgam of constructed elements, some of which may be very small artificial silicon crystals, created specifically to benefit humans. A natural crystal is an orderly pattern of matter that has existed for thousands or millions of years and which has been removed from its original site by humans. These days, a computer can be obsolete in less than a year. A crystal may remain in one form for longer than the human species exists on Earth. It would be presumptuous to assume a crystal has nothing better to do than what we tell it. If nothing else, programing a crystal will amplify whatever intent is placed within it so that it reflects back on the subtle levels of awareness. However, as a neutral mirror, without any participation of its own spirit or awareness, a programed crystal can be a devastating tool if misused.

There are two ways of programing crystals. The active method uses conscious thought-energy projected into the crystal. The passive method works by habituation or by using a crystal in the same way or in the same environment. This can happen quite naturally to our own crystals. Some we may use for healing, while others

ABOVE *Computers, operating systems, and programs quickly go out of date, but crystals are timeless energy powerhouses.*

we keep purely as personal meditation pieces. Crystals can also be placed consciously in a particular environment to imprint its energy upon the crystal's matrix.

Whether an active or passive programing method is used, that vibration of energy has to be in harmony with the crystal's own energy in order for it to work in a positive, life-enhancing way for both you and the crystal. As with all crystal work, it is important to remember that it is a joint effort between you and the stone.

Passive programing is easier to do and, by its very nature, it is a less intrusive method. It works by orienting the main energy of a crystal in a certain way. Using exposure to a distinct and coherent external influence, such as a color, a particular sound, a favorite scent, symbol, and so on, over time, that specific energy pattern is held within the memory – the energetic structures of the matrix. Thus a clear quartz that has been passively programed with blue light will work as clear quartz but in a blue sort of way.

ABOVE *By focusing light of a particular color onto clear quartz, the stone will pick up the qualities and energy of that color.*

PRELIMINARIES

The key to beginning the process of programing is to know your crystal completely. Attune to the crystal and feel whether in your mind you are completely happy with that crystal being modified, even if temporarily. Does it feel comfortable to work in this way with the crystal? Whichever method of programing you use, you should always attune to the stone and ask the crystal to receive the information or energy pattern.

Some crystals may have programs already, or be working on a particular energy level. This must be checked before stepping in.

1 Attune to the stone, using whichever exercises suit you best. This allows you to acquire a feeling for the crystal's energy.

2 Ask permission of the crystal before you attempt to place a program.

3 Wait for a response. If it feels negative or there is doubt, you can attune further and ask again. If the feeling is still negative or doubtful, don't continue.

4 Ask the crystal to open a part of its internal matrix to accept the program.

5 Wait until you feel a new openness in the crystal's energy.

6 If you are to use the passive mode, put the crystal in the appropriate place and leave it for a while.

7 If you are intending to use the active mode, you should work out the precise wording or the exact thought beforehand. Check and recheck its validity and correctness. It is essential that the vibration of your thought-energy must be in harmony with the crystal in order for it to work in a positive way.

8 Before focusing the thought into the crystal, allow the idea and the crystal to contact each other. Wait for a feeling of acceptance or resistance to the thought. Instead of using concentration or forceful focus, just float the thought into the crystal.

9 If there is harmony between thought and crystal, the next step is to then focus your awareness as closely as possible on the thought and project it into the crystal. Use your hands, heart, brow chakra, or any other points that you feel comfortable with as the connection point or projection point into the crystal.

10 Repeat this focus several times until you feel it is sufficiently established in the crystal.

11 Attune once more and check either mentally or with dowsing techniques that the program is settled and has been activated.

12 Visually and mentally close, seal, heal, and protect the crystal structure that carries your program. Check that all is OK.

13 Repeat the whole process once or twice more at different times to reinforce your intent.

BELOW *Crystals can be placed around the home to radiate positive influences into your environment.*

IDEAS FOR PROGRAMS

Any crystal will be able to accept programing. However, clear quartz is the favored stone simply because it has a broad range of functions and is more or less neutral. This enables quartz to work easily with a wider range of situations than most other crystals.

❖ A frequent suggestion is that newly acquired crystals can be programed so that they remain free of negative influences or can only be used for life-supporting ends. While these are noble sentiments, in almost all cases, the crystal structure itself will deal with most energy imbalances and will work to increase harmony and coherence. On the other hand, if a piece of crystal jewelry is worn often, it could be programed to become more efficient at self-cleansing. Jewelry can also be programed to enhance specific qualities, such as confidence, clarity of mind, protection from harm, health, and so on.

BELOW *Think about areas of your life where crystals could exert a benevolent influence.*

- reduce stress
- avoid fatty foods
- give up smoking
- learn to relax
- approach problems with clarity of mind
- diminish feelings of insecurity

BELOW *Charge a crystal with the essence of a special environment.*

❖ Where crystals are used for very particular purposes, whether programed initially or not, they will become more and more effective so long as they are regularly checked to see if they need cleansing.

❖ If you learn to listen to each crystal's wishes, you will never have a shortage of ideas for programing.

❖ Choosing the exact nature of a program does need careful consideration. The more precise and detailed the wording of the intent, the greater its effectiveness will be. Programing a crystal for world peace is expecting a little too much, but "peace around me," or "peace in this room," is fine. Likewise, the word "health" is very general, while "relief from headaches," "strengthening heart function," "reducing tension," and so on, is more focused.

❖ Try listening to the crystal itself, to see where it would appreciate its energies being directed. You may be surprised at the precise nature or the exact wording that pops into your awareness.

ABOVE *Any animal qualities you admire can be programed into a crystal.*

❖ A crystal can be programed with a piece of music that will continually radiate its qualities into a space. Likewise, a type of environment can be programed, such as a sunset on a long beach, a rainforest, even another galaxy. Use sounds, pictures, and other means to program a crystal. The energy of a favorite animal or plant, a spiritual teacher, or some other holy image can be programed into an appropriate stone, to energize and protect a space or individual.

❖ Some makers of flower essences, vibrational remedies prepared from plants, use programed crystals to absorb the vibrational characteristics of flowers, rather than having to pick them. The crystal is then put into spring water, which it charges with the plant's energy.

ABOVE *The active qualities of flowers can be transferred to crystals.*

Record Keepers

Record-keeper crystals are identified by perfect triangles etched or raised on one or more facets. They are said to be special crystals within which wisdom has been stored consciously by other beings. The triangular shape is a natural expression of how quartz grows and it might be that these formations allow clearer access to information present in many, if not all crystals.

Most record keepers need careful scrutiny to identify, and they tend to be of use to only one person at a time. Hunting for a record keeper is thus inappropriate unless the individual is in tune with the particular qualities of the stone.

Record-keeper crystals can reveal the history of the universe on physical and other dimensions. They can be teaching crystals for personal growth. Each stone will have a particular means of access but here is an exercise to try:

PROCEDURE FOR RECORD KEEPERS

1 Closely examine the crystal and especially the record keeper's triangle. Hold the shape in mind.

2 Close your eyes, quietening your breathing, perhaps repeat a mantra or say "Om" a few times to help your awareness settle down.

3 Imagine the crystal in front of you, and the triangular mark of the record keeper on your forehead.

4 See the crystal increasing in size until it is many times bigger than you.

5 Imagine you are moving closer to the crystal and be aware that you are looking for an entrance point. You may find yourself floating above or around the faces of the stone as if you were on an invisible escalator.

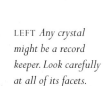

LEFT *Any crystal might be a record keeper. Look carefully at all of its facets.*

6 It is likely that there will be some kind of triangular door. Move over to the door and place your forehead against its surface.

7 If you are allowed to or ready, you will find yourself inside the energy form of the crystal and will then be able to receive information that will be of use to you.

8 When this process is complete, or you wish to leave, return to the door, place your forehead with its triangular mark to the door once more, and find yourself outside the crystal.

9 Move away from the crystal and become gradually aware of your body. Thank the crystal's energies and will it to return to its physical size.

10 Take time to record and assess the experiences you have had.

11 Visit the record keeper's crystal form often to attune your energies and to deepen the whole experience.

Many people consider the etched markings of some crystals to also indicate particular history or information within the stone. From a mineralogical point of view, these surface markings are a result of adverse conditions. But perhaps the evocative symbols and hieroglyphic-type markings can also put us in touch with more universal aspects of the self, freeing us to experience levels of awareness and information not usually available to the conscious mind. If you have a crystal whose markings you find fascinating, carry out the above exercise while visualizing the particular shapes

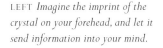
LEFT *Imagine the imprint of the crystal on your forehead, and let it send information into your mind.*

ABOVE *In traditional cultures, the shaman or medicine man interpreted events and conveyed their significance to the people. Interaction with the intuitive mind was a part of everyday life.*

instead of the triangular door. Traditional societies tend to view everything in their world as having important personal significance. Each event or unusual circumstance is examined for its meaning. There is a constant interaction between the individual and the world in which he or she moves. Contemporary society frequently sees coincidences, objects, and events as materialistic things rather than symbols of a deeper reality. This view might free us from the fear of powerful spirits, but it increases our profound sense of isolation and can be psychologically damaging. Our sense of play, of behaving "as if," allows other, deeper and more intuitive parts of our mind to enrich our experience of the world. Using the patterns, veils, etchings, and shapes of crystals to free the mind from its everyday organization can lead to an increase in well-being and a clearer view of reality.

Whether an experience is worthwhile and valid depends not upon how objectively real it might be, but on how much it improves one's enjoyment of life and sense of well-being.

Healing with Crystal Pendulums

Pendulum dowsing has a long history of use among healers of all types. As an assessment tool, learning to dowse is an essential skill for anyone wishing to work with crystals. It is well worth the time and practice in order to become confident and accurate in the use of pendulums. The skill needed for dowsing for information is largely one of mental attitude and correct procedure. There are also methods of using pendulums as tools for healing in their own right.

Amethyst

A pendulum is very simply a balanced weight on the end of a string or chain that allows movement. The actual swing or other movements of the pendulum are an amplification of minute physical or energetic changes within the muscles of the dowser. Like any other dowsing tool, the pendulum is an aid to recognizing changes in energy, so that they are shown in a clearly visible way.

Crystals interact dynamically with the human energy field, and when they are able to move through the aura, a powerful cleansing and balancing can occur. With the following techniques, the holder of the pendulum stays mentally neutral. No questioning is used or information sought. The pendulum is simply moved through the aura and left to swing in whichever way it wishes.

Any object moving through the auric field will have an effect of one sort or another. A crystal or gemstone is necessary to guarantee a beneficial healing effect. The most useful crystals to begin working with are clear quartz and amethyst. Both have a broad balancing effect on many systems.

ABOVE AND RIGHT
Begin by using clear quartz and amethyst for their broad balancing qualities.
Clear Quartz

FIVE-LINE CLEARING METHOD

1 Hold the pendulum lightly and firmly between your thumb and index finger. Keep your arm and shoulder relaxed and your body in a comfortable position. Your forearm should be held more or less level, with the wrist relaxed.

2 Before starting, consciously intend that the crystal pendulum will move away from the neutral swing only when it approaches an imbalance in the subtle bodies that can be corrected quickly and safely. This last point is important because it sets limits on a session that otherwise might last for a long time and release more stress than would be comfortable.

3 Start the pendulum swinging in a straight line, to and fro. This is known as the neutral swing. Any deviation from this simple swing will indicate that the pendulum is interacting with the energy fields in order to restore balance.

4 Move slowly in a line up the center of the body, beginning just below the feet, about 4 inches (10 centimeters) above the body. Whenever the pendulum swing moves away from neutral, just stay at that point until the swing returns to neutral. Occasionally the pendulum will seem to slow and stop, and then start to move in another direction. Make sure the pendulum has returned to a stable neutral swing before moving on.

ABOVE *Start off by guiding the pendulum into a neutral swing — a straight line to and fro.*

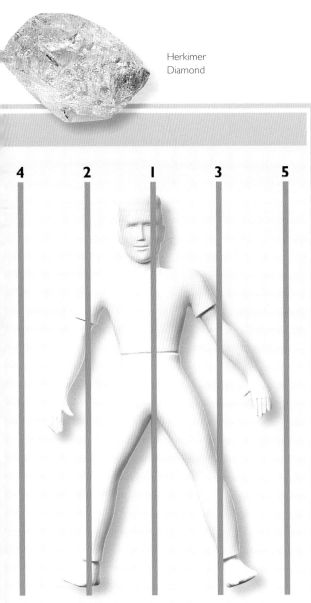

4 2 1 3 5

Herkimer
Diamond

ABOVE *Herkimer diamond and lodestone will repair energy fields. The five-line clearing can be fine-tuned by the intention of the pendulum holder.*

ABOVE *Move on to swing the pendulum over a series of lines traveling up the body. It is useful to mark on a diagram of a body those places where the pendulum has picked up and corrected imbalances.*

5 When you have traveled up the whole body and reached a point approximately 12 inches (30 centimeters) above the head, start again at the feet, this time holding the pendulum to one side of the body. A line following the outside edge of the legs and torso is ideal.

6 Repeat as before and then return to move up the other side of the body. The pendulum has now swept upward in three lines, covering all areas of the subtle bodies closest to the physical.

7 For the last two sweeps, the pendulum is held farther away from the physical body, but still parallel to the other lines. Here, it will be interacting mostly with the finest levels of energy within the auric field.

VARIATIONS

◆ The pendulum can be used to work even farther away from the physical body, creating profound clearing of the very fine subtle bodies – extend two further lines outward from the five lines, and extend farther above and below the feet and head.

◆ Changing the height of the pendulum swing will interact with different energy layers. If there is a significant imbalance closer to the body, raising the pendulum up might help to clear the subtle causes located in finer layers of energy.

◆ A pendulum made from a Herkimer diamond will detoxify energy fields effectively.

◆ Hold a lodestone stationary and move it slowly through the aura. Where it moves, there are electromagnetic imbalances, usually from environmental sources. Or keep the lodestone swinging in a rapid circle and move through the aura. This will disperse any buildup of electromagnetic static.

◆ Before starting the five-line clearing, think of the area or problem to be dealt with, such as the emotional body or the healing of an illness. The pendulum will then move only over relevant imbalances.

◆ Use the pendulum sweep to quickly assess which areas require work. Stone placements and other techniques can then be used to rebalance the body.

Massage Wands

Massage wands are a gentle and powerful way to introduce healing energies into the auric field. Wands are sometimes natural crystals that have had their bases smoothed and rounded, but most often they are cut from larger blocks of stone and are given a faceted point at one end and a rounded end at the other. This round end allows them to be used safely on the skin without scratching or irritating. The cool, smooth sensation they produce is extremely relaxing and they can be a useful adjunct to many forms of massage. Where there are areas of deep pain, lightly moving a massage wand over the area will help to relax and reduce the discomfort. Generally speaking, imbalances and tensions will be drawn out using small counterclockwise circles, but allow intuition and your body's own subtle senses to guide the movements of the wand.

ABOVE *Many crystal healers find that, as well as the natural crystals in their kit, shaped crystals serve useful purposes.*

Massage wands are also extremely effective tools for working within the subtle bodies. Their smooth, streamlined, highly polished shapes often seem to create less turbulence when moving through the aura than other shapes of stone.

WAND METHOD

The following method is an excellent way to become aware of your own intuitive skills while allowing profound healing on many levels. The deeper the healing work, the greater is the need for the healer to remain centered and grounded. It may be necessary to use a grounding stone or a grounding layout as a final procedure.

The principal purpose of this technique is to remove stress from the subtle bodies and align all energy fields. The wand is moved through the aura as is felt appropriate, but the following guidelines operate where personal intuition is absent:

1 Hold the wand comfortably with the rounded end closest to the body, point outward.

2 Starting near the patient's feet, make small counterclockwise circling movements with the wand 2–6 inches (5–15 centimeters) above the body.

3 The first part of this process is to slowly move up the body, unwinding any stresses and tensions. The speed at which you move or the order in which you proceed will be entirely up to you.

4 As you move the wand through the aura, you will experience a difference of quality in the movement of the wand or a sense of weight, lightness, stickiness, or even a difference within your own feelings. Wherever such changes are recognized, spend longer with the wand until it once again feels comfortable and smooth.

5 Often the movement of your hand will want to change. Allow the movement that feels most comfortable to you. In this method, nothing is wrong except ignoring intuitive modifications.

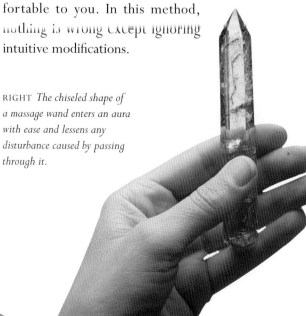

RIGHT *The chiseled shape of a massage wand enters an aura with ease and lessens any disturbance caused by passing through it.*

6 When the top of the head is reached, change the position of the wand so that it is held with the point facing the body. The movement used should now be small clockwise circles that recharge and energize the subtle bodies. Again variations may occur, although usually this second stage – moving from head back to feet – is a lot clearer and quicker to complete.

7 It is not very important in which hand the wand is held. Find the most comfortable position so that there is no physical strain in reaching over the whole auric field.

8 Make sure your patient is comfortable and ask them to let you know if they experience any strange sensations or if their mood or thoughts suddenly change. These will give further clues to the areas being released.

9 Be sure to make clear that any areas of imbalance identified will be on many different levels. One of the great strengths of crystal healing is that it can remove causes of potential illness long before it occurs on a physical level.

VARIATIONS

▲ Remember, working farther away from the body means that you will be interacting with the finest levels of awareness and thus potentially more powerfully. You can alter the height at which the wand is being held if you wish.

▲ This massage wand technique can be used to great effect to speed up localized healing. Follow the same procedures as with whole body sweeps.

▲ Different crystal wands will work well on different levels. A variety of wands can supply a huge range of working possibilities.

▲ The size and length of the wand will affect the number of levels of energy it will work with at any one time, but always remember that a very large or heavy wand will be much more tiring to use, and often much more fragile.

BELOW *Working on the top of the head. The use of massage wands can create deep states of altered awareness, so make sure the patient takes time to return to normal consciousness at the end of the session.*

Move the crystal in small, clockwise circles

Turn the point toward the head

Make sure the patient is comfortable

Emotional Stress

One of the greatest benefits of crystal healing is its ability to quickly and effectively reduce emotional stress. No matter what the level of an individual's health, emotional stress is a constant, energy-depleting, drain of life-force. Emotional stress includes the tiny everyday nuisances and pressures as well as the large-scale events like illness, accidents, and bereavement. Each stress, unless released, adds pressure to existing weaknesses in the body.

Emotional stress is not just something that upsets the mind. There is increasing evidence that emotional health is the best preventive for a whole range of serious physical diseases. Most complementary and alternative therapists recognize the repeated pattern of serious emotional stress preceding the onset of serious illness by a month or two. Emotional stress burdens the body so that it becomes less able to repair itself or to deal with invading microorganisms.

Emotional health is not a superficial concern. Life energy and life quality depend upon good emotional health. Emotional imbalance floods the physical body with excessive levels of hormones, prevents proper absorption of nutrients, and creates tension and restricted circulation in muscle tissue. Stress that arises from an emotional response gets locked into the physical body. Existing stress at fine levels of awareness in the subtle bodies further prevents the dissipation of more surface stress. Emotional stress builds up toxins, both chemical and energetic, and unless there is a way to clear the system, they continue to build up.

A stress is created whenever an event, sensation, or thought becomes caught or endlessly repeated in the memory of a cell, organ, or system. If we were hospitalized as a baby, it is likely that somewhere in our energy personality a little part of us is still stuck at that experience. All through our lives, we lose bits of ourselves as they get stuck in anachronistic time loops, locking up in tense muscles and erroneous belief systems energy that would otherwise be available to us now.

Reliving stressful events isn't necessarily helpful. Unless there is a mechanism for releasing the stress, it will probably remain unchanged and even become reinforced. Stress release using crystals doesn't require the conscious recall of an event. It can be likened to gently waking someone from a nightmare or a daydream. The energetic patterns of the crystals remind the stressed areas that the stress situation no longer exists in the present, encouraging relaxation and repair. Very often, working on the subtle bodies and the chakra system will release many levels of stress. Where there is a need to focus on rebalancing the emotions, several techniques can be very effective.

Before beginning any work to release stress, it is essential to make sure, if you are using pendulum dowsing or kinesiology, that it is an appropriate

LEFT *Unless there has been some active work to remove emotional stress from the system, it locks itself into the physical body, causing illness.*

time to work on the chosen areas. Stress can build up much like a wall, brick by brick. If you wish to remove the wall, it can be taken down slowly, safely, and neatly from the top, or the whole thing can be demolished all at once, creating a great deal of disturbance, more risk of injury, and taking much longer to clear away the debris.

We get used to the levels of stress that we carry around with us. It becomes familiar, a part of our make-up. We compensate for its presence. Removing a lot of stress too rapidly can unbalance our lives to such an extent that it becomes very uncomfortable. Working methodically with whatever healing is most appropriate at the time is, in all respects, the best approach.

In order to be permanent and effective, the release of emotional stress needs to be in agreement with the energy systems of the person who is being treated. What may appear to be an obvious stress factor that needs to be removed may not be the body's own priority issue. Emotional stresses

ABOVE *As if gently waking someone from a nightmare, the elimination of emotional stress using crystals must be carried out in harmony with the person's energy systems.*

tend to cluster together in pockets of associated events. The death of a pet or watching a tragic movie scene may trigger memories of loss, grief, and sadness that cause deep emotions to well up, apparently from nowhere, with no obvious bearing on the triggering event.

The body may need to disengage itself from some of its older, less raw emotional stresses before it feels comfortable addressing more current concerns. The anniversaries of stressful experiences also play an important role in their effective release. Somewhere at the back of the conscious mind is the memory of the exact time of each original stress. This floats to the surface as the anniversary nears, and it can be then that an effective stress release can completely release the trauma, even where no memory of the event seems to exist.

Emotional Stress Release Technique

Sometimes it can be useful to identify precisely an area of stress that needs to be released. The following technique, based on kinesiology, can use either dowsing or muscle testing.

1 Find a strong indicator muscle (see pages 102–105).

2 Hold lightly the frontal eminences on the forehead. These are the slightly raised bulges on each side of the forehead between the eyebrows and the hairline. Retest the indicator muscle. If it is now weak, this shows that emotional stress is present and it is appropriate to release it.

3 The next step isolates the area of the emotions in which the stress is stored. Test each of the following words by saying them aloud and testing a strong indicator muscle. One or more words will weaken the muscle, indicating the areas of stress. The categories are: Fear, Anger, Grief, Joy, and Sympathy.

4 Once the category has been found, next isolate the year in which stress is focused. Test by age, i.e. between 0 and 10, between 10 and 20, and so on, up to the person's present age. Sometimes other possibilities emerge, such as birth, gestation, conception, past or future lives.

5 Find the focus of the stress: self, family, relationships, vacation, school, work, pets, and so on. In all of this testing, the stressful area will weaken a strong muscle. Write down all the information.

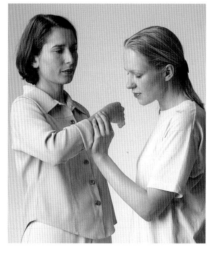

ABOVE *Begin by looking for a strong indicator muscle to enable you to identify the precise area of stress.*

ABOVE *Holding the forehead points can create an energetic link where emotional stress can easily flow between healer and patient.*

6 This information may be enough to allow the person to consciously remember the events, but it is not essential, as the stress will release automatically.

7 Once the information is found, repeat all the factors aloud. This will remind the body of the exact stress to be released.

8 The patient sits or lies comfortably and thinks through or around the events.

9 While the person is thinking, the healer lightly holds the forehead with the fingertips of both hands. Alternatively, two crystals can be lightly taped in place.

10 The release can be carried out in silence, or the patient can report memories and sensations. In either case, the healer should check how the patient is feeling at regular intervals. Make sure that both of you are comfortable before beginning, since it is important not to interrupt the process.

11 There is usually a noticeable change of mood when the stress has cleared. A retest of the strong muscle, with the stress factors spoken aloud, should remain strong if the stress has been fully released.

12 Test all five category words again. You may now be able to release other stresses. If there is time to work further, repeat the procedure until all category words test strong.

13 Remember that this technique will allow you to work only with stresses that the body is ready to release at the time.

LEFT *Work is one of the most prevalent causes of stress. Tell the patient to focus on his or her difficulties while you hold his forehead.*

BELOW *To assist with dispelling stress, circle a massage wand while tracking across the patient's forehead.*

It is a good idea to check whether further crystal work is needed, especially grounding and centering layouts. Where a lot of stress has been let go, check again the overall balance of the chakras and, if necessary, clear any energetic debris out of the auric field using a massage wand or crystal pendulum. In this case, amethyst quartz will do, or calming and gentle healing stones, such as carnelian, aventurine, jade, and smoky quartz, will help to soothe and integrate the subtle energy fields.

Drinking a little fresh water will help to re-establish electrical balance in the body and will also help to flush out any toxins that have been released from the process.

The healer using this technique should remain as mentally and emotionally neutral as possible, while of course remaining sympathetic and supportive throughout. To encourage this, make sure you continue to remain centered and grounded or wear some grounding crystals. Having a view from a window, a picture or a crystal on which the eye can rest is a good way to remain neutral and prevent tiredness or impatience.

In stressful situations, many people automatically hold the palm of one hand to their forehead. This immediately helps to reduce the anxiety. The technique can be done for oneself with or without finding the stresses involved. Simply hold the fingertips to the frontal eminences or hold a hand across the forehead.

Using a massage wand or crystal spheres can be another way to encourage this stress release. Work with the smooth surfaces of the crystal and lightly move over the skin of the forehead and face in small counterclockwise circles, paying particular attention to the sensitive areas around the frontal eminences.

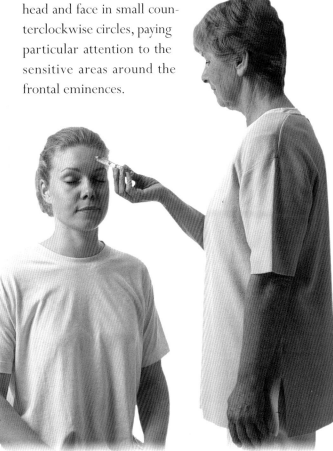

Whenever the body is rested and relaxed, it will take the opportunity to release surface levels of stress. During crystal healing, very deep relaxation often occurs, and this allows persistent, more chronic stress to begin to release. There are several recognizable signs of stress release that a crystal healer should be aware of, so that when they arise the patient can be reassured.

Relaxation naturally allows the breath to slow and deepen. A sign of release of stress, tension, or a rebalancing of energies is a very long, deep breath, a sigh, or a yawn. As a healing session progresses, there may be a series of phases where the patient moves deeper into calm states of awareness. Each successive stage offers the opportunity to release deep levels of stress. Involuntary muscle twitching and unconscious movements of a hand or foot can often indicate release of stress. Occasionally, the twitch is clearly linked to the event that caused the stress in the first place.

The clearest sign of stress release is a rapid fluttering of the closed eyelids. The patient may be aware or unaware of this movement, depending on how strong it is. At this point, it is a good idea to check that there are no feelings of discomfort. Of course, crying and sobbing are also indicators of release and, should they occur spontaneously, try to make the person as comfortable as possible. It is usually more comfortable for the patient to remove all stones and the healer to turn him or her onto one side rather than to remain lying on the back.

Make sure there are plenty of grounding stones at the legs and feet. This will allow a rapid clearing of released energy and help to prevent the stresses from settling back into the subtle bodies. If stress release becomes very disturbing by the conscious mind becoming involved in reliving or judging the events, then carry out grounding and centering exercises until calm returns.

PROCEDURE

Emotional stress release will automatically begin when stones are placed on the frontal eminences on the forehead. As the stress begins to clear, there may be a memory of the situation, but this does not necessarily happen. There may also be emotions that come to the surface. As the stress clears, the emotions will naturally dissolve. Use assessment techniques to find the most appropriate stones to use and how long they need to be in place. Once the stones have been removed, check that the process has been completed.

TENSION RELEASE LAYOUT

1 Place a rose quartz at the heart center and surround it with four clear quartz crystals with their points facing diagonally outward. This pattern will help to release emotional blocks from the heart and disperse them so they won't settle elsewhere in the subtle bodies. The clear quartz crystal will naturally transform the disharmonious energy imbalances into a more life-sustaining quality.

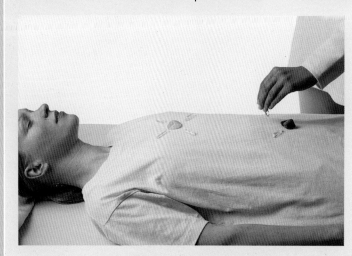

2 At the second sacral chakra, below the navel, place a tiger's eye stone. Surround this with four clear quartz crystals with points facing diagonally inward. This part of the pattern helps to give stability and grounding to the healing process by integrating the base, sacral, and solar plexus chakras. If the release is very strong, it is a sensible precaution to use extra grounding stones by the feet.

HEART CHAKRA CLEARING

Stress is very often caused by our relationship to other people, so the heart chakra is closely involved. To clear emotional imbalance from the heart chakra, try the following:

1 Put a rose quartz at the heart and use four clear quartz points placed on the main axes of the body. When the points are facing out from the central stone, imbalance will be quickly removed. When the points are placed facing inward, the crystals will help to stabilize and calm troubled emotional states.

3 When the mind needs quiet, an amethyst quartz can be put at the forehead or above the top of the head. In emotional states, amethyst is excellent for calming down thought.

2 A citrine quartz is placed, point downward, between the solar plexus and the sacral chakra. This acts as a gentle grounding stone, and reinforces self-confidence and security.

Layouts for Emotional Stress Release

There are some layouts of crystals that can be very helpful both to release stress and to encourage positive change. With most crystal layouts described here, a short session repeated on a regular basis every few days conveys greater benefit than spending a longer time once in a while. In this way, the body becomes accustomed to the new balance of energy and is able to better maintain it during everyday activity. The longer the healing session, the more time it takes to integrate the new information, and therefore the benefits of healing take longer to emerge.

PERSONAL POTENTIAL LAYOUT

This layout helps to clear emotional blocks so that suppressed or diverted skills can develop. The stones used are clear and rose quartz to cleanse the auric field and reestablish self confidence after emotional setbacks. If possible, this layout is best done lying on a yellow-colored cloth, which helps to stimulate positive solar plexus energies and mental clarity.

The rose quartz stones are all placed in contact with the body. One is set at the top of

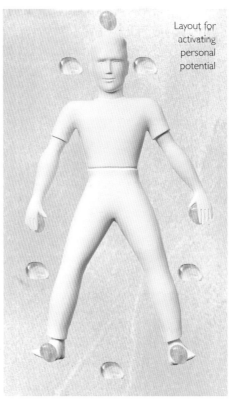

Layout for activating personal potential

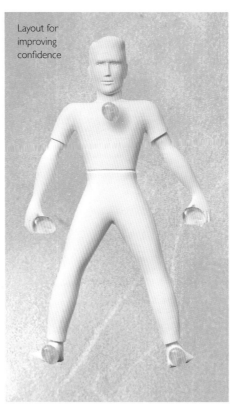

Layout for improving confidence

the head, one is held in each hand, and one is placed on each foot between the tendons of the first and second toes.

The clear quartz stones are placed next to the body on each side of the head, level with the ears, beside the legs at knee level, and one beneath the feet. Crystals with points should face inward.

Five or ten minutes spent regularly in this energy pattern will help to relieve stress.

CONFIDENCE LAYOUT

The placement of stones here will help to dissolve false inhibitions and stimulate motivation and drive.

Use a green cloth as a base color to focus the crystals' action on areas of balance, growth, and stress release around the heart chakra.

A rose quartz is placed at the base of the throat and one on each foot between the tendons of the first and second toes. Held in each hand is a clear quartz pointing away from the body. This both releases stress from the energy bodies and stimulates practical creativity and the desire to participate in the world.

Five minutes within these energies will help to establish their beneficial effects.

CALMING LAYOUT

Moonstone helps calm the emotions and reduce stress. It relates both to the solar plexus, where it calms the digestive system and reduces fears, and to the sacral chakra, where it encourages the balance of all fluids within the body and helps to dissolve emotional rigidity.

Using a blue cloth or background for this layout will emphasize the qualities of flow and peacefulness that the moonstones will direct into the subtle bodies.

Five moonstones of about the same size are used. If one stone is larger, place that at the top of the head, touching the scalp. On the front of the shoulders, in the hollow where arm meets torso, place a moonstone on each side. The remaining two stones are put on each hipbone. Some of these stones may need to be lightly taped in place.

This is a soothing healing pattern in which there is often an experience of great comfort. It induces a deep state of relaxation in which physical aches and pains can be relieved. Emotional worries tend to dissolve quickly from the mind. Occasionally, as the body releases stress and adjusts to the energies, there may be a sensation of pressure at the throat chakra. If it doesn't ease by itself, a light blue stone such as turquoise or blue lace agate will help the flow. It is easy to forget all sense of time in this energy net, so be aware that ten minutes will be ample to gain a healing benefit.

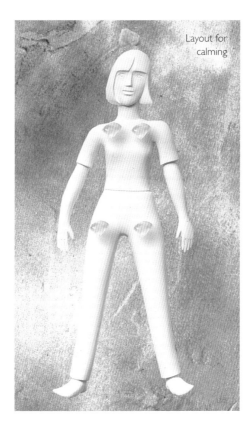

Layout for calming

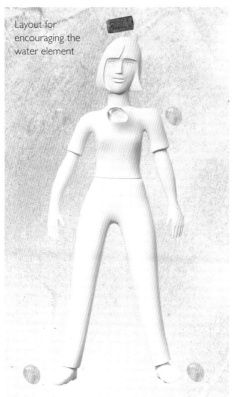

Layout for encouraging the water element

WATER ELEMENT LAYOUT

The quality of water symbolizes the flow and flexibility that we require if we are to be healthy and grow in life. Water is linked with the emotions, and both have the tendency to move outward until they reach a state of equilibrium. When this flow becomes blocked, pressure continues to build up, and, unless it is released, it can cause great destruction when it finally escapes.

Such emotional tension can feel as if one is at bursting point, full of desperation and with feelings circling in on themselves. This layout of crystals may help to release the internal pressure and establish a new state of balance.

Four rose quartz crystals are placed beside the feet and at the sides of the shoulders. This helps to free the blocks from the energy systems of the body, particularly those to do with emotional conflicts.

A clear quartz crystal is at the thymus gland at the base of the throat. This helps to strengthen the body's natural electromagnetic field and benefits the immune and endocrine systems.

A sapphire crystal is placed above the top of the head to balance the subtle bodies, encouraging a healthy link between physical, mental, and emotional systems, and specifically will ease depressive emotional states. Using a blue cloth or surface to lie upon helps to create a background energy of peacefulness and communication.

Meditation with Crystals

Meditation covers a wide range of activities and states of awareness. It can generally be defined as a means of turning attention away from the conscious mind to focus on other processes. Meditation is often thought of as doing nothing. It would be more accurate to say that meditation is doing something different.

The purpose of meditation can be as varied as the techniques. Relaxation and stress release are often reasons why meditation is suggested in the West, but these are really just the side effects of any successful meditation technique. Find a method with which you are comfortable and which provides the desired results. Everyone has different skills and tendencies that will help or hinder meditation. It is therefore a good idea to try out many different techniques, spending enough time with each one to become familiar with the process.

Crystal, and quartz in particular, can be useful in many different types of meditations. The orderly energy structure of crystal naturally imparts a stillness and order to the subtle body system, and this in turn helps to quieten the mind. One key to meditation is drawing the mind away from its normal analytical chatter. The visual appeal of crystals and gemstones, with their depth of color, shape, and play of light can be endlessly fascinating.

ABOVE *Gaze at the crystal for a few moments, then close your eyes and recreate the image. Open your eyes and repeat the process.*

Meditation and healing go hand in hand. In meditation, one is allowed to return to a more natural state of balance. With meditations that lead the mind along particular pathways, as in guided visualizations or guided meditations, the consciousness once more is focused away from everyday issues of the surface layers of the mind. Most anxiety, fears, and stresses are formed and given existence within the conscious mind. Problems are situations that haven't been resolved by normal thought processes. By slightly altering our way of thinking, a solution can automatically arise.

BELOW *Quartz is especially suitable as an aid to meditation, as it naturally calms the mind and focuses thoughts.*

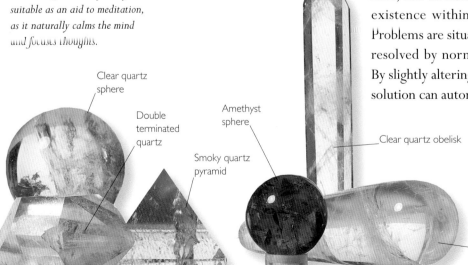

Clear quartz sphere

Double terminated quartz

Smoky quartz pyramid

Amethyst sphere

Clear quartz obelisk

Clear quartz massage tool

MEDITATION TECHNIQUES USING CRYSTALS

1 Adapting a traditional technique called Tratak, which uses a crystal instead of a lighted candle at which to gaze, can be a wonderful way of exploring the energy of a crystal as well as using it as a focus. The idea is to place a crystal at a comfortable distance away from you where your eyes can rest on it without strain. Begin by just gazing into the stone. Try not to blink. After a few minutes, close your eyes. In your mind's eye, try to recapture the image of the crystal. After a few minutes, open your eyes and gaze on the crystal again. You can repeat this procedure several times. Remember to take some time before returning to everyday activity when you have finished.

RIGHT *Setting out the stones into patterns is a relaxing way of interlacing the crystals' guiding energy with your thoughts.*

2 You can adapt the gazing technique further, by setting up certain parameters before you start the meditation. If you need help to solve a particular problem, you can think about that problem before opening your eyes to gaze on the crystal. Before beginning, create a calm and comfortable atmosphere in which to meditate. Remember to remain relaxed and let your thoughts flow. As the body relaxes and the mind calms, you may find a solution. Or, later in the day, you will suddenly see a way to deal with the problem.

3 This form of contemplation can also be used to find out more about the crystal and how it functions as a healing tool. It is a good idea to have several crystals on hand and to explore them, one at a time, to reveal the individual healing properties of each one. This technique also helps you to hone your own sensitivity to different crystals.

4 If you find it is particularly difficult to settle your mind, sit with a collection of stones and begin making patterns and shapes. This is not aimless, but an active form of contemplation that you may find quite revealing as well as very relaxing. If you have a lot of space, you can spread your designs out to fill the floor, and then sit at the center of the pattern for a few minutes.

5 Pick out two crystals that you feel are comfortable in your hands. A clear quartz in one hand and a smoky quartz in the other makes for an interesting starting point. Begin with the smoky quartz in the right and clear quartz in the left. Sit for a few minutes and then swap the stones, putting the smoky in the left and the clear in your right hand. Note the differences. Try this with other crystals, noting and using the combinations that make you happy, and use one of them for a few minutes each day.

Many exercises in this book, such as centering and grounding and attuning to crystals, can be used as effective meditations.

BELOW *Sit with a different crystal in each hand while you contemplate for a few minutes, then swap them.*

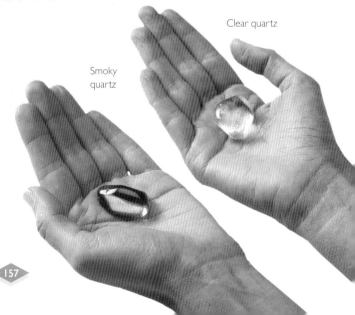

Clear quartz

Smoky quartz

Guided Meditation

CURTAINS OF LIGHT

This meditation is based on one suggested by David Tansley, a British radionics practitioner and well-known researcher into subtle energies. It can be used as a refreshing, cleansing, and revitalizing exercise after a crystal healing session, or as a daily meditation. It can be very protective and centering, and will encourage awareness of the whole self with its many different vibrational levels. Once learned, it can be worked through in a minute, quickly reminding us of our essential wholeness.

1 This meditation can be done seated or standing, whichever is more practical. Begin by finding a comfortable relaxed position with eyes closed. Take a moment or two taking slow, deep breaths. You may hold a crystal of clear quartz if you wish.

2 Visualize in front of you three concentric, circular curtains of light flowing down and disappearing into the ground. The outer curtain, nearest to you, is a sparkling, golden yellow. The next curtain is a beautiful soft rose pink. The third and innermost curtain is a clear electric blue. In the center of these three curtains of light, you can sense a bright source of radiant white light, a sphere of energy suspended in the air.

3 See yourself in profile standing in front of the curtain of golden yellow light.

4 Looking closely at the curtain, you can clearly see its downward movement, as if it were a waterfall of light.

5 In your mind make the sound, "Om," a traditional mantra, or word of power, that symbolizes the unity of creation.

6 Step through the curtain, and, as you do so, visualize the light flowing completely through your physical and etheric bodies. See the solidity of your form melt into a body of golden light. Feel all the impurities and toxins lodged in the etheric body drop away from you onto the outside of the curtain where they dissolve.

7 Now find yourself standing before the curtain of rose pink energies. This curtain represents your emotional body.

8 Once again, in your mind, sound the "Om" and step forward into the pink energy. Feel it sweeping through your emotional body, like water cleansing the fears, anxieties, and stresses. They all dissolve and drop away as you pass through the curtain.

9 Now you stand before the electric blue curtain that is the mental body. Silently chant "Om" and step forward, letting all negative thought patterns and outmoded beliefs drop away behind you. Feel the weight of negative thoughts fall away.

10 In front of you now is the floating orb of radiant white light. This is the highest level of your own being, your true self, the core of your consciousness. Experience the clarity and wholeness flood through you, bringing with it understanding, peace, and love. Here at your center, stress and pain are unknown. Absorb the light into your newly cleansed aura and feel yourself expanding in a beautiful radiance of colors filled with vibrant energy and love. Nothing inharmonious or negative can approach you now.

11 When you are ready, bring your awareness back to the three curtains of light. Step through each one in turn. First blue, then pink, and last the yellow. Add an extra radiance to each as you pass through. You are now outside the curtains again.

12 Remember the light at the center of your being and allow yourself to expand to the whole of the universe, vibrating the "Om." As your energies return, become aware of your physical body. Take a deep breath, stretch, and, when you are ready, open your eyes slowly.

ABOVE *Your meditation will take you through various stages, dispersing negativity and strengthening energies.*

ABOVE *This meditation exercise will take you on a magical journey through curtains of light, leaving you feeling both relaxed and energized.*

Goal Balancing

Goal balancing is one of the most useful methods available to the crystal healer. It can be used in a wide variety of circumstances and has the advantage of precisely focusing the healing processes in the desired direction.

Many complementary systems, among them crystal healing, work well when used as a preventative to reduce the likelihood of illness. Conventional medicine is structured to identify and treat symptoms of disease, and, as such, it has limited ability to work with wellness. Most doctors work from a state of disease, where the degree of disorder in the body has reached obvious levels.

With goal-balancing techniques, the crystal healer can work to reduce states of illness. More importantly, however, the healer can use them to help someone achieve any desired goal, whether it is a state of health, a lifestyle change, a long-cherished dream, or a state of mind.

SUGGESTED AREAS FOR GOAL BALANCE:

▲ Improve health conditions
▲ Reduce fears
▲ Improve creativity
▲ Find or clarify spiritual direction
▲ Improve emotional or mental states
▲ Clear particular stresses
▲ Become more effective at work
▲ Build confidence for tests and examinations
▲ Improve and understand relationships.

Working with goal balancing is very rewarding because it helps to remove blocks that are preventing someone from achieving their potential. Because the level of energy directed toward the goal is generally high, results become apparent quite quickly.

GOAL BALANCING BY CHAKRAS

1 Identify the goal as clearly as possible, once it has been established that a goal balance is appropriate. Sometimes the exact wording will be very important, and occasionally it may have peculiar grammar. What is important is that the stated goal is in a form the body recognizes and can work with. Be as precise as possible. "Perfect health" is a wonderful goal, but for most people it will take considerable change to achieve. "Tolerance of noise" or "restful sleep" are goals that are more likely to show noticeable improvements over a short period.

2 Once the goal has been clarified, say it out loud once again to reinforce it.

3 Perform a simple, single stone chakra balance with the intention of balancing the chakras for the stated goal. Each stone chosen will then not only bring a general balance to the chakra but will encourage those qualities in everyday life.

LEFT *Determine which areas of your life require improvement, and what your goals are.*

ROBERT FROST TECHNIQUE

This is a goal-balance technique based on a method devised by Robert Frost, a kinesiologist who has done extensive research into crystal energies. Muscle testing is ideal for this process, because it clearly shows the patient how their body is recognizing the energy characteristics of each crystal. Dowsing can also be used if necessary. The premise is that every individual at a subtle energy level can recognize the most useful stone to help with any problem. This method simply lets the body choose that energy pattern.

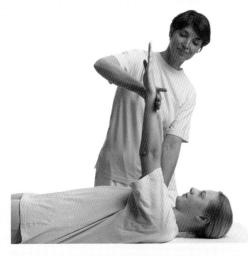

1 After centering and grounding, check the patient for a strong indicator muscle and run through the initial balance to check for switching (see page 104).

2 State the goal and check that it is appropriate for the present time.

3 Have a bag containing a good selection of different stones, one of each type.

4 Place the bag filled with stones on the navel area for a moment.

5 Remove the bag and muscle test to see if one or more of the stones in the bag will balance the person for the stated goal.

6 If the response is negative, other stones will need to be found. If the response is positive, remove about half of the stones and put them to one side.

7 Place the bag with the remaining half of the stone selection on the navel and leave there for a few moments.

8 Remove the bag and ask the same question. If the answer is yes, then you know one or more of the stones now in the bag will assist in achieving the desired goal. If the answer is no, you know that the selection you removed contains the required stone or stones.

9 Continue to divide the stones and retest until only one or two stones remain. These are the correct energies to help achieve the goal.

10 Finally, find out how they are to be used. If a stone should be worn, determine where on the body and for how long, day or night, and so on. If it should be kept elsewhere, find out the location. For example, should the stone be placed under a pillow, on a bedside table, or in the kitchen, car, handbag, etc.

Absent Healing

Sometimes it can be advantageous to be able to work on healing someone who is not physically present. This is known as absent or distant healing. The possible mechanisms for such work are unclear. Despite this, absent healing can work very effectively. However, it is not to be treated lightly. Because someone's physical body is elsewhere doesn't mean that the healer can ignore the normal safety measures. In fact, absent healing requires scrupulous adherence to the procedures of centering and grounding, and careful use of assessment and balancing techniques. Failure to do this can lead to an absorption of emotions, or even disease patterns, from the absent person.

ABSENT HEALING

The first rule of absent healing is to work only on someone who has given you permission to do so. This agreement ensures that the healer is not imposing in any way upon the free will of another, and that the patient is fully aware and cooperating with the healing energy. In the case of those who are unable to ask for themselves, or with young children and animals, checking the appropriateness of any healing can be made through dowsing, intuition, or meditation.

Thinking well of another person is the simplest absent healing of all. Gossip and other such negative character judgments not only depress the life force of the unwitting subjects, but also damage the speaker's energy structures as well. A blessing benediction and a careless curse can create endless ramifications of healing and disease. When asked by a student how to gain enlightenment quickly, one Master replied: "Just meditate regularly and never speak ill of others. Nothing else is required."

Asking permission may lessen the trap most healers will fall into at one time or another, and that is the need to bring about healing in order to lessen one's own pain at seeing the suffering of others.

This self-absorbed state is wholly understandable but needs to be recognized and balanced with dignified restraint. Otherwise, it can easily lead to a false martyrdom, sacrificing one's own health and life for the sake of others.

The second requirement of absent healing is the use of a witness. A witness is some object or substance that carries the energy pattern of the person being healed. It allows an accurate assessment of what is required, and it functions like a homing beacon for the healing energies. A witness is usually a small lock of hair, a drop of blood, a photograph, or a signature. An accurate natal astrological chart is a unique representation of an individual's energy characteristics and can make an ideal witness.

Lock of hair

Photograph

Signature

ABOVE *To perform absent healing, you will need to collect personal mementoes (witnesses) of the patient.*

ABSENT HEALING PROCEDURE

1 Begin by centering and grounding yourself. Tap yourself in. Check that your energies are balanced and that you are ready, willing, and able to do the proposed absent healing.

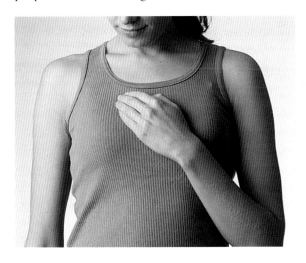

2 Check whether you need protection and support. This is much more likely to be necessary in absent healing work.

3 Hold the witness or touch it and allow time for your subtle perceptions to familiarize yourself with the energy pattern. One way is to put a pendulum into a circular swing. When it returns to a neutral swing, it indicates that the process is complete.

4 Use your skills to identify the best crystals to help heal and support the person. This step depends on whether any assessment is required or if healing energy is simply going to be given. At some stage, it will be necessary to determine what form the healing energy is going to take.

5 The crystals will then need to be placed on the witness and left somewhere undisturbed. Check to see how long the stones need to be in place. If several days or weeks are indicated, check again every day or so to see if any changes are needed.

How the crystals are arranged is up to your intuitive senses. A flat-based quartz crystal standing upright on or near the witness can act as an added transmitter.

A small mirror tile or a slice of agate can represent the aura of the subject and stones can be arranged on it.

ABOVE Use a pendulum to check that you have recognized the energy pattern of the witness.

When the process is complete, check your own energies once more. Use these methods to give yourself healing. A mirror or an outline sketch of a body with your name at the top will work. Place stones and work as if carrying out a normal crystal healing session.

Flat-based quartz

Lock of hair

ABOVE AND BELOW Place a mirror by the witness to represent the subject's aura, and arrange the crystals on it. A flat quartz crystal can be used as a transmitter.

Arranged crystals

Mirror tile

PART EIGHT

LIVING WITH CRYSTALS

Healing is not just about removing stress from the physical body. By making simple adjust-ments to our surroundings and the way we live, we can reduce the amount of stress that can easily build up without our noticing it. Crystals and gemstones can become very flexible tools for enhancing the life-giving qualities of our environment, wherever we may be.

ABOVE *Make crystals an integrated part of your existence and enjoy their life-enhancing qualities.*

Plants and Animals

PLANTS

Plants have a natural affinity with the mineral kingdom. They introduce new minerals into the food chain. It is their root systems that break up the subsoil and rock by which minerals are transported to the topsoil. Vast quantities of minerals are mined only to be ground up and added to fertilizers to improve crop yields. Unfortunately, this creates imbalances in ecosystems, which can lead to further impoverishment of the soil's fertility. Several authorities suggest that a more subtle application of crystal and mineral energies can increase the health and fertility of plants without degrading soil quality.

ABOVE *Rudolf Steiner made use of mineral and planetary influences.*

Rudolf Steiner, the founder of Anthroposophical medicine, established a garden and farm regime that used organic and mineral substances , which were made effective through combinations of planetary and stellar, influences together with positive intention and prayer.

Others, too, suggest that understanding the astrological correspondences of plants, and linking them with appropriate gemstones, can strengthen their growth and yield. For example, plants ruled by the energies of the sun such as corn, and sunflower would be energized by garnet and ruby. If these stones were placed near the plants, or if a gem remedy was used to water the soil, the mineral absorption would improve and the subtle energy of the plant – its life energy – would also increase.

LEFT *Grow towering sunflowers with a little help from a garnet or ruby placed nearby, or made into gem water for watering.*

Experimentation in the field has indicated that certain rocks and crystal formations attract or amplify electromagnetic frequencies that encourage localized plant growth. The presence of a quartz crystal can amplify plant growth and, as in humans, adds a beneficial energizing effect. Emerald, and beryl of any kind, is said to enhance all plants because it has a natural connection to the heart and the sun. A small beryl in a pot or flower bed will amplify positive qualities there.

CRYSTAL FERTILIZERS

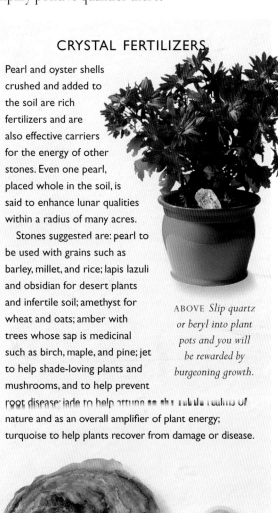

Pearl and oyster shells crushed and added to the soil are rich fertilizers and are also effective carriers for the energy of other stones. Even one pearl, placed whole in the soil, is said to enhance lunar qualities within a radius of many acres.

Stones suggested are: pearl to be used with grains such as barley, millet, and rice; lapis lazuli and obsidian for desert plants and infertile soil; amethyst for wheat and oats; amber with trees whose sap is medicinal such as birch, maple, and pine; jet to help shade-loving plants and mushrooms, and to help prevent root disease; jade to help attune to the subtle realms of nature and as an overall amplifier of plant energy; turquoise to help plants recover from damage or disease.

ABOVE *Slip quartz or beryl into plant pots and you will be rewarded by burgeoning growth.*

LEFT *Oysters and pearls act as a conduit for the energies of other stones when they are pushed into the soil.*

ANIMALS

Crystals can support your pets through times of illness. Like children, animals respond very well to subtle forms of healing.

Most owners are aware that pets are very sensitive to changes of atmosphere and can pick up frequencies far beyond the human range. This means they will sense the energy of crystals in an amplified manner as well. Caution is required when working in this way, however, so as not to disturb your pet unduly. Cats tend to be more fussy than dogs, and most will be wary if a lot of crystals are placed near them. It will be very obvious if an unwell animal does not appreciate this form of attention, but one that curls up and goes to sleep with crystals nearby has found that energy comfortable.

A massage wand or crystal pendulum can be an effective healing tool if your pet will allow you to use it. Work with it as you would on a person. Dogs and cats have chakras as well. Most four-legged animals have three main energy centers. They are at the top of the head, halfway along the backbone, and at the base of the tail. The whiskers, the ears, and the end of the tail are also areas that are especially sensitive to subtle frequencies.

If a particular crystal is needed by your pet, it can be placed safely in its bed or put into a small bag or pouch and securely attached to the collar. A tumbled stone can also be put in a silver spiral and suspended along with the name tag.

An effective method to give your pet a boost of healing energy is to use a gem water or gem essence. A few drops can be added to their drinking water or you could place a couple of drops on your hands and stroke it through their fur or around their auric field, from head to tail, two or three times. If you are concerned about their health, it is always wise to contact your veterinary practitioner.

LEFT AND RIGHT *The best-dressed pet sports its own personal crystal on their collar or on an attached pouch so that it may benefit from the healing energies. Alternatively, stroke some gem essence through the animal's fur.*

ANIMAL MAGIC

Animals are especially responsive to crystal healing treatment, probably because they have simpler, less convoluted mental barriers. Massage wands or pendulums work well, and particular crystals can be attached to their collars or placed in their beds.

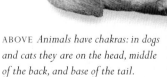

ABOVE *Animals have chakras: in dogs and cats they are on the head, middle of the back, and base of the tail.*

Carrying and Wearing Crystals

The earliest archeological evidence shows that mankind has always chosen to wear crystals, stones, and other magically precious items in order to absorb their beneficial properties. Today, wearing precious and semi-precious stones is widespread and popular. Wearing or carrying a crystal can be a helpful way to maintain the energy balance within the body.

CLEANSING

A stone will continue to be life-enhancing only so long as its own energy is kept clean. Placing your jewelry on a cluster of crystals overnight will help to remove any imbalances picked up during the day. This can be important when you have had a stressful day. Sometimes holding a stone under running water or cleansing it with incense or essential oil may be necessary.

Some stones will be more prone to energy exhaustion than others. Generally speaking, the softer the mineral, the more quickly it absorbs energy patterns, and the sooner it requires cleansing. Malachite, for example, is ideally suited to absorbing imbalances from painful areas of the body, but it will need recuperation after quite a short time.

The harder minerals like quartz, beryl, corundum, and diamond absorb energy to a lesser degree and will tend to cope for a longer time in stressed situations. However, when they do reach the limit, their natural broadcasting qualities will sometimes deflect disruptive vibrations into their immediate surroundings unchanged or even amplified. This is obviously not desirable.

Some minerals are effective at neutralizing strong, potentially damaging energy patterns, while not taking on the stress themselves. Crystals with parallel striations are useful in this respect. Tourmaline, topaz, rutilated quartz, tourmaline quartz, kyanite, kunzite, and particularly labradorite are excellent stones to wear in awkward, disruptive, or threatening situations.

Personal experience and clear observation of how one reacts in different circumstances is the only sure way to discover those crystals best suited to each person.

ABOVE *Crystals have long been made into charms, talismans, and amulets, redolent with mystical powers.*

PROTECTIVE CRYSTALS

Malachite

Blue Quartz

Tourmaline Quartz

Kunzite

Kyanite

Topaz

Labradorite

ABOVE *Malachite absorbs imbalances where you experience pain.*

ABOVE *Blue quartz also draws in energy, working over a longer period than malachite.*

ABOVE/RIGHT *These stones are good for dispersing negative energy patterns. They help ward off threatening situations.*

LEFT *The range of available minerals has greatly expanded from the traditional gemstones of diamond, ruby, emerald, and sapphire.*

WEARING STONES AND CRYSTALS

Stones often will change their appearance when they are worn. This can be a natural process, such as opal becoming more colorful as it warms up next to the skin, or turquoise becoming greener by absorbing skin oils or perfumes. Quartz crystal that is cloudy may become clearer over time, perhaps as the minute water or gas inclusions escape through small fractures, or inclusions of liquid may expand or contract with changes of temperature. Some crystals have had their natural color enhanced by heat or dyes and they can revert to their original appearance. Some crystals will fade when exposed to strong sunlight. Amethyst may do this, while others like kunzite may actually become more vivid. Sometimes, though, stones can change for no apparent physical reason. Very often in those cases, loss of color and an increase in fractures are a result of absorbing too much imbalance without the opportunity to restore equilibrium to the internal crystal structures. Such stones may never recover and are best given back to the earth and buried.

Stones are often worn around the neck in the form of pendants. Depending on the length of cord or chain, different chakra points can be affected. Near the throat, a stone will modify communication skills and artistic expression. Placed close to the thymus gland, it will help the body's immune system and the meridians. Worn at the heart, the emotions will be affected, and, depending on the stone, vulnerability can be reduced. A stone worn around the solar plexus will interact with personal energy reserves, motivations, and power.

The upper chakras can be significantly affected by wearing earrings of crystal. For example, tourmaline or diamond can help to alleviate structural tensions in the neck, jaw, ears, and skull bones.

Wearing gemstone rings can stimulate different meridian channels depending upon which finger they are worn.

CARRYING GEMSTONES

Where there is a need to carry a stone near a specific part of the body, a small bag or pouch can be attached to clothing using a safety pin.

At their best, crystals and gemstones can act as a support where the energy systems of the body need a little boost. However, they cannot replace long-term permanent change brought about through self-development and stress release techniques.

Every stone you carry in your auric field modulates your energy. Wearing more than one or two stones at a time will often confuse the energy messages to the body, reducing the efficiency of the crystals and potentially disrupting their natural balance. Use crystal jewelry as a healing tool and treat it as you would gemstones in a crystal healing session – with care and precision.

Finally, don't wear or carry crystals all the time. You may become energetically or psychologically dependent on them. Every so often, have a couple of days where you do not use any crystal jewelry.

BELOW *Wear one crystal at a time, or energies may interrupt each other.*

Crystals in the Home

The beauty of a cluster of crystals makes an effective decoration in all sorts of surroundings. The variety of colors and shapes offers a wide range of possibilities for creating an impressive highlight in any room in the house. Careful placement of crystals around the home can also have a beneficial effect, since crystals are able to alter the energy of a space quite dramatically, enlivening the atmosphere and neutralizing any negative effects.

ABOVE *A bowl of crystals makes an attractive focus in a room; it also works hard to enhance the atmosphere.*

Your home is an expression of your personality and how you like to be within yourself as well as how you would like others to see you. To add an element of harmony and natural beauty automatically creates a positive psychological and emotional effect. A careful examination of those areas of your home that do not feel so comfortable will give a good indication of areas that need attention. The underlying energy and atmosphere of these areas can be improved by the placement of some crystals.

There are no hard and fast rules as to what crystals should go where. Use your own judgment and experiment.

Clusters of crystals are certainly impressive and have the ability to retain their own energy integrity much more easily than small single crystals. This means that they will be able to transform more negative energy before they need to be cleansed again.

LEFT *If the telephone is a potential source of stress, position calming crystals by it to neutralize disruptive influences.*

Once you have acquired basic dowsing skills, it is a relatively easy task to discern what areas in your home could do with the presence of crystals.

There are many reasons why crystals may be needed. At the simplest level, they can reflect light and brighten up dark or shaded areas. Crystals hanging in the window can cast rainbows around the room as the sun shines in. Before the advent of Austrian lead glass, all chandeliers were made from clear quartz cut into faceted drops that would reflect and augment candlelight.

There are also many types of environmental stresses and natural earth energies that can create problems in the home. Crystals can be the easiest method to neutralize the potentially harmful effects of these stresses. If there are areas of your home that you tend to avoid, it is worth checking for these stress factors. The harmonizing quality of even a single, small, well-placed stone can make all the difference.

PLACEMENT

To find out where to place crystals to neutralize the effects of environmental stress, it is not necessary to know precisely what stresses are involved. Labeling energy as positive and negative is not helpful. An energy might be beneficial to one person while to another it might create serious health problems. Cats for example, seem to love sleeping on natural stress areas that most people would find disconcerting.

PLACEMENT EXERCISE

Draw a floor plan of your home with all the larger pieces of furniture in place. Make a separate plan for each floor. You do not have to be absolutely accurate – approximate measurements are good enough.

With a pendulum or muscle-testing techniques, check each room to see whether it would benefit from crystals placed somewhere.

Mark the locations where the crystals need to be placed and then return to identify what sort of stone is needed, whether more than one would be advantageous, etc. Use color coding as your initial guide.

Cleanse all the stones you are going to use before placement, and every so often check them again to see if further cleansing is required.

This process will not necessarily remove or alter the nature of the energies in your home, but it will make them easier and less stressful to the people who are living there.

BELOW *A crystal can be the focus for a special place of meditation or remembrance, charging it with life energy.*

RIGHT *Keep a crystal in the car to raise concentration levels and fight fatigue. Citrine quartz, clear quartz, and fluorite work well.*

PRACTICAL APPLICATIONS

❖ Keep a bowl of tumbled stones or a favorite crystal by the telephone to prevent draining of energy from difficult phone calls. Holding the crystals will prevent over-involvement or loss of perspective.

❖ A crystal cluster near a computer screen or TV will help to neutralize some of its electromagnetic fields. Cleanse the cluster regularly to reduce fatigue or irritability.

❖ A crystal can be the focus for a special place of meditation or remembrance. It will help to cleanse and charge an atmosphere with life energy.

ABOVE *A crystal cluster by a TV will help to neutralize strong fields.*

ABOVE *Test each room in your home to see if it would benefit from crystals, and mark the positions on a plan.*

Crystals and Environmental Stress

One of the most significant factors affecting health today is the problem of environmental stress. The human body has evolved over millions of years, adapting to its environmental conditions, learning to recognize potentially harmful substances and how to remove them from body tissues. Only in the 20th century have technological advances introduced a wide range of completely new factors to which the immune system has not had enough time to adjust.

Some everyday substances, like electricity, plastics, radio, and microwaves, may have possible harmful effects. Petrochemicals, organophosphates, and radiation are demonstrably damaging to human tissue, yet they are now inescapable all over the world. These substances may not in themselves create illness, but they do increase the stress loading on our systems. This means that susceptibility to disease increases as the level of available life-energy is decreased. Social and cultural patterns often lead us to spend time in environments we might naturally prefer to avoid completely.

ABOVE *Power lines are the source of vast electromagnetic fields, which are energy-draining and detrimental to our health.*

ELECTROMAGNETIC ENERGY

The planet Earth has a natural electromagnetic energy called the geomagnetic field. All life has developed within this field and removal from it causes serious physiological problems. Even astronauts are equipped with special generators to mimic the exact frequency of the geomagnetic field while they are in space. Man-made materials such as metal girders, concrete, electric wiring, and plastic can reduce this ambient earth energy by shielding it or setting up stronger electromagnetic resonances that may interfere with the natural frequencies.

Increasing evidence suggests that high voltage electricity cables greatly increase psychological instability and the likelihood of serious immune system disease or autoimmune reactions, from allergies to cancer, in those who spend many hours close to very strong electromagnetic fields.

Microwave radiation, as used in ovens, defense communications, and mobile telephones, is a high-frequency energy that heats and eventually disrupts cellular structure and chemical reactions in the body, including DNA and genetic material.

ABOVE *Organophosphates in sheep dip put farmers at risk for many years before it was discovered that they are harmful.*

Manufacturers tend to say that dosage is so low as to be harmless. Some scientists have their doubts, however.

Every electrical device in the home creates a powerful electromagnetic field around itself, even when turned off. In someone who is energetically run down or especially susceptible, this can create a problem of entrainment. Entrainment is when the natural frequencies of the body become enmeshed with a stronger set of frequencies from an outside source. It may be described as equivalent to situations where you are trying to count in sequence and someone else is shouting random numbers in your ear, or when you are trying to sing next to someone who is out of tune. The stronger pattern, whether appropriate or not, will win.

There are some clear indications of susceptibility to electromagnetic stress, such as multiple allergic reactions made particularly worse in metal surroundings, sensitivity to thunderstorms, difficulties with fluorescent light, static electricity from clothes or car doors, intolerance to water, or a tendency to make electrical apparatuses break down or malfunction. A pendulum of magnetite or lodestone held steady will rotate in front of any part of

ABOVE *Cellular phones use low amounts of microwave radiation which may disturb chemical reactions in the body.*

the body under electromagnetic stress. Muscle testing will clearly indicate problem areas at work or in the home. Modern offices with artificial lighting, tinted windows, air conditioning, nylon carpeting, metal furniture, and multiple computers can be disastrous for the human energy system.

By amplifying personal energy fields, many crystals can help counteract the effects of environmental pollution, although they will need cleansing regularly. In very electrical environments, plastic buckets of salt water will help to neutralize electrical resonance buildup; and clearing the aura with a pendulum of lodestone, magnetite, or copper every day will help to restore natural frequencies. Simply move the pendulum in a circular motion and pass it through all of the auric fields several times.

Use the assessment procedure for protection and support (see pages 48–49) or a goal balance (see pages 160–161) in order to identify which crystals will be helpful in neutralizing some of the most damaging effects.

ABOVE AND LEFT *Often, the cause of a problem cannot be avoided, but by regularly using crystal healing techniques, and by careful placement of stones, some of the most damaging effects of modern technology can be neutralized.*

Crystals and Astrology

The concept of birthstones is a simple way of labeling precious and semiprecious stones. In Ayurveda, the ancient Indian system of healing, a complex system of relationships exists between gemstones and planets. Nowadays, Western and Eastern systems have merged to give gemstones for each month, each planet, and each zodiac sign.

The reasons for attributing a stone to a particular sign can be various. Even a stone's color may link it to a planet. For example, copper minerals tend to be green, and both the color green and the metal copper are said to be related to the planet Venus.

With so many possible ways to establish connections, it is very limiting to state that there can only be one or two gemstones worn as birthstones. It is more appropriate to choose a stone that feels intuitively comfortable or that draws your attention.

Each planet at the time of birth forms a unique relationship with all other planets, dependent not only on when but also on where you were born. The energies of the universe, represented by the 12 signs of the zodiac, are modified by any planet that happens to be between the Earth and the constellation at the time of birth, hence the Moon in Scorpio, the Sun in Leo, and the like.

The angles each planet makes in relation to others also alter personal energies in a natal chart. Some may amplify certain tendencies; others can create awkward juxtapositions of energy. The natal chart presents us with a toolbox of energies or a series of skills that we can develop or ignore.

HEALING WITH ASTROLOGICAL LAYOUTS

The planets and signs continually circle around us, creating an ever-changing pattern of cosmic energies, which sometimes create a sensitive time when they interact with our own natal chart details. Most times these transits pass by unnoticed, but occasionally they trigger periods of turbulence. If you suspect the influence of transits, carry or wear a piece of natural native copper. If this reduces the pressure you feel, it may indicate an active transit. Copper helps to reduce the effects of difficult transits and amplifies positive astrological placements. Dowse a stone placement for the planets to help you to understand these energies in a positive way. When dowsing, you need to have full astrological or astronomical information. A goal-balancing technique (see pages 160–161) may also be helpful.

BIRTH ENERGY LAYOUT

One of the most powerful ways to experience your own birth chart energy is to create one large enough in which to place gemstones.

1 First, work out intuitively or through dowsing or muscle testing, the most appropriate stones for each planet and sign.

2 Lay the twelve stones representing the zodiac constellations in a large circle on the floor.

3 Inside this circle, create a second circle with stones that represent the planets, and place them in their appropriate signs according to your natal chart.

4 Dowse, intuit, or muscle test which is the most appropriate direction to lie inside the pattern.

5 Spend a short time inside the crystal energies a few times a month to familiarize yourself with this layout.

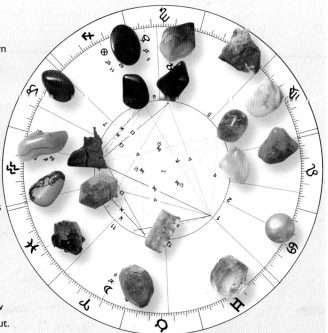

ASTROLOGICAL CORRESPONDENCES FOR PLANETS AND SIGNS

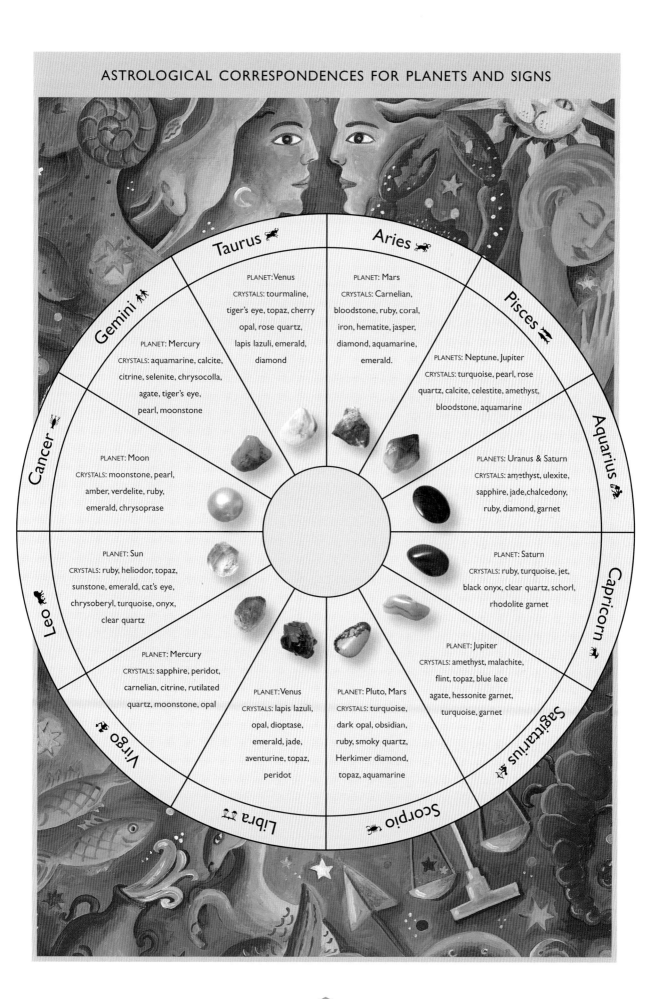

Taurus
PLANET: Venus
CRYSTALS: tourmaline, tiger's eye, topaz, cherry opal, rose quartz, lapis lazuli, emerald, diamond

Aries
PLANET: Mars
CRYSTALS: Carnelian, bloodstone, ruby, coral, iron, hematite, jasper, diamond, aquamarine, emerald.

Gemini
PLANET: Mercury
CRYSTALS: aquamarine, calcite, citrine, selenite, chrysocolla, agate, tiger's eye, pearl, moonstone

Pisces
PLANETS: Neptune, Jupiter
CRYSTALS: turquoise, pearl, rose quartz, calcite, celestite, amethyst, bloodstone, aquamarine

Cancer
PLANET: Moon
CRYSTALS: moonstone, pearl, amber, verdelite, ruby, emerald, chrysoprase

Aquarius
PLANETS: Uranus & Saturn
CRYSTALS: amethyst, ulexite, sapphire, jade, chalcedony, ruby, diamond, garnet

Leo
PLANET: Sun
CRYSTALS: ruby, heliodor, topaz, sunstone, emerald, cat's eye, chrysoberyl, turquoise, onyx, clear quartz

Capricorn
PLANET: Saturn
CRYSTALS: ruby, turquoise, jet, black onyx, clear quartz, schorl, rhodolite garnet

Virgo
PLANET: Mercury
CRYSTALS: sapphire, peridot, carnelian, citrine, rutilated quartz, moonstone, opal

Libra
PLANET: Venus
CRYSTALS: lapis lazuli, opal, dioptase, emerald, jade, aventurine, topaz, peridot

Scorpio
PLANET: Pluto, Mars
CRYSTALS: turquoise, dark opal, obsidian, ruby, smoky quartz, Herkimer diamond, topaz, aquamarine

Sagittarius
PLANET: Jupiter
CRYSTALS: amethyst, malachite, flint, topaz, blue lace agate, hessonite garnet, turquoise, garnet

Divination with Crystals

Throughout the centuries, quartz crystal has been used as a way to reveal what is hidden either in the past, the present, or the future. Many tribal peoples specifically kept crystals for this purpose, feeling that the very nature of the stone allowed the mind to see beyond the physical into the realm of the spirits.

Perhaps the oldest form of oracle is geomancy, where a number of stones are cast and the resulting patterns interpreted as an answer. In classical geomancy, there are sixteen arrangements or figures, each with a particular meaning. In Africa, Greece, and medieval Europe, geomancy, the oracle of stones, was very popular.

Crystals can be used in two ways: scrying and divination. Scrying, an Old English word meaning "to see or understand," is primarily a way to access the unconscious, or subconscious, mind. A crystal, or some other polished surface, is used to amplify or act as a screen for knowledge held in symbolic form within the mind. Scrying requires practice and a degree of discipline, but once the skill is acquired it can be used in many situations.

Divination uses the arrangement or pattern of objects and their interpretation according to pre-arranged guidelines or rules. The unconscious mind still plays an important part in the interpretation, but the process can be more objective. Divination with crystals usually takes the form of a certain number of different stones being randomly chosen

ABOVE *For thousands of years, geomancy has been used in many cultures to gain insight into the past, present, and future.*

or cast onto a cloth divided into sections. The information available to the crystal diviner depends upon the meaning that the stones and cloth have been given. The more detailed the meanings, the more precise the answer can be. A diviner can make up new rules and meanings to suit each question so long as his or her mind is completely clear about how to interpret the fall of the stones.

The easiest way to attribute meanings is to use either the basic color of each stone as a guide or to use its healing qualities. For example, amethyst is violet and so is concerned with the imagination, fantasy, delusion, and achieving potential. Amethyst is a calming stone and works well with the mind, anxieties, headaches, and the like. Sugilite is also a violet color, but could be interpreted as being more to do with group activity, socializing, and integrating. This can also be an effective way to memorize the different functions of color and crystals.

LEFT *Stones can be cast onto a cloth, and a reading taken from the positions in which they fall.*

SIMPLE CHOOSING METHOD

1 From a wide selection of different stones and crystals, ask a friend to choose four that attract her attention.

2 The first stone chosen represents her physical state. The second stone represents her emotions, the third is her mental state, and the last choice indicates her spiritual aspirations at that time.

3 There is no need to tell your friend what each choice represents, so long as it is clear in your own mind.

4 If you decide beforehand that the selection will show what energies your friend needs in each area of her life, it will be easier for you to interpret. Therefore, a blue stone as the first choice might show the need for peace and quiet or for

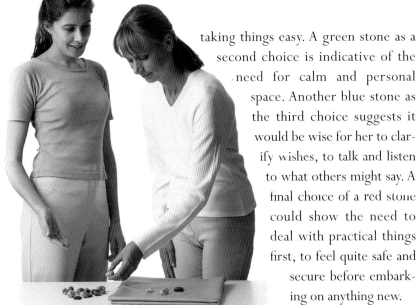

ABOVE *Ask your friend to select four stones that appeal to her, then interpret their meaning.*

taking things easy. A green stone as a second choice is indicative of the need for calm and personal space. Another blue stone as the third choice suggests it would be wise for her to clarify wishes, to talk and listen to what others might say. A final choice of a red stone could show the need to deal with practical things first, to feel quite safe and secure before embarking on anything new.

Intuition comes fully into play when the diviner selects one sense from the many possible meanings of each crystal or placement. Skill comes with practice and confidence. Go with your initial idea and try not to let your analytical mind confuse you with all the other possible alternatives.

USING A CASTING CLOTH

Tossing or placing stones on a marked cloth can give a great deal of information about a situation. The design can be simple or very complicated. Areas where stones fall or are placed are important to the person at that time. Empty areas are not significant to the question.

Design One

Draw three concentric circles on a piece of paper. The innermost circle represents deepest wishes, or causes. The next circle is present activities, and the outermost ring is what needs to be done.

Design Two

An area is divided into 12 segments based on the astrological houses. Each area represents an aspect of a person's life. Where stones fall is interpreted in that light. The 12 segments will represent:

1 the self and personality

2 possessions, feelings, and beliefs

3 associates, everyday communication, short journeys

4 home, security, roots, and mother or females

5 creativity, leisure, and risk-taking

6 health, self direction, and personal path

7 personal relationships and partnerships

8 areas of change and transformation

9 higher thought, learning, spiritual growth, and long journeys

10 career, outer persona, and the father figure or males

11 social groups and friends

12 hidden factors, behind-the-scenes activity

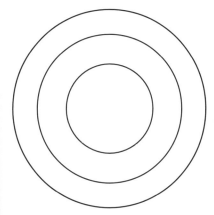

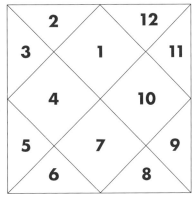

SCRYING WITH CRYSTALS

The objects that are used in scrying are various, but all have a quality of watery reflection and smoothness. Water, ink, oil, silver, mirrors, glass, gemstones, jet, obsidian, and clear quartz can all work effectively.

Jet

Whatever object is chosen, the skill is to gaze through or beyond the surface as if looking through a window at the world beyond.

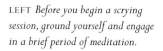

Obsidian cabochon

Scrying will only work when the mind has moved into the necessary state of awareness, a neutral receptiveness in which the mind is open and waiting to receive impressions in the form of sight, hearing, smell, or other sensory information.

The conscious awareness still needs to be present; otherwise, what occurs will not be remembered or understood. But it takes a back seat and simply watches rather than constantly chattering, interpreting, and analyzing.

Here is the advantage of using a quartz crystal for scrying. Clear quartz will naturally take your mind to quieter levels of functioning where there is less surface chatter and a greater coherence of the brain waves. This is exactly the state required to notice the energy patterns of the finer subtle bodies. The mind dives down into itself, leaving the familiar clear coordinates of time and space experienced as an individual wave, and enters the deep ocean of consciousness where collective and universal currents are to be found.

Where quartz will quieten and balance the mind, allowing an expansion of awareness, a surface such as polished obsidian will work in the opposite way. Obsidian has no crystalline structure. It is amorphous. Gazing into an obsidian crystal can be compared to the effects of white noise where all sound frequencies exist but none predominates, leaving the mind unable to focus on any one sound. This, too, can create the necessary void or neutrality to become aware of the unconscious images.

The best scrying tool is one with no internal forms. This is rare in quartz spheres since most will contain veils or fractures. However, a small perfectly clear sphere can often be more effective than a large one filled with interesting patterns, and will certainly be more affordable. Obsidian spheres, cabochons, or disks are usually less expensive than those of quartz. Experiment with different materials to see which enable you to reach a state of neutral awareness most effectively. Even a natural crystal with a large flat side or facet might be enough. Glass spheres are a lot less expensive, but they also must be free of bubbles and do not hold the mind as effectively as quartz.

Clear Quartz

LEFT *Before you begin a scrying session, ground yourself and engage in a brief period of meditation.*

PROCEDURE

1 Center and ground your energies.

2 Spend a few minutes performing some sort of quiet meditation – perhaps a simple breathing exercise or chanting a mantra.

3 Place the crystal in a position in which you will see no reflections.

If you are using an opaque reflective surface, such as an obsidian ball or slice of polished jet, make sure that there are no surface reflections and look through the surface as if you were staring into the depths of a dark pool.

4 You might prefer to work at night or in a darkened room – the less distraction the better.

5 A black or dark blue cloth can be put around the crystal to reduce reflection and glare. In addition, some people draw a cloth over their head and shoulders to cut out more light.

6 Take a minute or two to formulate your question clearly in your mind.

7 Focus the gaze into the center of the crystal or through it, not on the surface.

8 Most people will eventually start to see clouds or mist of different colors. When they appear, it is important not to focus on them or the necessary state of mind will vanish. Just continue to look through the crystal.

9 With practice, images will appear and sometimes sounds or smells may be noticed. It will require a careful balance and concentration to register these sensations without losing focus.

10 Remember that what appears is your unconscious mind's response to the particular question. The more precise the question in the first place, the easier it will be for you to interpret the images.

11 If you begin by focusing on a particular time or place, it will be easier to remain emotionally and mentally neutral. Like dowsing, scrying as a technique is more reliable when personal hopes and wishes are not involved.

12 Set yourself a time and place for practice, and when the time is up, remember to ground and center yourself properly.

BELOW *Block out intrusive distracting light by using a dark cloth, or by working in a darkened room.*

PART NINE

CRYSTALS – A LONG TRADITION IN HEALING

Many think that the current interest in crystals is a peculiar quirk of the times, an ephemeral fashion with little basis or substance.

The following brief survey shows that, on the contrary, crystals have been recognized for their special qualities ever since humans first walked on the Earth. They have been regarded as powerful tools for knowledge and healing in nearly every culture and civilization, on every continent, right up to the present day.

ABOVE *Crystals and healing: a modern partnership that is as old as time.*

The Stone Millennia

If the whole of human history were scaled down to a year, only in the beginning of July would the simplest stone tools be found. As the year progresses, these tools become refined and specialized until finally, on the last day of the year, late in the afternoon, agriculture would begin and shortly after that, the Bronze Age. That evening, the Iron Age and Christianity would emerge, and only as the year came to a close would the Industrial Revolution burst forth. Just before the stroke of midnight the twentieth century with its development of petrochemicals and electronic industries begins. Such a view of time really puts the human relationship with stone into a proper perspective.

For these many thousands of years, humanity has familiarized itself with the uses and properties of stone – not only by making stone tools but also over long periods of living surrounded by stone in cave dwellings. Understanding and taking advantage of the feel of different pieces of rock, stone, and crystal would have been a natural skill to encourage and pass down the generations. Flint was the main tool for the whole of the Stone Age. Great skill is evident in the making and shaping of these pieces. The Solutrean culture of southwestern France, about 20,000 years ago, produced exquisitely made laurel-leaf blades of such skill and quality that it is suspected they may have performed a special ritual function. It has been shown that much of this flint was fire-hardened, indicating that our ancient ancestors knew a lot about the nature of stone. Flint is formed of microcrystalline quartz compressed from the skeletons of minute sea creatures. Heating flint simply shatters it, as its crystal structure and trapped water expand quickly. Only when heated to the right temperature for the right length of time will flint become tougher, sharper, and easier to work. Placing the flint in the embers of a dying fire packed in clay provided the ideal conditions. In the Neolithic period when the ice caps were retreating again, stone is associated with ritual burials. Jade was especially valued for making ceremonial axes polished to a mirror finish. Obsidian, also, has been found in Neolithic sites made into razor sharp blades and mirrors. Both in the Old and New Worlds, these materials continued to be

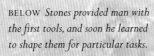

BELOW *Stones provided man with the first tools, and soon he learned to shape them for particular tasks.*

sacred for many thousands of years. Jade became the most highly regarded stone of Imperial China as well as in South America and the islands of the Pacific. Amber has been found associated with burial sites of the megalithic and Neolithic periods. Easily worked, translucent, and richly colored, amber is found around the Baltic Sea, which became the focus for trade routes that covered the whole of Europe. Perhaps the most sacred stone of all, with a history that goes back 100,000 years, is red ocher, the earthy iron ore often associated with hematite and magnetite. Red ocher was mined over thousands of years at sites in South Africa. Millions of tons of material was removed by hand, using simple stone-digging tools like antler picks. When the mine eventually became exhausted, the shafts and holes were carefully filled again. From Africa to France to Wales, red ocher has been found in the graves of Neanderthal peoples, and later, in the

ABOVE *Beautiful stones in glowing colors, together with metals, were fashioned into ceremonial art and decorative objects such as this Peruvian funerary mask.*

burials of Cro-Magnon man, or modern Homo sapiens. From Australia to North America, red ocher is a substance associated with life energy, power, and the sacred. About 8,000 years ago, the first metals were used. Initially, copper in natural nugget form was beaten into shape to use as tools and weapons. Only a thousand years later, the skills of metal casting were learned. Copper was then mixed with tin to produce the much harder alloy, bronze. During the Bronze Age, both gold and bronze were high status symbols of importance and power. Trade in raw materials was extensive and enabled many cultures to become rich and influential. All this was to change dramatically around 1200 B.C.E. with the collapse of the Hittite Empire in the high lands of what is now eastern Turkey. The Hittites had developed the technology of smelting iron. With the collapse of their society, this closely guarded secret spread into Europe, with iron replacing bronze as the primary material for all tools and weapons, and giving a clear advantage to people like the Celts, who learned the secrets. From that day to this, iron has been one of the most important resources of mankind.

Snowflake Obsidian

LEFT *The earliest cave art was painted with sticks dipped in colors made from ground-up minerals.*

Australia and Southeast Asia

Australian aborigines see crystals as sacred. They are an essential part of the initiation rites of healers and shamans. Quartz crystals, called wild stones, are associated with the Rainbow Serpent, an important mythological figure of Northern Australia linked to water, rain, fertility, and the iridescence of mother-of-pearl. The supreme god Baiame is the source of many healers' and magicians' power, and is connected with quartz crystal. The throne Baiame sits on is made of clear crystal, fragments of which are said to have fallen to earth where they can still sometimes be found. Here are the associations with rainbows, water, rain, clouds, and heaven that link to quartz crystals as belonging to the upper world of the spirits and ancestors. They are considered solidified light. In the Australian Euahlayi tribe, it is Baiame himself who performs the initiation of young healers. He sprinkles them with sacred powerful water made from liquefied quartz. In order to become a

ABOVE *The Aborigines associate quartz crystals with the Rainbow Serpent, a fertility god, depicted here in this painting by Michael Nelson Tjakamarra.*

shaman, it is necessary to be filled with the solidified light of quartz crystal. This process fills the shaman with the substance of the sky, enabling him to journey whenever there is need. The Wiradjuri shamans put rock crystals into their apprentices' bodies and make them drink water in which crystals have been placed. This is said to enable the apprentice to see spirits. He is then led to a grave where the dead come and give him magical stones. A snake appears as an ally and leads the apprentice into the earth where he is further empowered by more snakes. He is then ready to be taken by the shaman to Baiame, the Supreme Being, where, in a place of light, with crystals glittering from the walls, he is given some crystals and shown how to use them. He is then returned to his campsite and left in the top of a tree. These descriptions may sound peculiar to us but tribal peoples are so used to working with altered, non-ordinary realities that they are talked about matter of factly, like everyday experiences.

Clear Q

LEFT *An Indonesian shamans' ceremony. In Borneo, shamans keep crystals or "light stones" in a special box. These are used to cure illness.*

Only in the urbanized West does a dream mean the same as "not real." These initiations largely take place in spirit journeys, but the abilities and healing skills learned there can be of real value to the tribe in everyday reality. On the Malay peninsula, the healer also uses quartz crystals that have been cut from the sky and given to him by the spirits of the air. The shaman might also make them from magically solidified water. Because they come from the sky, the crystals are able to show the healer and shaman things that are happening here on Earth. Like North American shamans, Malaysian healers use crystals to see where the sickness is in the patient and how it can be removed.

In Borneo, the shaman has "light stones" that are able to show whatever is going on in the patient's soul and can lead the shaman to where the lost soul is trapped. These "light stones" (*Bata ilau*) are kept in a box with other magical objects. When someone becomes ill, it is because their soul has flown from the body, so the shaman needs to find the soul and return it to its home. The healing ritual is carried out at night. First, crystals are rubbed over the patient's body and then, while onlookers chant rhythmically, the shaman dances until he falls exhausted and his spirit flies off to retrieve the lost soul. The Wotjobaluk of Australia say that a supernatural being called Nagatya comes and initiates the medicine man. He opens up the man's belly and puts in rock crystals that give magical power.

ABOVE *To become a shaman, the candidate undergoes a ritual where quartz crystals are used to prepare him for office. Magic crystals are absorbed into his body. This aboriginal shaman sports extensive body painting.*

The Aranda of central Australia say that the candidate is taken by spirits into their caves where all his internal organs are removed and replaced by "atmongara," or fragments of quartz. Among different tribes sometimes one large stone is acquired, sometimes many in different parts of the body, but in order to become an effective healer and shaman the person must, at least in part, become crystalline.

A medicine man can also be created by other experienced elders. Taken to a solitary place, the candidate goes through a long ritual where the old men rub his body with rock crystals, press quartz into his scalp, pierce a hole under one fingernail, and make an incision in his tongue. His body is then decorated with symbols representing the spirits of the Dreamtime surrounded by lines that symbolize the magical crystals now in his body.

Quartz Clusters

Rose Quartz

Clear Quartz Rock Crystal

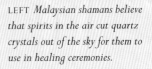

LEFT *Malaysian shamans believe that spirits in the air cut quartz crystals out of the sky for them to use in healing ceremonies.*

185

North American Native Traditions

Among the native tribes of North America, crystals are held in high regard as objects of great healing and spiritual power. They are considered different from other stones and were known to some as wii-ipay, or "living rocks." Native burials as old as 8,000 years have been found to contain quartz crystals.

Present-day Yuman or Paipai shamans keep quartz crystals with them in deerskin pouches. As a protector and guardian, the stone's advice is sought continually in order to understand and work with the world of the spirits. Rattles used in dance and healing ceremonies to summon helpful spirits are often filled with small, round pebbles of quartz.

ABOVE Ceremonial rattles were sometimes filled with small quartz crystals to summon spirits.

Among the settled tribes of the northern and eastern coasts, crushed quartz was spread over fields that didn't get much sunlight. Quartz was linked with the sky, light, and the sun, so by this means solid light could be sprinkled where none of the sun's rays could reach, ensuring a successful crop. A quartz crystal was used for distant healing among the shamans of the Tsimshian people on the Northwest Coast. During the night, the spirit of the crystal was sent out in order to bring back the soul of the sick person.

The Cherokee name for crystal means "light that pierces through," and quartz was seen as a primary tool for revealing information and conveying messages. Sometimes the crystals would be positioned so that they caught the sun's first rays. Where the light from the stone fell indicated the required answer. To reveal the outcome of a hunt, or a war party, or the future of a community, the holy man would, after appropriate ritual, gaze into the stone. Healers would warm a crystal over a fire and then lay it over a patient's body, looking through the quartz to determine the main areas of illness. Next, the crystal would be placed in sunlight to reveal the cause of the illness and, by turning the crystals to look through the different faces, the means to a cure were found. Crystals were also rubbed between the healer's hands and then placed on a patient's body to remove pain. It is said that very often the whole body would vibrate and shake until the pain left, leaving it relaxed and peaceful.

One traditional way to wake up or activate a crystal was to strike its non-pointed end lightly on a rock standing in a stream or in the ocean. It has recently been found that striking a rock does impart it with a peculiar charge that remains and influences the energy around it.

The coastal Miwok near San Francisco had a very large quartz crystal of great power. On special occasions, it was woken up by a shaman who would go to a particular rock in the Pacific Ocean and strike the crystal as hard as possible. Tribal tradition was that if the crystal shattered, the world would end.

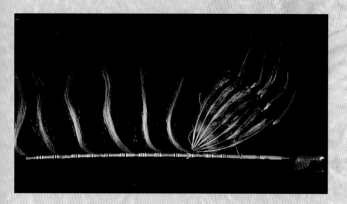

LEFT *Catlinite, or pipestone, was excavated for carving into the bowls of sacred pipes.*

LEFT *Turquoise forged a link between the earthly and the spiritual, and was used on religious artifacts.*

Turquoise was a stone held in the highest regard by Central American Indians such as the Aztecs, Toltecs, Mixtecs, and Mayans. It was used exclusively for decorating the images of their gods and for offerings. The tribes of the Southwest United States also value turquoise for its protective and strengthening qualities. Turquoise is seen as a link between heaven and earth, as the deep blue of the sky buried within the ground, so it is an ideal offering to the spirits. For example, after a successful hunt, a little of the animal's blood is mixed with crushed turquoise as a thanks offering to its spirit.

The Apaches considered turquoise an essential part of the shaman's equipment, and hunters also wore the stone to protect themselves and to improve their chances of success. Of special significance to all the tribes of North America is a quarry in Minnesota where, for centuries, people have dug out pipestone – a rich, red, soft stone also known as catlinite, from which the bowls of their sacred pipes were carved. Pipestone is considered to be the blood of the earth and the people. The bowl represents the earth, and the stem symbolizes the heavens, so when the two are joined in ceremony, the sacred smoke becomes the means of communication between the worlds of spirit and matter, while honoring and uniting all beings. In the same manner as all other sacred stones, quartz, turquoise, and pipestone have enabled generations of tribespeople to maintain their strong links with the spirits and their ancestors, thus helping to uphold their way of life.

LEFT *Shamans used crystals for diagnosing and curing illness, and also to find answers to questions.*

Central and South America

We know little about the highly developed civilizations that grew up in Central and South America in the thousand years or so before the arrival of the Europeans. Even the Aztecs at the time of the Spanish conquest knew little about the people who had built and deserted the magnificent cities like Teotihuacán.

It is clear from what remains of these Central and South American cultures that stone-working was a valued craft. Turquoise, obsidian, and jade objects have been found, as well as a few gold artifacts that escaped being shipped to Europe to be melted down.

It is clear that mica played an important role in the ritual procedures of the builders of Teotihuacán. The large central Pyramid of the Sun was originally capped with mica that no doubt would have reflected sunlight like sheets of glass. More mysterious is the nearby so-called Mica Temple where, on lifting the stone blocks covering

ABOVE *A turquoise chimli, or sacrificial knife. This is an example of the intricate craftwork employed to make ceremonial items.*

the floor, archeologists found two massive slabs of mica, each ninety feet square (8 square meters). Over a thousand years ago, the builders traveled 2,000 miles to Brazil in order to mine this stone. On their return, they laid it down and covered it from sight. Obviously mica served much more than a decorative function. Jade is also found to be associated with religious and royal sites. At the Mayan city of Palenque in Mexico, there is a famous building known as the Temple of Inscriptions. Here the Sun Lord Pacal was buried in 683 C.E., a well-loved ruler who had died aged eighty. His tomb beneath the temple has striking similarities in design to Egyptian pyramid architecture. Two carved jade figures were found at the entrance. The king was found wearing jade ornaments, including jade rings on his fingers and a necklace of jade beads around his neck. He wore earrings made from mother-of-pearl and held a piece of jade in each hand as well as one in his mouth. His face was covered with a death mask decorated with a mosaic of jade, obsidian, and white shell. It appears that the Mayas, like the Chinese, associated jade with the continuation of existence beyond physical death.

Quartz beads are often found in Central American burials, but rarely have large finds been made. However, a Mixtec grave found at Monté Alban in Central America was filled with many gold ornaments, pottery, and precious stones. The body had been buried wearing crystal beads, crystal earrings, and a crystal lip-plug, all the insignia of the

LEFT *The Sun Lord Pacal was buried here in the Temple of Inscriptions, Palenque, Mexico, with an assortment of crystals — thought to facilitate the journey to the next world.*

highly regarded astronomer caste of Mixtec society. The most unusual find was a unique carved goblet or drinking vessel of clear quartz.

Farther south, among the tribespeople of the Colombian rainforests, quartz crystal is regarded as condensed solar energy in which a shaman can detect many different colors or energies that can be manipulated and balanced in order to ensure continuing harmony and abundance within the environment. Indeed, the hexagonal shape of quartz crystal reflects for the Tukano and Desana people the model of order and organization for every level of their existence. The crystal is an important blueprint because within the regular hexagonal form exists the constantly changing colors and patterns of light symbolizing the energies of dynamic change within the order of existence. The skill of survival in the rainforest is to balance the forces of chaos and change with the need to establish continuity of food sources, families, and so on.

Among the Kogi and Muiska of the Colombian Highlands, quartz crystal and emerald have a similar religious importance. There also, the crystals are connected to solar energy, fertility, and order, and also with the healing ability of color. In the mountains of southern Peru, high in the Andes, the Q'eros still use special stones in healing rituals. In their culture as well, everything is seen as being alive, imbued with spirit.

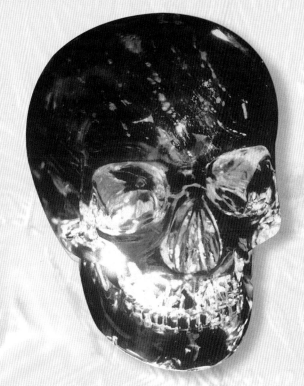

ABOVE *A crystal skull discovered in Central America – crystals' changing colors and reflections of light mirrored the need to live in harmony with the energies of the universe.*

The shaman-priests learn how to use power-stones. They are kept carefully wrapped in cloths specially made for the purpose to help retain the stones' power. These healing stones may look no different than garden or beach pebbles, but for the healer who has meditated and worked with them for many years, they are imbued with universal energy that can be called on to remove illness. Placed on the body or moved through the subtle bodies, the spirit of the stones works in harmony with the chants and intentions of the shaman.

RIGHT *The Kogi consider quartz and emerald to have religious significance, affecting fertility, healing, and order.*

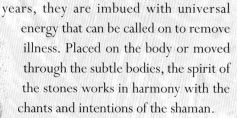

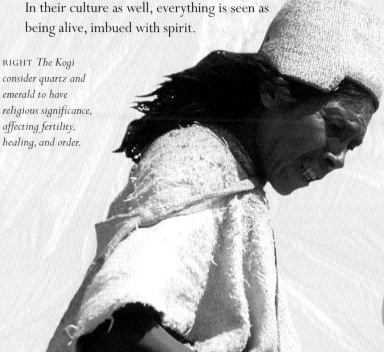

The Use of Gemstones in Tantra and Ayurveda

The use of gemstones for healing has the longest recorded history in India and may have influenced European systems via Greek and Arab trade contacts. The origin of gemstones is described in many ancient texts. In one text, the light that spreads out from the Creator of the Universe is reflected and transmitted to Earth through each of the planets. These rays are collected by gemstones and radiated into their surroundings to energize anyone nearby.

In another text, gems were said to be created from light emanated by the planets, each having one of the colors of the rainbow. These light rays combined and merged to create all physical matter.

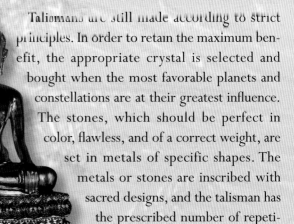

ABOVE *The ultimate goal of healing in these traditions is the end of all suffering — complete Realization and enlightenment.*

Other descriptions include a supernatural being who offers himself for sacrifice in order to save the balance of creation and whose remains are then converted into the "nine gems of eighty-four types." His blood becomes rubies, his teeth pearls, his eyes blue sapphires, and so on. As a logical progression, gemstones were seen as being able to help specific parts and tissues of the body.

Gem powders and oxides are used to make sacred images and ritual patterns that contain beneficial energies. Crystals and gemstones are also used to make religious statues, prayer beads, and amulets because they are more powerful than most other materials, conferring greater benefit.

LEFT *A phur-bu, a silver and rock crystal ritual dagger used by Tibetan lamas to demarcate protective boundaries.*

Talismans are still made according to strict principles. In order to retain the maximum benefit, the appropriate crystal is selected and bought when the most favorable planets and constellations are at their greatest influence. The stones, which should be perfect in color, flawless, and of a correct weight, are set in metals of specific shapes. The metals or stones are inscribed with sacred designs, and the talisman has the prescribed number of repetitions of mantra recited over it. Talismans developed from practices where deities and planetary energies were invoked using patterns of gemstones to create complex colored thangkas and mandalas. These would act as a focus for contemplation and meditation.

Early writings state that gemstones absorb and transmit the energy of the planets and are able to absorb negative energy, transforming it for use in the body. Astrologers and healers elaborated the system so that they could compensate for the deleterious effects of the planets' positions in someone's natal chart. A skillful astrologer will consider all planetary placements as well as favorable constellations and will balance this with the needs of the client. The most beneficial stone will be selected after scrutiny of the natal chart.

ABOVE *A Nepalese claw amulet inlaid with turquoise. Rules about the wearing of gemstones usually dictate that they are worn separately.*

There are many traditional prohibitions regarding the wearing of gemstones, and rarely are stones able to be worn together. However, there is one arrangement that includes all nine planetary gemstones made into a ring or necklace. Based on a traditional design, it balances all influences together. The nine gems, the navratnas, are those with planetary influences. The remaining 75 other traditional ratnas or gems are mostly semiprecious stones used in medicine and healing. In Ayurveda, these stones are associated with the three energies of the body,

the three doshas, which are *pitta*, *vata*, and *kapha*, representing the qualities of heat, air, and water. Health is maintained while the doshas are in balance; illness comes about through an imbalance in one or more doshas. Gemstones are powdered, mixed with honey or cream, and given by mouth to balance the doshas. Gem waters are also used. A copper or silver vessel is filled with water and the appropriate gemstone placed in it overnight. In the morning, it is divided into three doses to be taken during the day.

AYURVEDIC GEMS OF THE NINE PLANETS

There are many ways to determine which gemstone will be the most beneficial. The stone representing the sign in which the Moon is placed is often used. The Moon represents the psyche and the underlying drive of a person. Some astrologers, however, prefer to check whether the Moon is in a supporting position in the first place and, if it shows weakness, will suggest a stone that will support the Moon's energy. Wearing a gemstone increases the energy of its related planet, so if the planet is not in a good position, the situation can be made worse. A skillful astrologer will select the most beneficial stone after careful scrutiny of the natal chart.

Planet	Gem	Substitute Gem
SUN	ruby (manikya)	garnet, star ruby, red spinel, red zircon, red tourmaline, rose quartz
MOON	pearl (mukta)	moonstone, quartz
MARS	coral (prawal)	carnelian, red jasper
MERCURY	emerald (markat)	aquamarine, peridot, green zircon, green agate, jade, green tourmaline
JUPITER	yellow sapphire (pushpraga)	yellow pearl, yellow zircon, yellow tourmaline, topaz, citrine
VENUS	diamond (vajra)	white sapphire, white zircon, white tourmaline
SATURN	blue sapphire (neelmani)	blue zircon, amethyst, blue tourmaline, lapis lazuli, blue spinel
RAHU	hessonite (gomed) [zircon]	hessonite garnet
KETU	cat's eye	tiger's eye (vaidurya) [chrysoberyl]

Rahu and ketu are lunar nodes associated with eclipses.

The Biblical Tradition

The Bible contains references to crystals and gemstones in many places. Sometimes the writer uses familiar stones as an effective way to describe color. In other places gemstones are used to suggest great riches and wealth. There are specific instructions for religious vestments and the stones they should contain. Finally, there are descriptions of transcendent visionary experiences of heaven and the spiritual realms.

In Exodus, Chapter 28, the Lord gives very detailed instructions on how to make "the breastplate of judgment" for the High Priest to wear:

"And thou shalt make the breastplate of judgment with cunning work …and thou shalt set it in setting of stones, even four rows of stones: the first row shall be of sardonyx, a topaz, and a carbuncle….And a second row shall be an emerald, a sapphire, and a diamond. And a third row a ligure, an agate, and an amethyst. And a fourth row a beryl, and an onyx, and a jasper: they shall be set in gold in their enclosings."

In the Book of Job, precious gemstones are used to emphasize both the richness of the Earth and the order placed upon it by the Creator, and as a metaphor between material and spiritual riches.

ABOVE *Ezekiel was an Old Testament Prophet. Some of his descriptions of visions referred to crystals.*

"Surely there is a vein for the silver And a place for gold where they fine it. Iron is taken out of the earth, And brass is molten out of stone…. As for the Earth….The stones of it are of the place of sapphires: and it hath dust of gold… ." "And where is the place of understanding? Man knoweth not the price thereof…. It cannot be gotten for gold… .It cannot be valued…. with the precious onyx, or the sapphire. The gold and the crystal cannot equal it… no mention shall be made of coral, or of pearls: For the price of wisdom is above rubies. The topaz of Ethiopia shall not equal it, neither shall it be valued with pure gold."

The visions of Ezekiel and of John in Revelation use crystals and gemstones to communicate the richness and opulence of the experience. Ezekiel's vision of the heavenly beings is awesome:

"And I looked and, behold, a whirlwind came out of the north…and a fire infolding itself…as of the color of amber…The appearance of the wheels and their work was like unto the color of a beryl…And the likeness of the firmament upon the heads of the living creature was…the color of the terrible crystal, stretched forth over their heads above…And above the firmament that was over their heads was the likeness of a throne, as the appearance of a sapphire stone…"

The striking visions of John the Divine, as described in the Book of Revelation, were represented extensively in art throughout the Middle Ages in Europe. "I looked, and, behold, a door was opened in heaven: and the first voice which I heard…said, 'Come up hither, and I will show thee things which must be hereafter.' And immediately I

was in spirit: and, behold, a throne was set in heaven, and one sat on the throne. And he that sat was to look upon like a jasper and a sard stone; and there was a rainbow about the throne, in sight like unto an emerald."

This vision and its language remarkably parallels the initiatory experience of an Australian shaman journeying to the celestial crystalline world of Baiame. The next vision perhaps had the clearest influence on medieval religious thought. John's description of a new heaven and a new earth, couched in the language of crystals, legitimized the lavish use of precious gems and metals in the Church. This allowed a burgeoning of creativity within the whole spectrum of religious life.

"And there came unto me one of the seven angels…and he carried me away in spirit to a great and high mountain, and showed me that great city…descending out of heaven…and her light was like unto a stone most precious, even like a jasper stone, clear as crystal… and the building of the wall of it was of jasper: and the city was pure gold, like unto clear glass. And the foundations of the wall of the city were garnished with… precious stones.

"The first foundation was jasper; the second, sapphire; the third, a chalcedony; the fourth, an emerald; the fifth, sardonyx; the sixth, sardius; the seventh, chrysolite; the eighth, beryl; the ninth, a topaz; the tenth, a chrysoprase; the eleventh, a jacinth; the tenth, an amethyst.

"And the twelve gates were twelve pearls; every several gate was of one pearl: and the street of the city was pure gold, as it were transparent glass."

RIGHT *Charlemagne, a medieval king. In the Middle Ages, religious thought drew on John's vision to sanction abundant use of precious stones in the Church.*

The Atlantis Legends

The legend of Atlantis and other civilizations of the distant past carry little credence in academic circles, yet in several books about crystals and crystal healing, Atlantis is talked about as if its historical existence is widely accepted. Some writers believe that linking crystals with Atlantis is all the validation the therapy needs to establish its credentials.

Only in the last two hundred years of Western scientific thought has the theory of evolution been advanced as a model for the processes of change. Implicit in the concept is the very Victorian idea that the present is the epitome of enlightenment and progress. This is only one view of time and history. Other, older cultures have a model where cycles of time all but obliterate previous worlds.

As yet, no clear evidence for advanced civilizations such as Lemuria and Atlantis have been found, although increasing research suggests the date for antiquities such as the Sphinx in Egypt is far older than most historians would currently believe. In many museums around the world, there are anomalous artifacts, things found in the wrong places for the current acceptable view of history. Finally, there are reports from the Bimini Atoll near the Bahamas that much more than the already recorded submerged walls are being found.

For the present, Atlantis remains a powerful myth. All the same, it is a myth worth examining. Whether described as an island in the Atlantic or a planet now destroyed, the stories are often similar. The channeling of Edgar Cayce described huge crystals, initially used for communication between dimensions, that were developed to generate power and energy throughout Atlantis. The Firestone, or Great Crystals, were housed in a dome which could concentrate the sun's rays into the crystals thus creating tremendous energy.

Some say the selfish manipulation of these crystals precipitated the changes that destroyed the civilization. Other sources describe development of the use of crystals from an earlier civilization

BELOW *In the legendary civilization of Atlantis, crystals were used to generate energy and for healing.*

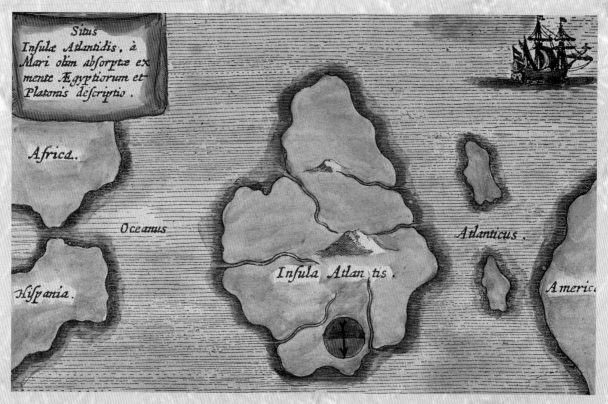

called Lemuria. Here the inhabitants dwelled close to nature and experienced a multidimensional consciousness in time and space where awareness of both physical and subtle dimensions existed simultaneously. Gemstones were used to focus and modify consciousness, assisting the physical energies of the body much like a kind of subtle nutrition, and also amplifying thought.

Atlantis developed from a Lemurian colony and tended toward a higher technologically structured society. The harmony with the natural surroundings became disturbed causing new health problems. Gemstones came to be used in specialized healing techniques as well as in the modification of the genetic codes of humanity. There are descriptions of special healing chambers with walls made of quartz crystal in which people could enter to receive healing from large wand-like crystals or alternately go deep into meditation and experience higher forms of consciousness.

Healing priests are also mentioned, who were able to bring about new states of awareness using crystals such as amethyst, diamond, quartz, and jade. Alongside technical advances like flying machines, long-distance communications, and genetic engineering, there were those who worked with the nonphysical dimensions and the inhabitants of subtle realms of the planet. Special groves were created in order that those who wished could spend time in communication with these realms' invisible beings and learn to share information between kingdoms.

These areas were created around hot springs and healing streams with numerous fountains and cascades to cleanse and maintain large arrangements and structures of crystal that allowed communication to take place. These crystal groves are said to have contained quartz crystals supplemented with emerald, ruby, lapis lazuli, pearl, amber, gold, and silver.

ABOVE According to the Atlantis legends, crystal groves were created close to streams to create a healing environment.

The Atlantis legends are a complex mixture of the inspiring images of a Golden Age and precautionary messages of a runaway science that eventually creates a series of self-destructive catastrophes.

Psychologically, Atlantis plays out all our hopes and fears concerning humanity's ability to control natural processes. Teaching a way to behave by example can be a true myth for today's world. And although myths cannot be located with certainty on any map, they loom large in the powerful depths of the psyche, despite any number of rationalizations and exposures to ridicule.

Lapis Lazuli

Emerald

Ruby

Amber

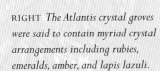

RIGHT The Atlantis crystal groves were said to contain myriad crystal arrangements including rubies, emeralds, amber, and lapis lazuli.

PART TEN

GEMSTONE DIRECTORY

This directory is to help you to identify some of the most useful crystals and minerals used in crystal healing. Because so much depends on the interaction between the energy of the mineral and the make-up of the individual, it is unwise to attribute specific healing properties to a stone. General tendencies are given here which, together with information that can be surmised from other characteristics such as the crystal system and color, can help the crystal worker to ascertain what might be happening at energetic levels during a healing session.

This directory is by no means an inclusive survey; there are thousands of minerals known, and several dozen new ones identified each year. Although every mineral has a potential for influencing health and well-being, the delicacy, rarity, or toxicity of some makes them impractical for general healing.

ABOVE *Find out all about the qualities and healing properties of the crystals that you choose.*

How to Use the Directory

CHEMICAL FORMULA

The chemical formula of a mineral shows the complete makeup and relationship of elements within a crystal or rock. From this formula, it is easy to see how simple or complex a mineral may be. The formula also identifies similarities between different minerals, and in a few cases, where different minerals have exactly the same constituents arranged in different patterns.

CRYSTAL SYSTEM

Each crystal system tends to modify energy in particular ways, so the external shape that reflects the internal structure of a crystal will give some indication of its qualities as a healing tool.

HARDNESS

The hardness of a mineral shows first how delicate it may be. Softer stones will tend to get easily damaged by careless handling. However, even hard minerals may be brittle and fracture easily. Keep hard and soft minerals stored separately to minimize damage. Soft stones tend to be better at absorbing energy than hard stones, which are effective amplifiers and broadcasters of energy.

Hardness is measured by the Mohs Scale, which was devised to aid identification of minerals. It is a relative scale that indicates degree of hardness by a higher number. A sample with a high number will scratch all stones of a lower number.

BELOW According to the Mohs Scale of 1–10, gypsum and calcite are soft minerals that fracture easily, whereas topaz and quartz are hard crystals.

LUSTER

Luster is the way light reflects from the surface of a gemstone. These are various descriptions but the most frequently used are:

ADAMANTINE like a diamond, very hard and brilliant.

VITREOUS like glass, shiny but without brilliance.

PEARL like pearls, a soft light, perhaps with iridescence.

SILKY an uneven rippling play of light, usually caused by long crystal structures irregularly arranged beneath the surface.

GREASY feeling moist, slippery, or slimy to the touch, may look as if it is wet.

RESINOUS a dull, sticky-looking surface, like amber or violin resin.

EARTHY dull and nonreflective, like soil.

METALLIC shiny, reflective, like metal.

MOHS SCALE

▲ TALC (1) – the softest mineral, scratched by every other mineral and easily marked with a fingernail.

▲ GYPSUM (2) – can be scratched with a fingernail using a greater pressure than 1.
(A fingernail will mark any mineral with a hardness below 2.5.)

▲ CALCITE (3) – can be scratched by a sharp coin.

▲ FLUORITE (4) – can be scratched with a penknife blade.

▲ APATITE (5)- can be scratched with difficulty using a steel point.

▲ FELDSPAR (6) – will easily scratch glass.

▲ QUARTZ (7) – will scratch most common surfaces.

▲ TOPAZ (8) – can scratch quartz.

▲ CORUNDUM (9) – easily scratches topaz and quartz.

▲ DIAMOND (10) – the hardest natural substance.

Topaz

Quartz

Gypsum

Calcite

LUSTER

❖ Luster describes the way in which light is reflected away from a gemstone - the following examples are taken from main categories of luster.

Earthy Magnetite

Silky Tiger's Eye

Adamantine Diamond

Greasy Blue Calcite

Metallic Copper

Vitreous Tourmaline Quartz

Pearl Opal

Resinous Amber

COLOR

The colors listed under each mineral in this directory are those commonly seen. Many minerals show a different color, or have no color at all (allochromatic) in a pure form. The actual color of a mineral is determined by a scratch test where a sample is drawn across a plain unglazed porcelain tile. The color of the dust left behind is the true color of the mineral.

BELOW *To identify a crystal's true color, scratch it across a plain porcelain tile and examine the color of the remaining dust.*

CHAKRA AND SUBTLE BODY

Where there is a clear relationship between a stone and a chakra or subtle body, it is indicated in the directory. This in no way limits the possible uses of a crystal, as its particular qualities may make it valuable in many different placements and situations. Indications of chakras and subtle bodies are simply other associations that may help to suggest the type of energy with which a stone is most likely to work well.

As far as possible, the illustrations in this section include natural and polished examples of each mineral, as well as common variations in shape and color to help clear identification.

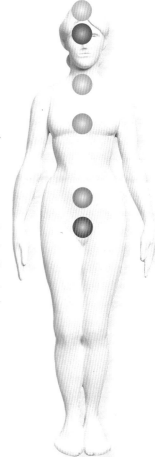

RIGHT *The directory will suggest which stones are most appropriate to use for balancing particular chakras or subtle bodies.*

Gemstone Directory

MALACHITE

CHEMICAL FORMULA: $Cu_2CO_3(OH)_2$

CRYSTAL SYSTEM: *monoclinic*

HARDNESS: *3.5 to 4*

LUSTER: *adamantine, silky, dull*

COLOR: *green with dark green or black layers.*

CHAKRA: *heart*

SUBTLE BODY: *etheric, emotional*

Malachite draws out emotional imbalances. It is a very absorbent stone that will need regular cleansing when used in healing. Don't use salt, as it will damage the surface. It is especially protective from environmental pollutants to the heart chakra and to the physical body.

Malachite

AMBER

CHEMICAL FORMULA: *fossil resin similar to* $- C_{10}H_{16}O + H_2S$

CRYSTAL SYSTEM: *amorphous*

HARDNESS: *2*

LUSTER: *resinous*

COLOR: *yellow, brown, red, sometimes green*

CHAKRA: *solar plexus*

SUBTLE BODY: *mental*

Amber helps to warm and enliven. Some may find its energy too stimulating, but it can be an excellent aid to nervous disorders and in detoxification.

The latter is an effect of its resin and sulfur content. Amber can introduce the strengthening combination of sunlight with tree energies into an underactive, dull condition.

RUBY

CHEMICAL FORMULA: $Al_2O_3(+Cr)$

CRYSTAL SYSTEM: *trigonal*

HARDNESS: *9*

LUSTER: *vitreous to adamantine*

COLOR: *red*

CHAKRA: *heart*

SUBTLE BODY: *mental, spiritual*

Ruby balances the heart at every level. It can enhance the physical function and the circulatory system, and because the heart chakra is central to the subtle energy systems, it can help the whole self. Confidence, security, self-esteem, and balanced relationship as well as positive states of mind are increased.

Ruby

Amber

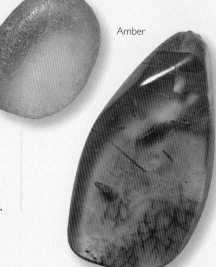

SELENITE

CHEMICAL FORMULA: $CaSO_4.2H_2O$

CRYSTAL SYSTEM: *monoclinic*

HARDNESS: *2*

LUSTER: *vitreous to pearl*

COLOR: *transparent, white, yellow, brown, red, blue-gray*

CHAKRA: *sacral, throat, crown*

SUBTLE BODY: *emotional, soul, spiritual*

Selenite has a wonderful moonlight luminescence, hence its name. It is one of the very best shifters of energy and can remove negativity from the auric field rapidly. The quality of frictionless flow and rapid cooling and organizing energy means that selenite is excellent at removing blocked and stagnant energy. It brings clarity to the mind and is effective in expanding consciousness. Selenite is extremely soft and easily scratched by a fingernail, so gem-quality stones need careful handling. The crystals are also extremely sensitive to water and humidity. They will bend even when held in the hand and may slide apart and disintegrate in water.

Selenite

Calcite

Blue Calcite

CALCITE

CHEMICAL FORMULA: $CaCO_3$
CRYSTAL SYSTEM: *hexagonal*
HARDNESS: *3*
LUSTER: *vitreous, pearl, silky*
COLOR: *colorless, allochromatic, black, blue, gray, brown, green, yellow, red*
CHAKRA: *all*

Calcite of the appropriate color can clear and energize all chakras. It has a fast, multidirectional quality and is a good remover of stagnant energy. It can quite easily shift levels of awareness. Spheres and eggs can be useful meditation tools.(See also: Coral)

EMERALD

CHEMICAL FORMULA: $Be_3Al_2Si_6O_{18}$
CRYSTAL SYSTEM: *hexagonal*
HARDNESS: *7.5 to 8*
LUSTER: *vitreous*
COLOR: *bright green*
CHAKRA: *heart*
SUBTLE BODY: *etheric, emotional, astral*

Emerald is a stone of harmony. It encourages peaceful growth and abundance. The heart

Emerald

chakra is strengthened by it. This stone will aid cleansing processes, help remove hidden fears, and calm a troubled mind. Emerald can be a useful meditation stone. (See also: Aquamarine, Beryl)

Peridot

PERIDOT

CHEMICAL FORMULA: $(Mg, Fe)_2 SiO_4$
CRYSTAL SYSTEM: *orthorhombic*
HARDNESS: *6.5 to 7*
LUSTER: *vitreous to greasy*
COLOR: *yellow-green*
CHAKRA: *heart, solar plexus*
SUBTLE BODY: *all*

Peridot is an effective cleansing stone said to be able to gradually remove all toxins from the body. It increases clarity of mind and optimism. It can help with visualization skills. It is a good protecting stone.

FLUORITE

CHEMICAL FORMULA: CaF_2
CRYSTAL SYSTEM: *cubic*
HARDNESS: *4*
COLOR: *purple, blue, green, yellow, clear*
LUSTER: *vitreous*
CHAKRA: *brow*
SUBTLE BODY: *etheric*

Fluorite supports healthy bone tissue and physical structures of all organs. Fine levels of awareness and information from other dimensions are able to be easily assimilated with fluorite. Also this stone helps to balance coordination at physical levels, so it is useful for improving learning skills, dexterity, and balance. Fluorite encourages order and structure.

Fluorite Octahedra

Fluorite (with Iron Pyrites)

PEARL

CHEMICAL FORMULA: $CaCO_3$ +
conchiolin + H_2O
CRYSTAL SYSTEM: *amorphous,
orthorhombic*
HARDNESS: *2.5 to 3.5*
LUSTER: *pearl*
COLOR: *white, pink, brown, black*
CHAKRA: *sacral, solar plexus*
SUBTLE BODY: *etheric,
emotional*

Pearl can balance the
emotions and increase
tolerance and flexibility. The
nervous system relaxes,
especially where there has been
irritation or frustrated energy.
Aspects of solar plexus
function, such as balance of
physical energy, assimilation of
nutrients, and self-assurance are
all influenced by pearl. Many
glandular functions can be
regulated with pearl.

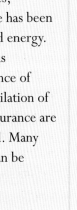

Pearl

AMETRINE

Ametrine
works well
with headaches,
tension, and
stress-related
illnesses such as
digestive upset and
ulcers, balancing the
energies of the solar
plexus and the head.

Ametrine also combines insight
with clear thinking, so this is a
useful stone for study. (See also:
Citrine, Amethyst)

Rhodonite

RHODONITE

CHEMICAL FORMULA: $MnSiO_3$
CRYSTAL SYSTEM: *triclinic*
HARDNESS: *5.5 to 6.5*
LUSTER: *vitreous*
COLOR: *pink to dark pink with
brown or black areas*
CHAKRA: *heart*
SUBTLE BODY: *emotional*

Rhodonite is said to be useful
for those people using mantras,
increasing the mediation's
effectiveness and their
sensitivity to the practice. Its
color suggests a balancing of
the heart chakra, especially
where practical aspects of the
emotions are concerned. Like
many pink-colored stones,
rhodonite is an
emotional
balancer and
a remedy for
negative states
like anxiety and
confusion.

Ametrine

Indicolite (Blue
Tourmaline)

INDICOLITE (BLUE
TOURMALINE)

CHEMICAL FORMULA: Na
$(Mg,Fe,Li,Mn,Al)_3Al_6(BO_3)Si_6O_{18}$
$(OH,F)_4$
CRYSTAL SYSTEM: *trigonal*
HARDNESS: *7.5*
LUSTER; *vitreous*
COLOR: *blue, blue-green*
CHAKRA: *throat, brow*
SUBTLE BODY: *all*

Indicolite is the hardest variety
of the tourmaline. The blue
coloration is caused by
manganese and iron.

Indicolite works well with the
throat center and its associated
organs, the thyroid gland,
lungs, larynx, and bones of the
neck. The deep blue varieties of
this mineral will activate the
properties of the brow chakra,
increasing flow of information,
perception, and intelligence.
Like all tourmalines, the
striations along the length of
indicolite crystals speed energy
flow, helping to clear blockages
and restoring equilibrium. (See
also: Tourmaline)

COPPER

CHEMICAL SYMBOL: *Cu*
CRYSTAL SYSTEM: *cubic*
HARDNESS: *2.5 to 3*
LUSTER: *metallic*
COLOR: *copper, red*
CHAKRA: *base, sacral, solar plexus, heart*
SUBTLE BODY: *all*

Copper's main action is to reduce inflammation and is well known as an aid in rheumatism and arthritis. Like many metals, it works effectively in balancing brain functions. It is strengthening on every level and helps the flow of energy, particularly in the nervous system. The buildup of tensions, frustration, and nervous energy can be released by this metal. Copper effectively balances all astrological influences, easing the effects of difficult transits and aspects by helping us to integrate them efficiently.

JASPER

CHEMICAL FORMULA: SiO_2
CRYSTAL SYSTEM: *trigonal*
HARDNESS: *7*
LUSTER: *dull to vitreous*
COLOR: *red, yellow, green, blue, brown*
CHAKRA: *base, sacral, solar plexus, heart*
SUBTLE BODY: *etheric*

Jasper

Copper

Jasper is an earthy, grounding stone. The red variety is gently energizing and can be of use in balancing the base chakra. Other varieties will work with other chakras: yellow with the solar plexus, green with the heart, etc. The many varieties and patterns of jasper make each piece unique. Very often in a healing situation, one specific stone will be particularly useful because of its combination of shape and color.

KUNZITE

CHEMICAL FORMULA: $LiAlSi_2O_6$
CRYSTAL SYSTEM: *monoclinic*
HARDNESS: *6.5 to 7.5*
LUSTER: *vitreous*
COLOR: *pink, lilac pink (spodumene: clear; hiddenite: green)*
CHAKRA: *heart, throat*
SUBTLE BODY: *etheric*

A great heart chakra cleanser and protector, kunzite can help remove negativity and unwanted thought

Kunzite

forms. Its clarity and subtle coloration can create a meditative space. The cardiovascular system can be aided with kunzite, and its high lithium content is supportive with thyroid problems. Life energy and self-esteem are enhanced. Kunzite acts rather like a dynamic rose quartz. The degree of violet color will determine how much the brow and crown chakras are involved.

SCHORL (BLACK TOURMALINE)

CHEMICAL FORMULA:
$Na(Mg,Fe,Li,Mn,Al)_3Al_6(BO_3)Si_6.O_{18}(OH,F)_4$
CRYSTAL FORMULA: *trigonal*
HARDNESS: *7 - 7.5*
LUSTER: *vitreous*
COLOR: *black*
CHAKRA: *base*
SUBTLE BODY: *etheric, astral*

Schorl is an effective grounding stone. It stabilizes the energy of the base chakra and helps link personal energies to those of the planet. It has been used to counteract the effects of jet lag. Schorl helps to realign the bones of the skeleton and can be helpful where there are pulled and strained muscles. This stone is one of the most useful protecting stones, energizing the wearer at the same time as deflecting disharmonious vibrations. (See also: Tourmaline)

Schorl

Kyanite

BLOODSTONE

CHEMICAL FORMULA: SiO_2

CRYSTAL SYSTEM: *trigonal (microcrystalline)*

HARDNESS: *7*

LUSTER: *vitreous*

COLOR: *green with red spots*

CHAKRA: *heart, base*

SUBTLE BODY: *etheric*

Traditionally, bloodstone stemmed the flow of blood from wounds, and it can be used in healing where blood and circulation need support. Both heart and base chakra are stimulated, so bloodstone is a good physical energizer and motivator. It also helps to bring spiritual qualities into practical everyday life. (See also: Chalcedony)

Bloodstone

AGATE

CHEMICAL FORMULA: SiO_2

CRYSTAL SYSTEM: *trigonal*

HARDNESS: *6.5*

LUSTER: *vitreous*

COLOR: *variegated colors in concentric bands*

As a quartz, agate has a general strengthening effect on the subtle anatomy, and, depending on the colors displayed and the distinct patterning it takes, will help to clarify and reveal underlying levels of information. Agate slices are commonly sold as decorative ornaments and can be useful as a meditation tool, a focus, and in absent healing.

KYANITE

CHEMICAL FORMULA: Al_2SiO_5

CRYSTAL SYSTEM: *triclinic*

HARDNESS: *4 to 7 (depending on direction)*

LUSTER: *pearl, vitreous*

COLOR: *blue, blue-black*

CHAKRA: *throat*

SUBTLE BODY: *all*

Some find that kyanite will never accumulate negative energy. It can be used to balance all chakras and subtle bodies. Kyanite has the essence of the blue vibration. It brings calm, tranquility, and allows access to all levels of awareness. Meditation can also be easier with this stone.

GARNET

CHEMICAL FORMULA: $X_3Y_2 (SiO_4)_3$ *where x = calcium, iron, manganese or magnesium and y = chromium, aluminum, iron or titanium.*

CRYSTAL SYSTEM: *cubic*

HARDNESS: *6.5 to 7.5*

LUSTER: *vitreous*

COLOR: *red, brown, orange, green*

CHAKRA: *mostly base*

SUBTLE BODY: *etheric, astral*

Garnet

Red garnets are the finest energizing stones for the body. They are able to accelerate and amplify the actions of other nearby stones. The actions will vary depending on the stone color, but will always concentrate and focus energy toward practical support for the systems involved. Multi-faceted garnet crystals are easy to find and tend to be slightly larger than most tumbled stones. River-tumbled garnet pebbles appear black until a light shows up their blood-red color.

Agate

LABRADORITE

CHEMICAL FORMULA: $(Na, Ca)Al_{1-2}Si_{3-2}O_8$

CRYSTAL SYSTEM: *triclinic*

HARDNESS: *6 to 6.5*

LUSTER: *vitreous*

COLOR: *gray with iridescence of green, yellow, orange, peacock blue*

CHAKRA: *all*

SUBTLE BODY: *all*

Labradorite allows many different levels of energy and awareness to be used in the body. With it, ideas and intuitive knowledge are easy to access. It is a good stone to use for seeing new solutions and opportunities in life. It is able to shift energy to multidimensional levels and so can work with every chakra and subtle body. Labradorite is one of the best stones for protecting the aura. The ever-changing play of light prevents negativity from attaching anywhere.

Labradorite

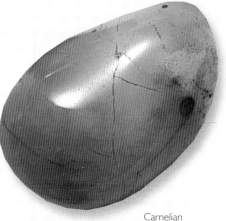

Carnelian

CARNELIAN

CHEMICAL FORMULA: SiO_2

CRYSTAL SYSTEM: *trigonal*

HARDNESS: *7*

LUSTER: *vitreous*

COLOR: *red-orange*

CHAKRA : *sacral*

SUBTLE BODY: *etheric*

Gently warming, carnelian is a good all-round healing stone. Very stabilizing, it works particularly well with the second, sacral chakra. Some may find the energy a little too strong, but the addition of other cooler stones will regulate the energy. (See also: Chalcedony)

SMOKY QUARTZ

CHEMICAL FORMULA: SiO_2

CRYSTAL SYSTEM: *trigonal*

HARDNESS: *7*

LUSTER: *vitreous*

COLOR: *brown, smoky gray, black*

CHAKRA: *base, sacral, solar plexus*

SUBTLE BODY: *emotional, mental, astral*

Smoky quartz acts as an effective, usually gentle, grounding stone. It is quietening and calming with an even energy that can regulate and temper crystals of a more volatile nature. It will gently dissolve negative states of mind.

While clear quartz broadcasts energy, smoky quartz absorbs and stores energy and information. Life energy is stabilized and enhanced, giving protection to the whole being.

Smoky Quartz

AMETHYST

CHEMICAL FORMULA: SiO_2 *(quartz variety)* $+ Fe$ *(iron)*

CRYSTAL SYSTEM: *trigonal*

HARDNESS: *7*

LUSTER: *vitreous*

COLOR: *violet*

CHAKRA: *brow, crown*

SUBTLE BODY: *emotional, mental, spiritual*

Amethyst is a wonderful healing stone whose activity focuses on calming and stabilizing. It can be used effectively as a meditation stone and works well with the brow and crown chakras. Amethyst will aid the healing process wherever it is needed in the body.

Amethyst

Lodestone

Magnetite

MAGNETITE (AND LODESTONE)

CHEMICAL FORMULA: Fe_3O_4

CRYSTAL SYSTEM: *cubic*

HARDNESS: *5.5 to 6.5*

LUSTER: *metallic, dull*

COLOR: *black*

CHAKRA: *all*

SUBTLE BODY: *all*

Magnetite and lodestone (which is magnetite with polarity) are both excellent balancers of the energy systems. They can temporarily align the actions of all the chakras and subtle bodies, allowing the release of stress. They also help to align the energy bodies to the electromagnetic field of the planet. This is both grounding and sustaining to our life force.

The more obvious magnetism of lodestone, usually identified by iron filings adhering to it, stimulates the electrical properties of the body.

MOLDAVITE

CHEMICAL FORMULA: *various silicates*

CRYSTAL SYSTEM: *amorphous*

HARDNESS: *5*

LUSTER: *vitreous*

COLOR: *green*

CHAKRA: *heart, throat, brow, crown*

SUBTLE BODIES: *all higher bodies*

As a healing tool, moldavites are excellent amplifiers of other stones. They work primarily with the higher faculties of the mind, encouraging the development of subtle senses, intuition, and an appreciation of the scale and beauty of creation. Those sensitive to subtle energy might find this stone takes time to get used to, because not everyone likes the expansive heat that is often felt on first contact with it. Moldavite works well with the heart, throat, brow, and crown chakras. Communication with different aspects of creation is quite a common experience using this stone for meditation. Holding a moldavite to the light and gazing through the surface patterns that often resemble a planet's surface can be a powerful way to activate the brow chakra.

Large pieces more than an inch big are rare and expensive, but small fragments are fine for healing purposes. If it is not green, it's not moldavite. Other tektites – brown, black, and opaque – are much less expensive.

If you are sensitive to this stone, make sure you have tourmaline or some other grounding stone nearby. Moldavite works well with clear quartz, which stabilizes its dynamic qualities. With other minerals that activate subtle skills and perceptions, very deep levels of awareness can be reached. Try it with celestite, danburite, sugilite, or apophyllite. Aquamarine, meteorite, diamond, lapis lazuli, and opal have also been reported to be good combinations. (See also: Tektite)

Moldavite

Topaz

HEMATITE

CHEMICAL FORMULA: Fe_2O_3
CRYSTAL SYSTEM: *trigonal*
HARDNESS: *5 to 6*
LUSTER: *metallic or dull*
COLOR: *metallic gray/black or red*
CHAKRA: *sacral and solar plexus*
SUBTLE BODY: *etheric*

Hematite is for most people one of the most effective grounding stones. Its high iron content supports the circulatory system and blood, and temperature regulation. Hematite can help with detoxification processes. It has a steady energizing effect upon physical levels, although its high metallic luster can be used as an aid for soul travel and astral projection. Hematite jewelry can be used as a general grounding and protecting aid for the aura, though care needs to be taken as it is quite brittle and can shatter easily.

Green
Tourmaline

TOURMALINE

CHEMICAL FORMULA:
$Na(Mg,Fe,Li,Mn,Al)_3Al_6(BO_3)Si_6$
$O_{18}(OH,F)_4$
CRYSTALS SYSTEM: *trigonal*
HARDNESS: *7 to 7.5*
LUSTER: *vitreous*
COLOR: *red, pink, yellow, green, blue, violet, black, multicolored, colorless*
CHAKRA: *all*
SUBTLE BODY: *all*

All tourmalines have a powerful healing effect on the body, as these stones help to harmonize the subtle systems such as meridians, chakras, and subtle bodies. Single color tourmalines can be used to balance the appropriate chakra. Multicolored tourmalines, such as watermelon tourmaline, containing areas of red and green, are ideal for the heart chakra; cat's eye and tourmaline quartz can be used at the brow and crown chakras. (See also: Indicolite, Tourmaline Quartz, and Schorl)

TOPAZ

CHEMICAL FORMULA: Al_2SiO_4
$(F.OH)_2$
CRYSTAL SYSTEM: *orthorhombic*
HARDNESS: *8*
LUSTER: *vitreous*
COLOR: *orange, pink, yellow, white, blue, white, gray, green, brown, clear*
CHAKRA: *solar plexus*
SUBTLE BODY: *etheric*

Topaz relaxes tension held in the body and helps to stabilize the emotions. Confidence increases. A long topaz crystal can be a powerful healing tool, and as a wand it can focus healing energy into the physical body. The energy of golden topaz works well with the crown chakra, where the flow of peace and harmony can charge the chakra system. Blue topaz works at the throat chakra and can bring a stabilizing universal energy into the body.

Hematite

Chrysoprase

Jade

CHRYSOPRASE

CHEMICAL FORMULA: SiO_2
CRYSTAL SYSTEM: *trigonal*
HARDNESS: 7
LUSTER: *resinous to vitreous*
COLOR: *apple green*
CHAKRA: *heart, sacral*
SUBTLE BODY: *etheric*

Chrysoprase is the most valuable variety of chalcedony. It is unmistakable for its bright green color. This mineral has been found useful for sleeplessness and insomnia. It is deeply calming both physically and emotionally, and may also be of use where there are sexual difficulties.

Chrysoprase is a popular stone for carving, although the rich color fades in sunlight. The variety known as prase is less brilliant and forms distinct quartz crystals with a greasy tinge. (See also: Chalcedony)

MOSS AGATE

CHEMICAL FORMULA: SiO_2
CRYSTAL SYSTEM: *trigonal*
HARDNESS: *6.5*
LUSTER: *vitreous to greasy*
COLOR: *clear with green and brown inclusions*
CHAKRA: *heart*
SUBTLE BODY: *emotional, mental*

Moss agate helps establish personal space and the possibility of expansion and growth. Physically, it can free constricted and congested areas by acting on the lymphatic system. It increases security and optimism, and helps to encourage the desire to explore and experience more of life. It also attunes to the realms of nature and encourages plant growth. (See also: Chalcedony)

Blue Quartz

BLUE QUARTZ

CHEMICAL FORMULA: SiO_2
CRYSTAL SYSTEM: *trigonal*
HARDNESS: *6.5 to 7*
LUSTER: *vitreous to waxy*
COLOR: *blue, blue-gray*
CHAKRA: *throat, heart*
SUBTLE BODY: *all*

Blue quartz works well with the organs and functions of the upper body. It can help to detoxify, cleanse, and repair. Excellent for throat problems, blue quartz also strengthens the immune system and reduces fear. Self-expression and creativity are enhanced.

JADE

Jade is, in fact, two distinct minerals: nephrite and jadeite. Jadeite is a deeper green color and is known as imperial jade.

CHEMICAL FORMULA:
$NaAlSi_2O_6$ *(jadeite)*
$Ca_2(Mg,Fe)_5Si_8O_{22}(OH)_2$ *(nephrite)*
CRYSTAL SYSTEM: *monoclinic*
HARDNESS: *7 6 to 6.5*
LUSTER: *waxy to vitreous*
COLOR: *allochromatic, colorless to rich green*
CHAKRA: *heart*
SUBTLE BODY: *astral, emotional, etheric*

Jade is a useful stone for the heart chakra. It helps to stabilize and integrate the personality, particularly instinct and the relationship of the body to the earth. This creates a sense of belonging, sensitivity, security, and effective action. With increased integration of mind with body, healing processes become more efficient.

Jade

Moss Agate

Cherry Opal

AQUAMARINE

CHEMICAL FORMULA:
$Be_3Al_2Si_6O_{18}$

CRYSTAL SYSTEM: *hexagonal*

HARDNESS: *7.5 to 8*

LUSTER: *vitreous*

COLOR: *blue*

CHAKRA: *throat*

SUBTLE BODY: *etheric, mental*

Aquamarine is an excellent booster for the immune system. It works well in the thymus and throat areas, but can prove useful with many body systems, particularly where cleansing is needed. Like many light blue stones, it encourages optimism and inspiration, and can be helpful with creative expression and communication. Its links to the immune system can prove useful in combating chronic infection. (See also: Beryl, Emerald)

Aquamarine

OPAL

CHEMICAL FORMULA: $SiO_2.nH_2O$

CRYSTAL STRUCTURE: *amorphous*

HARDNESS: *6*

LUSTER: *vitreous to pearl*

COLOR: *various*

CHAKRA: *mainly sacral, solar plexus, and crown*

SUBTLE BODY: *emotional body*

CHERRY OPAL

sacral and crown chakras

Found in shades of pink, red, and orange, Cherry Opal is helpful in tissue regeneration, particularly with blood disorders. It gently increases energy levels and can help to lift moods.

COMMON OPAL

Common opal contains no iridescence or fire and can take on many colors – from milky white, gray, green, purple to brown or clear. It has a more gentle energy than other opals and will focus its activity on the appropriate chakra color. Common opal stabilizes the emotions and feelings of self-worth. Even without the play of color, common opal, like other varieties of opal, allows awareness of finer dimensional levels of reality.

DARK OPAL

emotional and mental bodies, sacral chakra

Dark-colored opals of brown, black, or gray-blue activate and balance the energies of the sacral chakra. It has been found to be one of the best stones to help premenstrual tension or menstrual cramps, bringing almost immediate relief when held or placed in a hip

Common Opal

pocket. All opals work well at bringing emotional balance, and this variety will help with all sorts of sexual tension that has an emotional basis. Sensitivity is increased, and newly released emotions are assimilated.

DENDRITIC OR TREE OPAL

An opaque, common opal with impurities that form mosslike patterns. It can help patterns of growth and the ability to organize and plan. All physical systems with branching structures like lungs, nerves, and blood can be helped, especially when constriction is present. Tree opals also connect well with nature.

Dark Opal

FIRE OPAL

Fire opals are deep orange and red in color, and are usually found in small veins within a matrix rock.

An energizing, warming stone, it encourages recovery after emotional upsets and burn out or draining situations. Like all opals, fire opal works well with the fluid systems of the body and focuses on the emotional aspects of the self.

WATER OPAL

Hyalite, also known as jelly opal or water opal, is a colorless, clear opal with rainbow colors and veils suspended within the stone.

The ephemeral, otherworldly appearance of this gem can emphasize subtle spiritual qualities of the emotions and the emotional body. It helps to stabilize mood swings, eases the flow of life energy through the meridians and nadis, and makes a link between the sacral and crown chakras, which encourages enhanced meditative experiences.

Water Opal

WHITE OPAL

White opal is milky and is similar to common opal, although it does contain some colors. This stone is able to energize the crown chakra and bring clarity to the mind and a still calmness where necessary. Opals with an interplay of colors, like other multicolored stones, express and balance the energies of the crown chakra extremely well.

Rhodochrosite

RHODOCHROSITE

CHEMICAL FORMULA: $MnCO_3$
CRYSTAL SYSTEM: *trigonal*
HARDNESS: *3.5 to 4.5*
LUSTER: *vitreous, pearl*
COLOR: *pink, apricot, cream, red*
CHAKRA: *base, sacral, solar plexus, heart*
SUBTLE BODY: *emotional, mental, astral*

The range of delicate colors — from red to pink and orange with cream — helps to balance the energies of the first, second, and third chakras and has a positive effect on clearing stress from the heart chakra. Its main function is the stimulation and enhancement of self-worth and confidence, releasing tension from the emotional, mental and astral bodies. When there is pain and disease, rhodochrosite can help to remove negative perceptions, particularly where issues of abuse or sexuality are present.

AZURITE

CHEMICAL FORMULA: $Cu_3(CO_3)_2 (OH)_2$
CRYSTAL SYSTEM: *monoclinic*
HARDNESS : *3.5 to 4*
LUSTER: *vitreous, chalky*
COLOR: *blue to dark blue*
CHAKRA: *throat, brow*
SUBTLE BODY: *etheric, mental*

Large crystals of azurite are often very dark, almost black, and very shiny with an electric blue edge. This stone can reach to deep levels of consciousness and draw out memories or old stresses to be released in healing. Its deep blue stimulates all fine communication skills, creativity, and flow. It shifts all states from physical to subtle, toward integration and understanding. As a crystal, it is very soft, so it needs care in handling.

Azurite-malachite is a natural mix of these copper oxides. This gem is excellent for the digging up and clearing out of deep levels of imbalance.

Azurite

Lapis Lazuli

Citrine

BERYL

CHEMICAL FORMULA:
$Be_3Al_2Si_6O_{18}$
CRYSTAL SYSTEM: *hexagonal*
HARDNESS: *7 to 8*
LUSTER: *vitreous*
COLOR: *clear, yellow, pink, blue, green*
CHAKRA: *all*
SUBTLE BODY: *all*

Beryl quietens the mind, particularly where it is over-analytical or anxious. This helps relaxation on a physical level.

Heliodor (yellow beryl) works well with crown and solar plexus chakras, helping the quality of wisdom and discrimination.

Bixbite (red) energizes the base chakra and helps with practical issues such as completion of projects and creative flow.

Goshenite (colorless) helps the energy of the crown chakra and has a stabilizing influence at times when change is seen as difficult.

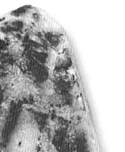

Morganite (pink) cleanses and balances the heart chakra. Yellow Beryl The second chakra also is activated by this gem. Calm, creativity, and self-worth can increase with its use.
(See also: Aquamarine, Emerald)

LAPIS LAZULI

CHEMICAL FORMULA: *(Na, Ca)$_8$ (Al.Si)$_{12}$ O$_{24}$ (S, SO$_4$)*
CRYSTAL SYSTEM: *cubic*
HARDNESS: *5.5*
LUSTER: *vitreous to greasy*
COLOR: *deep blues with white and gold*
CHAKRA: *throat, brow*
SUBTLE BODY: *etheric, mental*

Lapis lazuli works well with the throat and upper chest areas. It is a very effective cleanser. It can be a little uncomfortable for some people, as it draws out tension and anxiety from deep within the energy bodies. An archetypal blue stone, lapis lazuli will activate every aspect of communication and expression and, for those who like the energy, can be a great meditation stone.

CITRINE

CHEMICAL FORMULA: SiO_2 with *inclusions*
CRYSTAL SYSTEM: *trigonal*
HARDNESS: *7*
LUSTER; *vitreous*
COLOR: *yellow, golden brown, orange brown*
CHAKRA: *solar plexus (sacral, base, crown)*
SUBTLE BODY: *causal*

Citrine is a warming, stimulating stone that, depending on its color, is able to gently ground the energies of the base chakra, energize the second chakra with orange, or balance the yellow vibration of the solar plexus.

Citrine can bring a sunny warmth to the subtle anatomy. Emotionally, it can increase confidence and link to the source of personal power. This stone can also help the mind to integrate better with intuition and spiritual energies. Where there is depression or lack of energy during the winter months, citrine can help to supply sunny energy. (See also: Amethyst, Quartz)

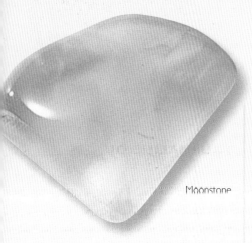

Moonstone

Clear Quartz

BLUE LACE AGATE

CHEMICAL FORMULA: SiO_2

CRYSTAL SYSTEM: *trigonal*

HARDNESS: 6.5

LUSTER: *vitreous to greasy*

COLOR: *bands of blue, white, gray*

CHAKRA: *Throat*

SUBTLE BODY: *emotional, mental*

Blue lace agate is a type of chalcedony quartz. It is a cooling, calming stone that can be used anywhere where there is a buildup or excess of energy. Unlike many other blue stones, it has an easy, gentle energy that is uplifting and nurturing. (See also: Chalcedony)

MOONSTONE

CHEMICAL FORMULA: $KAlSi_3O_8$

CRYSTAL SYSTEM: *monoclinic*

HARDNESS: *6 to 6.5*

LUSTER: *vitreous*

COLOR: *pearly white, cream, yellow, blue, sometimes with cat's eye or rainbows*

CHAKRA: *sacral, solar plexus*

SUBTLE BODY: *emotional*

Moonstone is an excellent stone to use for stabilizing the emotions and releasing tension caused by emotional stress. It helps to relax the energies of the solar plexus and so can help in disorders of the upper digestive tract, particularly if they are stress-related. All fluid systems of the body are brought to better balance by this stone. Menstrual cramps and other blocks and constrictions of the female reproductive organs can be relieved with moonstone. It also enhances intuition, creativity, and empathy.

Blue Lace Agate

Clear Quartz

QUARTZ

CHEMICAL FORMULA : SiO_2

CRYSTAL SYSTEM: *trigonal*

HARDNESS: 7

LUSTER: *vitreous*

COLOR: *transparent, white*

CHAKRA: *all*

SUBTLE BODY: *etheric, emotional*

Clear quartz contains no impurities, so appears completely colorless and transparent. This stone amplifies and strengthens the whole auric field, and the etheric and emotional bodies in particular. It brings calm and clarity. Quartz will amplify the energies of other stones placed nearby. For thousands of years it has been considered the main tool for contacting the spirit worlds. It is an ideal stone for contemplation, meditation, and healing. (See also: Amethyst, Citrine)

VERDELITE (GREEN TOURMALINE)

CHEMICAL FORMULA:
$Na(Mg,Fe,Li,Mn,Al)_3Al_6(BO_3)Si_6O_{18}(OH,F)_4$

CRYSTAL SYSTEM: *trigonal*

HARDNESS: *7 to 7.5*

LUSTER: *vitreous*

COLOR: *green*

CHAKRA: *heart*

SUBTLE BODY: *all*

Green tourmaline (verdelite) is found in Afghanistan, Italy, and southern Africa, but mainly in Brazil. It is sometimes called Brazilian Emerald. Technically, verdelite is where there is only a green coloration.

Green tourmaline is a good balancer for the heart chakra. It also works well with the thymus gland and can strengthen the immune system. Along with schorl, the black variety of tourmaline, verdelite will realign pulled and strained bone and muscle tissue. With it, there is a greater strengthening of the auric field to the energies of the planet, increasing confidence, security, and a sense of belonging. (See also: Tourmaline)

Verdelite
(Green
Tourmaline)

Rutilated
Quartz

RUTILE/ RUTILATED QUARTZ

CHEMICAL FORMULA: TiO_2

CRYSTAL SYSTEM: *tetragonal*

HARDNESS: *6 to 6.5*

LUSTER: *adamantine, metallic*

COLOR: *yellow, orange, deep red, brown*

CHAKRA: *all*

SUBTLE BODY: *all*

Most rutilated quartz contains golden threads or strawlike rutile crystals, but where the crystals are very closely packed and fine, a star-shaped luminescence, or asterism, can appear on the stone's surface. Rutile quartz is an efficient energy shifter and is particularly useful for repairing torn and broken tissues. It can act as an integrator at all levels of energy.

TOURMALINE QUARTZ

All colors of tourmaline can be found embedded in quartz, but the black variety, schorl, is the most common. Schorl is an effective grounding and protecting stone, closely linked to the planet's energies. This is combined with the quartz that amplifies those characteristics and adds its own cleansing and clarifying nature.

Tourmaline quartz is one of the best stones for strengthening and protecting the subtle energy fields from outside influences. Order and coherence is given from the quartz, while the tourmaline grounds and deflects environmental disturbances.

Tourmaline quartz speeds and integrates energy patterns and works well with crown chakra energies, although it will help to align all subtle bodies and chakras. (See also: Tourmaline)

Tourmaline
Quartz

Rubellite

RUBELLITE (RED TOURMALINE)

CHEMICAL FORMULA: $Na(Mg,Fe,Li,Mn,Al)_3Al_6(BO_3)Si_6.O_{18}(OH,F)_4$

CRYSTAL SYSTEM: *trigonal*

HARDNESS: *7 to 7.5*

LUSTER: *vitreous*

COLOR: *pink, red*

CHAKRA: *sacral, heart*

SUBTLE BODY: *emotional, astral*

Depending on the depth of color, rubellite can be a stimulating or a calming stone. In general, it balances the personality where there is too much aggression or passivity. Rubellite is energizing to the sacral chakra, increasing creativity on all levels. Where green is intermixed with the pink, as found in watermelon tourmaline, it is a perfect balancing stone for the heart chakra.

CELESTITE

CHEMICAL FORMULA: $SrSO_4$

CRYSTAL SYSTEM: *orthorhombic*

HARDNESS: *3 to 3.5*

LUSTER: *vitreous to mother of pearl*

COLOR: *clear, gray blue, sky blue*

CHAKRA: *throat, crown*

SUBTLE BODY: *soul*

Celestite, also called celestine, has a cooling, spacious, uplifting energy that works well with clearing the throat chakra and allowing a lightness and relaxation to enter into heavy, sad, or desperate situations. It does seem often to be able to open new perspectives on finer levels of reality. Inspiration, meditative states, and heightened intuition align celestite to the brow and crown chakras.

GOLD

CHEMICAL SYMBOL: *Au*

CRYSTAL SYSTEM: *cubic*

HARDNESS: *2.5 to 3*

LUSTER: *metallic*

COLOR: *yellow, orange*

CHAKRA: *heart*

SUBTLE BODY: *emotional, mental, spiritual*

Many consider gold to be the finest stone. It works mainly at the heart center. Like most other precious metals, gold is excellent for balancing the functions of the brain and nervous system. It works

Celestite

alongside all bioelectric functions of the body, and strengthens the immune system and major glands. Gold helps to stabilize electrical functioning at cellular levels, resulting in less energy waste and the reduction of stress factors.

Obsidian

OBSIDIAN

CHEMICAL FORMULA: *igneous rock containing feldspar, quartz, ilmenite, magnetite*

LUSTER: *vitreous*

COLOR: *black, greenish-black, gray, red-brown*

HARDNESS: *6*

CHAKRA: *base, sacral, crown*

SUBTLE BODY: *mental*

In addition to being an effective grounding stone, obsidian can help to reveal deeply buried imbalances so that they can be dealt with by other crystals. Physically, it can help to balance the digestive system, and likewise emotionally, it can help us digest truths we find hard to accept. Obsidian, traditionally used in scrying, will help to reveal the truth. It's a useful stone for protection, too.

Sapphire

SAPPHIRE

CHEMICAL FORMULA: $Al_2O_3(+Fe$ & $Ti)$

CRYSTAL SYSTEM: *trigonal*

HARDNESS: 9

LUSTER: *subadamantine to vitreous*

COLOR: *blue, violet-blue*

CHAKRA: *solar plexus, heart, throat, crown*

SUBTLE BODY: *emotional, astral*

Sapphire has a tradition of stimulating the higher mind and communication on subtle and spiritual levels. Personal expression increases, which benefits the heart and throat chakras. Sapphire is a calming, regulating stone, reducing tension in the solar plexus and helping to balance the glandular system as well as overactive elements in the body.

CORAL

CHEMICAL FORMULA: $CaCO_3$

CRYSTAL SYSTEM: *hexagonal or trigonal*

HARDNESS: 3

LUSTER: *dull to vitreous*

COLOR: *red, white, pink, golden, blue, black*

CHAKRA: *heart*

SUBTLE BODY: *etheric*

Coral has a positive value for the heart, blood, and circulatory systems and physical structure is also strengthened. Primarily, coral is an emotional balancer. The color will modify its characteristics: red gives energy and practical support, pink gives sensitivity and support for the heart chakra, blue activates communication skills, and the black variety protects and grounds. (See also: Calcite)

Aventurine

AVENTURINE

CHEMICAL FORMULA: SiO_2 with *inclusions*

CRYSTAL SYSTEM: *trigonal*

HARDNESS: 7

LUSTER: *vitreous*

COLOR: *brown, green, blue*

CHAKRA: *heart*

SUBTLE BODY: *etheric, emotional, mental*

Green aventurine is an ideal stone for balancing the heart chakra. It promotes tranquility and a positive outlook on life. Aventurine has an activating and cleansing effect, and helps stabilize the etheric, emotional, and mental bodies. Shiny inclusions are the best way of distinguishing aventurine from similar stones.

Aventurine

Sapphire

Coral

SODALITE

CHEMICAL FORMULA: $Na_4Al_3Si_3O_{12}Cl$

CRYSTAL SYSTEM: cubic

HARDNESS: 5.5 to 6

LUSTER: vitreous to glassy

COLOR: blue with white veining

CHAKRA: throat, brow

SUBTLE BODY: emotional, mental

Sodalite

Sodalite works at the throat and brow chakras, where it clarifies perceptions and helps communication. It cools and stabilizes emotions and thought processes and can bring the necessary flow of energy for expansive states of awareness. It is said to work well with the lymphatic system and hence with cleansing the body and enhancing the immune system. Its high sodium content will help fluids in the body.

TIGER'S EYE

CHEMICAL FORMULA: SiO_2

CRYSTAL SYSTEM: trigonal

HARDNESS: 7

LUSTER: vitreous to silky

COLOR: yellow to brown

SUBTLE BODY: astral, causal

Tiger's eye is a helpful stone that can integrate the functions of the base, sacral, and solar plexus chakras. This instills confidence, practicality, and gentle grounding. It helps to integrate the individual into society so as to become comfortable in social situations. Its fibrous quality allows tiger's eye to direct and clear energy from blocks. The blue variety — hawk's eye — acts on the brow chakra and throat and will access intuitive information, symbolic interpretation, and psychic skills. The red variety will create practical motivation.

ROSE QUARTZ

CHEMICAL FORMULA: SiO_2

CRYSTAL SYSTEM: trigonal

HARDNESS: 7

LUSTER: vitreous

COLOR: pink, rose, peach, violet pink

CHAKRA: heart, throat

SUBTLE BODY: emotional, mental, astral

Rose Quartz

This stone's color is from impurities of titanium or manganese oxides. Rose quartz is a powerful healing stone. Small pieces can be calming and healing in all aggressive conditions. Personal issues that are very often at the root of emotional and mental tensions can be eased with rose quartz. Usually it is considered to be a gentle stone, but where there is considerable stress, rose quartz can release imbalance very rapidly, which may cause some discomfort. At the heart chakra, it is best used with balancing green stones.

Tiger's Eye

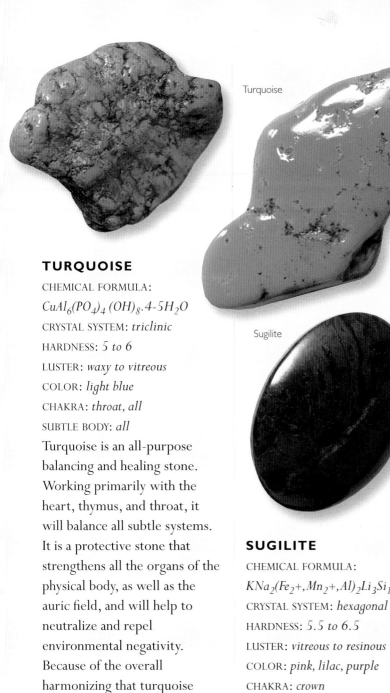

Turquoise

Sugilite

Sugilite

TURQUOISE

CHEMICAL FORMULA:
$CuAl_6(PO_4)_4(OH)_8.4-5H_2O$

CRYSTAL SYSTEM: *triclinic*

HARDNESS: *5 to 6*

LUSTER: *waxy to vitreous*

COLOR: *light blue*

CHAKRA: *throat, all*

SUBTLE BODY: *all*

Turquoise is an all-purpose balancing and healing stone. Working primarily with the heart, thymus, and throat, it will balance all subtle systems. It is a protective stone that strengthens all the organs of the physical body, as well as the auric field, and will help to neutralize and repel environmental negativity. Because of the overall harmonizing that turquoise allows, there is an increased flow of energy and information that calms, cools, and can enhance intuition and psychic skills. It has a natural connection to the spirit worlds.

SUGILITE

CHEMICAL FORMULA:
$KNa_2(Fe_2+,Mn_2+,Al)_2Li_3Si_{12}O_{30}$

CRYSTAL SYSTEM: *hexagonal*

HARDNESS: *5.5 to 6.5*

LUSTER: *vitreous to resinous*

COLOR: *pink, lilac, purple*

CHAKRA: *crown*

SUBTLE BODY: *astral, causal*

Sugilite can be a useful healing tool for the crown chakra and the activities of the brain and nervous system. Coordination of left-right hemispheres is encouraged, and energy flow within nerve cells is improved. It has been found a useful

stone where there is tension between spiritual and physical levels of reality and helps sensitive individuals to integrate better with their everyday surroundings. Like other purple stones, sugilite can bring the fine aspirations of spiritual life into a practical working focus.

CHRYSOCOLLA

CHEMICAL FORMULA:
$Cu_2H_2Si_2O_5(OH)_4$

CRYSTAL SYSTEM: *monoclinic or orthorhombic*

HARDNESS: *2 to 4*

LUSTER: *vitreous to waxy*

COLOR: *green, turquoise, light to mid-blues*

CHAKRA: *heart, throat*

SUBTLE BODY: *emotional and mental*

This stone's strong colors suggest effective use in the throat and chest areas. It is relaxing physically and emotionally. Stability in growth processes is encouraged by chrysocolla.

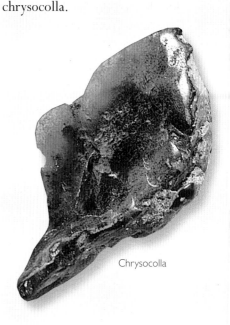

Chrysocolla

Glossary

CHAKRA — spinning vortex of subtle energy.

CHATOYANCY — play of light, silk-like rippling, caused by light refracting off parallel microcrystals.

CHI — Chinese term for life energy flowing through the universe, concentrated within channels within the body.

CONCRETION — a mass of mineral matter found generally in a rock whose composition is different and produced by deposition from aqueous solution in the rock.

CRYSTAL — a mineral exhibiting regular planes and faces reflecting its internal organization of atoms.

CRYSTAL SYSTEM — a characteristic grouping of atoms that produce crystals with similar axes of symmetry and geometrical form.

DOUBLE-TERMINATED — a crystal that forms faceted points at both ends.

DOWSING — various ways to access and indicate unconscious knowledge or sense data — for example, pendulum, rod, hand-scanning, muscle-testing.

ELECTROMAGNETIC STRESS — any strong field, either electrical or magnetic, that disrupts normal states within the body.

AFFIRMATIONS— statements that emphasize positive states and emotions, helping to move self-limiting or erroneous beliefs or concepts.

AURA — general term for the personal electro-magnetic field and subtle bodies around the physical body.

ASTERISM — a star of light appearing on a crystal's surface caused by internal microcrystals. A true asterism will move around with a light source.

CABOCHON — a method of cutting gemstones, usually semi-precious stones, with a flat oval base and a domed surface.

CENTERED/CENTERING — the state of being aware and focused within the physical body with a clear, calm mind.

ENTRAINMENT — where one system in a state of vibration or energy overrides another system's own vibrational frequency, causing resonance.

ESSENCES — (or vibrational essences) preparations of water charged with the energy signature of the gemstone, flower, or other object placed within it while exposed to sunlight.

GROUNDING — techniques that allow excess and out of balance energies to flow from the body.

HOLISTIC — viewing the body, mind, and emotions as an integrated system where change in one inevitably affects the whole.

IGNEOUS — rock formed from molten material. Called intrusive if it solidifies before reaching the earth's surface.

INCLUSION — a solid foreign body enclosed in a mineral mass, often in the form of another crystalline mineral, gas, or water droplets.

INDICATOR MUSCLE – a muscle used in kinesiology that shows by its function, a yes/no response to a question put by the tester.

KINESIOLOGY – also known as muscle-testing. A way of assessing energy flow through muscle tone and correcting energy imbalances.

LATTICE – the regular pattern of atoms composing the internal structure of all crystals.

MATRIX – the base rock from which crystals grow.

MERIDIAN – subtle energy channel running close to the surface of the skin, along which can be found sensitive places such as acupuncture points.

METAMORPHIC – a rock changed or modified by heat and pressure.

MINERAL – a single chemical compound. Minerals can be a single element like diamond, or a complex combination of atoms like tourmaline.

NADIS – nonphysical channels throughout the body carrying energy from each chakra.

RESONANCE – the effects of one system or body beginning to vibrate at the same rate as another already in a state of vibration. See: Entrainment.

ROCK – sometimes a single mineral, most often a combination of different minerals and crystal structures.

SCHILLER – twinkle or sparkle in a stone created by light reflecting off microcrystals.

SEDIMENTARY – rock formed from layers of dust and fine material, compressed by its own weight and water.

SHAMAN – a general term for those skilled in working with the spirit worlds, particularly for healing and helping the tribal group.

STRONG-INDICATOR MUSCLE – the foundation of accurate muscle-testing. A muscle that effortlessly resists gentle pressure.

SUBTLE BODY – nonphysical aspects of consciousness that surround and interpenetrate the physical body.

SWITCHING – where the meridian system becomes unstable through stress, making muscle testing unreliable.

TAPPING IN – finger tapping around specific areas to bring the meridian system into balance. For grounding and centering.

TERMINATION – the natural end facets of a crystal, usually meeting in a point.

VIBRATIONAL HEALING– a general term for nonphysical healing modalities, including crystal healing, color healing, sound healing, and vibrational essences.

WITNESS – a link by which a healer assesses the energy state of a person not physically present, usually from a sample of hair, photograph, or signature.

Index

Index

random intuitive layout 108–9
ratnas 191
recharging 53
record-keeper crystals 142–3
red 57, 58, 89, 93
red ocher 57, 183
refraction 57
relaxation 152, 156
repetitive stress injury 136
rhodochrosite 210
rhodonite 202
rings 169
RNA 35
rock cycle 10–11
rose quartz 21, 52, 53, 216
   confidence layout 154
   heart chakra 79, 153
   personal potential layout 154
   tension release layout 152
   water element layout 155
rubellite 214
ruby 56, 77, 200
rutilated quartz 75, 168, 213
rutile *see* rutilated quartz

S
sacral chakra 59, 70–1, 74–5, 89, 93,
   152, 155
sahasrara 84
salt method 24
sapphire 56, 155, 215
Saturn 191
scepter quartz 30
schorl (black tourmaline) 42, 119,
   130, 203
scrying 32, 176, 178–9
Seal of Solomon 53
sedimentary rocks 10, 11, 218
selenite 23, 137, 200
self-cleansing 140
self-healing 53
self-massage 126
self-testing 105, 123
sensitivity exercises 106–7
sexual chakra *see* sacral chakra
shamans 184–5, 186–7, 189
sight 49
sight focus 46
single crystals 20, 21
skeletal quartz 29
smell 49
smoky quartz 22, 29, 42, 43, 52, 79,
   151, 205
   circuit rebalancing 130
   emotional body layout 117
   meditation 157
sodalite 119, 216
solar plexus 60, 70–1, 76–7, 89, 93,
   155, 169

soul body 115, 120, 121
sound 49
sound cleansing 25
sound focus 46
South America 188–9
Southeast Asia 184–5
specimen samples 20
spectrum layout 91
spheres 21, 137, 151
spiritual body 115, 120, 121
spiritual growth 88
Star of David 53
Steiner, Rudolf 166
stock bottle 27
storage 22–3
streak test 57
stress 36, 37, 146, 148–55
   base chakra 72
   environmental 170, 172–3
   figure eight circuits 130
   mental body layout 118
   solar plexus chakra 76
subtle bodies 29, 113–21, 146, 199,
   218
subtle sight 106
sugilite 176, 217
Sun 191
sun and water method 24
support 48–9
surrogate testing 105
svadhisthana 74
switching 101, 104, 218
symmetry 16–17

T
tabular crystals 30
talismans 190
Tansley, David 158
Tantra 190–1
tapping in 47, 49, 101, 102, 218
telephone 171
Temple of Inscriptions 188
tension release layout 152
Teotihuacán 188
terminations 42, 218
tetragonal system 16
therapy localizing 128
throat chakra 62, 65, 70–1, 80–1, 89,
   93, 155, 169
Tibetan healing 130
tiger's eye 42, 77, 152, 216
time-link crystals 33
topaz 168, 207
tourmaline 168, 169, 207
   base chakra 73
   black tourmaline 42, 115, 119,
    130, 203
   blue tourmaline 202
   green tourmaline 79, 213

tourmaline quartz 168, 213
toxic stones 26
trans-channeling crystals 32
transmitter crystals 32
Tratak 157
tree meditation 44
tree opal 209
triboluminescence 14
triclinic system 17
trigonal system 17
Tsimshian people 186
Tukano 189
tumbled stones 21, 22
turquoise 52, 53, 65, 166, 169, 187,
   188, 217

U
upper circuit 130

V
vata 191
Venus 191
verdelite (green tourmaline) 79, 213
violet 64, 93
   brow chakra 89
   crown chakra 89
   divination 176
   mineral dyes 57
visualization 25, 49, 92, 134, 136
visuddha 80
voice focus 46

W
wands
   laser 30
   massage 21, 146–7, 151, 167
water element layout 155
water imaging 44
water opal 210
wearing crystals 168–9
wellness 36–7
white 56, 66, 89, 120
white opal 210
wild stones 184
window crystals 33
Wiradjuri shamans 184
witness 162, 163, 218
worked crystals 20–1
Wotjobaluk 185

Y
yellow 60, 93
   mineral dyes 57
   personal potential layout 154
   solar plexus chakra 89
yin and yang 135
Yuman shamans 186

Acknowledgments

The following have provided inspiration and guidance for particular methods of working:

Centerline breathing: Katrina Raphaell, Uma Sibley

Recharging body and spirit, general re-energizing, crystals and breath: Baer and Baer *Crystals of Light*.

Minor chakras: David Tansley, *Radionics and the Subtle Anatomy of Man*, G.L.Paulson, *Kundalini and the Chakras*.

Color Meditation: channeled via Barbara Brennan, *Hands of Light*.

Body Overview: Katrina Raphaell, *Crystal Healing*.

Subtle body, stone placement derived from suggestions in channeled material in Gurudas, *Gem Elixirs and Vibrational Healing Vol.I*.

Information about meridians: Gerber, *Vibrational Medicine*.

Balancing Meridians with quartz crystals: from Baer and Baer, *Crystals of Light*.

Meridians, end-points, and emotional connotations: John Diamond, *Life-Energy*.

Meridian Massage as taught by kinesiologist Pamela Wilkinson.

Hand-held crystals: Jonathan Pawlik and Pamela Chase, *Newcastle Guide to Healing with Crystals*.

Guided Meditations: "Curtains of Light" derived from David Tansley, *The Raiment of Light*.

Goal Balancing – as discovered by Robert Frost.

Bibliography

BAER, R. and BAER, V., *Windows of Light* (Harper and Row, 1984)

BONEWITZ, R., *Cosmic Crystals* (The Aquarian Press, 1983)

COWAN, D. and GIRDLESTONE, R., *Safe as Houses?* (Gateway Books, 1996)

DIAMOND, J. *Life Energy* (Dodd Mead & Co., 1985)

ELIADE, M., *Shamanism* (Penguin, 1989)

GARDNER, J., *Color and Crystals* (The Crossing Press, 1988)

GERBER, R., *Vibrational Medicine* (Bear & Co, 1988)

GURUDAS, *Gem Elixirs and Vibrational Healing*, Vol I (Cassandra Press, 1989)

JOHARI, H., *The Healing Power of Gemstones* (Destiny Books, 1988)

JUDITH, A., *Wheels of Life* (Llewellyn, 1987)

LILLY, S. and LILLY, S., *Crystal Doorways* (Capall Bann, 1997)

MELODY, *Love is in The Earth* (Earth Love Publishing House, 1991)

PAULSON, G. L., *Kundalini and the Chakras* (Llewellyn, 1991)

PAWLIK, J. and CHASE, P., *The Newcastle Guide to Healing with Crystals* (Newcastle Publishing Co., 1988)

RAPHAELL, K. *Crystal Enlightenment* (Aurora Press, 1985)

ROBINS, D., *The Secret Language of Stone* (Rider, 1988)

SIBLEY, U., *The Complete Crystal Guidebook* (Bantam, 1986)

TANSLEY, D., *Radionics and the Subtle Anatomy of Man* (C W Daniel, 1972)

TANSLEY, D., *The Raiment of Light* (Arkana, 1984)

Useful Addresses

Simon and Sue Lilly
Institute of Crystal and Gem
Therapists MCS
PO Box 6
Exeter
Devon EX6 8YE
U.K.
+44 (0)1392 832005
email:
icgt@greenmantrees.demon.co.uk

Affiliation of Crystal Healing
Organisations (Represents ten schools
within the U.K.)
PO Box 34
Manchester M60 2EZ
U.K.
+44 (0)161 278 0096
email: info@iacht.com

Crystal Academy of Advance Healing
Arts (Katrina Raphael)
PO Box 1334
Kappa
Kauai, Hawaii
96746 U.S.A.
(001) 808 823 6959
email:
http://crystalacademy.cncfamily.com